PLACING HISTORY

REIHE
KULTUR.WISSENSCHAFTEN

Herausgegeben vom Bundesministerium für
Bildung, Wissenschaft und Kultur

BAND 7

SUSAN INGRAM
MARKUS REISENLEITNER (HG.)

Placing History

THEMED ENVIRONMENTS, URBAN CONSUMPTION AND THE PUBLIC ENTERTAINMENT SPHERE

ORTE UND IHRE GESCHICHTE(N): THEMENWELTEN, URBANER KONSUM UND FREIZEITÖFFENTLICHKEIT

TURIA + KANT
Wien

Bibliografische Information Der Deutschen Bibliothek
Die Deutsche Bibliothek verzeichnet diese Publikation in der Deutschen Nationalbibliografie; detaillierte bibliografische Daten sind im Internet über http://dnb.ddb.de abrufbar.

Bibliographic Information published by Die Deutsche Bibliothek
Die Deutsche Bibliothek lists this publication in the Deutsche Nationalbibliografie; detailed bibliographic data is available in the internet at http://dnb.ddb.de.

ISBN 3-85132-354-8

A – 1010 Wien, Schottengasse 3A/5/DG 1
info@turia.at • www.turia.at

Inhalt / Contents

Introduction / Einführung

Introduction / Einführung

Whether it is hotels that imitate Venice or Egypt, shopping malls that recreate Parisian boulevards or ›ethnic‹ restaurants, North American, and increasingly European, urban landscapes are increasingly becoming themed environments. The term »themed environment« is used more and more often to describe the postindustrial transformation of urban landscapes into entertainment hubs, places to play at home while consuming the exotic in the form of ethnic restaurants, themed shopping malls and nostalgic, historically oriented reconstructions of problem neighborhoods. These developments are, on one hand, fervently denounced as infantilizing and »inauthentic«; on the other hand, they offer invaluable assets for tourism's promotion of »place images« and often form the basis of local identity projects.

This volume sets out to explore and approach this new urban economy from different angles. A cultural phenomenon as pervasive, popular and visually arresting as themed environments has to be understood as resulting from a wide variety of converging traditions, developments and discourses. At the same time, these are contested places, sites where histories and communities are produced, negotiated, contested and obliterated at the crossroads of vectors of colonialism, national identity and urban experience – with noticeable consequences for the built environment. Despite their attempts to render the cityscape legible and contain the meaning of places, to perform, orchestrate, regulate and discipline encounters, often with an exoticized other or past, and generally at the expense of public space, randomness and contingent encounters, themed environments in urban settings are nowhere as transparent as they try to appear to be. Highly complex phenomena, they come in a bewildering variety and rely (consciously or unconsciously) on different strategies in their creation and assembly of symbolic sites. Thus the contributions collected here share an interest in the specifics of how these places are assembled, how to approach individual instances of themed environments as specific junctures of mass entertainment, identity negotiation, social hierarchy, public space, theatrical spectacle, visual pleasure and a consumption-based leisure industry in order to understand their traditions and explain their particular appeal.

While the contributions collected here cover quite a lot of territory, both literally and metaphorically, they share a fundamental belief in the importance of history for these spatial practices, history not simply understood as the linear emergence of a phenomenon motivated by social or economic developments, but history as a context which inscribes particular ideological and political discourses that are circulated, mediated, modified and contested at particular sites. So while many contributions here lead us back in time, they do not do so in search of an origin, emergence, or even genealogy, but rather in an attempt to explore what crystallizes at particular junctures, in particular sites. In this sense, themed environments, understood as a subset of spatial practices, emerge as the intersections of many histories, histories which make themselves felt even if they are submerged. Theming makes histories (and images associated with those histories) travel, but these travels – through time and space – never follow straight routes, and never arrive at the same place, even if it is the same site.

The volume begins with some of the theoretical concepts useful for exploring those public sites where theming predominates as a form of entertainment, drawing attention to the quote marks that increasingly need to be put around »public.« The quest for these specific histories leads us back to the end of the eighteenth and the early nineteenth century, when entertainment in urban environments emerges as a key factor in negotiations over public space, cultural hierarchies and the role of consumption. The first contribution introduces, in the context of Vienna, the notion of a »public entertainment sphere« as a critique of Habermas's concept as well as an attempt to explore notions of hegemony for the topic, relating it to the social as well as symbolic structures that had an impact on it, while the second contribution on London during roughly the same period identifies changes in the way public entertainment is consumed. Focusing on specific public spaces, such as streets, pleasure gardens, music halls and the Crystal Palace, this contribution looks at how they functioned to contain conflicts and enact class segregation and distinction. In many ways the importance of context-specific studies is borne out by juxtaposing these two cities: what emerges in London is not simply a model, an earlier stage of tendencies also visible in Vienna. Rather, in thus denying any shortcuts in relating phenomena of theming to the abstract linearity of modernity's march through Europe, London and Vienna appear as twisted mirror images, in which leisure is subordinated to consumption against a backdrop of discourses of authority and paternialism which make themselves felt in identifiable ways. The aim of looking into eighteenth- and nineteenth-century forms of public entertainment must not be considered a kind of attempt to find a mythical »origin« of themed environments, a task both hopeless and less than useful; rather, identified here are key moments of intricacy and ambiguity in which cultural practices, tied to practices of place and spatial meaning, are re-articulated in the public realm. At specific moments in the history of these two cities, negotiations over the utilization of space as both a site of identity formation and leisure-oriented entertainment become re-articulated as negotiations over cultural hierarchies, the accessibility of public space, and imaginings of the exotic other.

That this exotic other need not necessarily be located elsewhere but can also materialize as a »temporal elsewhere,« a magical past constructed out of cultural tradition, is shown in the following two contributions. One of the most prominent characteristics of themed environments is the way they rely on, and cross-fertilize, imaginings that originated or are prominently promoted in other genres of popular and high culture. A recurrent topos of historical escape is provided, in the context of European popular culture, by the Middle Ages, which provide a setting for chivalry and romance from the early popular literature in the nineteenth century to Disney's Sleeping Beauty phantasmagoria. The contribution »*Once upon a time…*« traces the specific function of medieval imagery, the cultural and political implications of the libidinal energies and investments bound up in motifs of the Middle Ages, and the particular structural patterns of fantasy facilitated by this particular period and its traditional associations. It addresses the question of how traditions inform the meanings attributed to themes in a specific case that baffles by its pervasiveness and longevity. While some of these functions have arguably been taken over by the fantasy genre recently, the Middle Ages still provide a powerful counterfoil to modernity.

It is also a motif that travels extraordinarily well, from the Old World to the New, and back. At the American world fairs – seen by many as prototype theme parks –, Europe was very much a fairytale land far, far away, while at the same time not relinquishing its claims to the present and presenting stiff industrial and commerical competition. These competing visions of Europe had to somehow be brought together in an approachable imagery at the fairs, reflecting the conflicts inherent in the paternalist and the capitalist discourses of public entertainment. How these negotiations affected the process of theming and in turn created powerful place images is explored in the next contribution, which looks at the contradictory representations of Austria at the American world fairs at the turn of the century as both medieval and modern. Relating these displays to the »double and split time« of national representation Homi Bhabha elaborates in his work on nationalism reveals the key to be location. Whereas the official pavilions were bastions of modernity and progress, the medieval emerges as a theme on the margins, on the profit-driven »Midway« amusement zones, in architectural forms that link the escapist fantasies of the early nineteenth-century *Trivialromane* with Disney's dreamworlds a century and a half later.

From the material substantiation of castles in the air, we turn to the shape given by the Old World to its fantasies of the faraway. While Vienna was being marketed successfully as »Altwien« on both sides of the Atlantic, the exotic themes to enjoy the same kind of success in Vienna itself were Buffalo Bill's Wild West Show and »Venice in Vienna.« The next contribution details the tension in the Viennese »public entertainment sphere« between the local dominance of performance, with a particular emphasis on the *Prater* and the theater, and global discourses of representation and construction employed and/or mobilized by entertainment corporations and managers. One of the negotiations to be found here which deserves our special attention are the ways audiences are represented and imagined in a tradition of entertainment industries that enclose the other for digestible consumption – representations of audiences that are more often than not as fictional as the material prepared for them – harboring potent strategies of social control and engineering which are often translated into the concrete architectural structures of these environments.

How theming took root by hearkening back to a tradition in urban entertainment is also explored in the next contribution, which revisits the Crystal Palace. While earlier contributions trace how the particular spatial organization of knowledge about faraway places brought together enlightenment and entertainment, spectacle and speculation, nationalism and empire, and integrated it with what can be seen as the hallmark of public entertainment in urban capitalist societies: consumption, attention here is focused more closely on the dynamic of education and amusement as it is mediated by nostalgia for the non-industrial premodern. By attending to the confluence of recreation and the re-creation of exotic (and again: medieval) settings, the study suggests that the growth of themed entertainment and shopping complexes needs to pay particular attention to the circumstances of their being built and, more generally, to the larger histories of the (often eclipsed) conurbations in which they are located.

The next contribution to this volume provides precisely such an accounting: of Canada's best-known northern »indoor« city. Thick descriptions of a worn-out, kosher pizza-joint in »the« mall and of a Scouting group with deeded, permanent privileges to use particular rooms in a church show that even the most tightly assembled enclosed spaces allow pockets of resistance which both affirm and contest the dominant place images produced by themed environments. Both cases detail how the builders as well as the actors enact resistance in particular ways, a constant tension and negotiation that opens up and closes possibilities for political agency.

While these articulations invariably happen in urban environments, the final four contributions deal specifically with what happens when a city itself, or a particular urban neighborhood or district, are themed. The very special history of Dawson City, Yukon, provides a test case for the almost complete transformation of an urban into a themed environment. A town in the far north of Canada that boomed when gold was discovered there in the late 1890s, it verged on becoming a ghost town in the 1950s and 1960s until it was rearticulated exclusively as a national heritage site and tourist center. This contribution explores how the cultural negotiations and contests between European and North American themes characteristic of a turn-of-the century urban environment were streamlined into movie- and literature-inspired motifs of an Arctic frontierland for foreign, primarily German, tourists.

That the remaking of urban space can never be as complete and as successful in real places as in the controlled environments of shopping malls and small isolated communities is suggested in the ensuing discussion of multicultural theming in the contemporary Netherlands. Contestations over the cultural meaning of public architecture predictably set in when theming meets the lifeworlds and needs of real immigrants in four contemporary projects which aim at exoticizing the environment under the auspices of consumption and often target derelict neighborhoods in an attempt of gentrification, while occasionally aiming at providing places of identification and a sense of belonging for immigrants. The article explores the tensions and negotiations brought out by these clashes and fundamentally queries the paternalist as well as the market discourses motivating these projects.

While developments in the Netherlands incorporate aspects of themed environments in an attempt to deal with the challenges of migration multiculturalism, the next contribution turns to a very different strategy of creating place images in a city which cheerfully embraces its museum-like qualities. Vienna's long-established tradition of declaring itself the »Capital of Music« (something also exploited at the World Exhibitions) provides a powerful metaphor for an ongoing transformation of public space that capitalizes on these notions. In this place image (like in any other), several strands of cultural negotiations are articulated: music as a battlefield of national culture, art music as a particular form of bourgeois cultural value, and the contemporary emphasis on fun and entertainment characteristic of the public entertainment sphere and its commercialization by leisure industries. As much as these projects rely on unifying metaphors, they are nonetheless torn apart by the multiplicity of meanings inherent in music that they try to contain. Gentrification, tourism, and the almost-forgotten postwar struggle to create a whitewashed image of Austrian nationhood can, as is argued here, hardly be brought together in a period when the cultural values and hierarchies on which these themes rely are themselves contested. In a twist inspired by a musical installation that uses web metaphors, the contribution challenges the function of urban space as a site of containment. In a time when media flows locate more than urban space, musical metaphors that rely on those flows seem to query the very site in which themes are contained.

The subject of the final contribution of this volume is the city where »it all comes together,« the urban environment that has become paradigmatic for the postmodern city. This contribution traces the emergence of Los Angeles as an urban environment out of a theme that was meant to sell the place quite literally, and explores competing themes that have possibly contributed to making it a real place.

*

This volume has many roots. What started out as two research projects funded by the Cultural Studies Program of the Austrian Ministry of Education turned into a much wider undertaking, assisted by the School for Advanced Studies in London and the Wolfsonian-FIU in Miami Beach, and culminating in a highly rewarding panel at the 4th International Crossroads in Cultural Studies Conference in Tampere, Finland. It was difficult for such a polyvocal undertaking to be brought together in the established and traditonal forms of academic writing, since neither a monograph nor a traditional edited volume seemed adequate to the way the project had developed (no monograph could have covered the territory we thought should be addressed, but we also did not want to lose the core commonalities that had developed in our thoughts and discussions over the years.) This book should be understood as a collective attempt to explore the issues at stake in very specific contexts, which had to be addressed by different people and different disciplines, with many of our ideas and analyses developing through discussion and co-operation even if we looked at geographically as well as topically widely dispersed topics. We hope that this common ground and common agenda are reflected in the pages that follow.

Thus the following pages, perhaps more than usual, have been the joint efforts of many people, without whom they would not have been possible. We would like to thank Ilse König and Christina Lutter from the Austrian Ministry of Education, who facilitated this project in the first place, were (as always) open to modifications and the haphazard reorganizations necessitated by the vagaries of globetrotting academic careers, and provided many helpful hints and suggestions whenever we had a chance to get together, in places as far apart from each other as the sites covered in this book. Our thanks also to Karl Vocelka and his marvellous IEFN (Institut für die Erforschung der Frühen Neuzeit) team for providing office space in Vienna, a forum for presenting the project at several stages of completion, and above all their wide and inspiring knowledge and sociability; Paulus Ebner and Markus Feigl for the work they did on a preliminary study which inspired this project, and Hubert Christian Ehalt from the Vienna City Council for funding this study; Dennis Sweeney (University of Alberta) and Geoff Eley (University of Michigan) for valuable input on the concept of a »public entertainment sphere« and an inspiring panel at the GSA in Houston; Nicholas Blaga and Frank Luca at the Wolfsonian-FIU for all their help in the library and Joseph Patrouch and Felice Lifschitz for introducing us to this collection; Susanne Pils from the Wiener Stadt-und Landesarchiv for her energetic support; Christa Müller from the Austrian National Library and Erika Banski from the Library of the University of Alberta; the librarians of the Special Collection of Senate House and the British Library; the School of Advanced Studies at the University of London for their assistance of Susan Ingram's work on London; Shannon Olson and her colleagues at the Yukon Public Archives in Whitehorse for making our work in the far north both pleasant and productive; the Getty Center and the Public Library in Los Angeles; and all the students and colleagues with whom we had a chance to discuss our work and who provided valuable insight and criticism.

Public Entertainment and the Construction of a Public Entertainment Sphere in Nineteenth-Century Vienna: Creating a Middle-Class Audience in Urban Entertainment Spaces

MARKUS REISENLEITNER

The development of an urban, public entertainment and leisure culture has been seen in the context of changes in the urban landscape around the turn of the last century, when full-service entertainment firms took control of a public entertainment industry (Snyder, Leach). On the North American continent, Coney Island was promoted as »a mingling of individuals of all ranks and classes, college and factory workers dining next to each other, the disregarding of character or station, equality being taken for granted joyfully« (Weinstein 2). This trend has been interpreted as proof of the »commercialization of leisure« (Hannigan 17), which »created a national consumer market for the ›culture of desire‹« and »needed to convince less affluent patrons that they were being transported to magical realms (the amusement park, the movie palaces) beyond the orbit of everyday constraints of class and gender, and at the same time reassure bourgeois pleasure-seekers that these new public amusements were safe and physically and morally ›clean‹« (Hannigan 18).

This interpretation seems to fit assumptions about the emergence of a mass culture in the industrial era, which, being of a decidedly urban character, is regarded as being produced for the sole purpose of entertainment and commercial success, resulting in a largely passive audience of spectators thus distracted from any kind of serious political engagement. Critical Theory's interpretative framework elucidates this process in terms of the commodification of culture through ›culture industries,‹ the emergence of which apparently coincides with the emergence of what I will call a *public entertainment sphere*, characterized by its location in urban culture, by mass participation and commodification. »Urban spectacle has been understood as a defining quality of

›modernity‹ generally construed« (Schwartz 3). This public entertainment sphere is conceived of as a sharp counterpoint to elite culture, while retaining (or promoting) a character of respectability that supposedly lures, and creates, a middle-class audience in discourse.

This situation obtains extraordinarily well in Vienna around the turn of the last century, a city in which social tensions are supposed to have been bridged and defused by leisure and entertainment. Social boundaries were supposedly transcended by social integration through entertainment institutions like the *Prater*, the *Heuriger*, the (suburban) commercial theaters and other forms of public entertainment, particularly outside the city walls, while the inner city, insulated from this form of mass culture, signified the boundaries of the elite culture (cf. the contributions in Horak).

It is noteworthy that such claims to, and manifestations of, a class-transcending public entertainment sphere are not necessarily those produced by forms of entertainment culture new to an urban landscape transformed by the impact of modernity and industrialization at the end of the nineteenth century, but rather seem to be based on an indigenous tradition of popular culture and entertainment. In Vienna, one can find a similar rhetoric employed for public entertainment spaces already a century earlier in the rhetoric of enlightened absolutism. Arguably these phenomena can be traced back to the Enlightenment, and it is the (temporal) coincidence that suggests a connection to the concept of a public sphere theorized (and idealized) by Jürgen Habermas. Habermas's pivotal investigation provides the background against which I want to explore the dominant discursive strategies employed in Vienna during the nineteenth century, first by official institutions but increasingly also by a budding (commercial) entertainment sector intent on promoting such public spaces of entertainment as safe, middle-class environments while at the same time defining and normalizing a ›respectable‹ audience for (consumable) urban entertainment and setting limits to or even suppressing sub-cultural expressions and carnivalesque, deviant and subversive behavior.

Let me start with an example that seems particularly obvious: Joseph II's allowing the ›plebs‹ public access to a huge area of meadows and parkland within walking distance of the city center, the *Prater*, which had formerly been reserved for aristocratic hunting. The following announcement is indicative of the paternalistic intentions of the Emperor:

> *Künftighin und von nun an zu allen Zeiten des Jahres und zu allen Stunden des Tags, ohne Unterschied jedermann in den Bratter sowohl als auch in das*

> *Stadtgut frey spazieren zu gehen, reiten und zu fahren, und zwar nicht nur in der Hauptallee, sondern auch in den Seitenalleen, Wiesen und Plätzen (die allzu abgelegenen Orte und dicke Waldungen, wegen sonst etwa zu besorgenden Unfugs und Mißbrauchs alleinig ausgenommen) erlaubet, auch Niemandem verwehrt seyn soll, sich daselbst mit Ballonschlagen, Kegelscheiben und anderen erlaubten Unterhaltungen eigenen Gefallens zu divertieren.* (*Wienerisches Diarium* 9 April 1766)

A wide variety of spectacles (animal chases, *Völkerschauen*, dioramas) became concentrated in this newly open, accessible space, whose supposedly class-transcending character as an affordable opportunity for the social mingling of individuals of all ranks and classes was repeatedly emphasized in advertisements and other forms of promotion. The discourse of public entertainment created a public culture and an idiom of popular entertainment within the urban environment that offered opportunities for identification beyond class distinctions by tying it to a public sphere of entertainment within a shared urban space, luring a wide cross-section of society while employing subtle strategies of internal distinction and external exclusion to maintain social difference and less subtle strategies of policing and control. Thus a visit to the *Prater* was prohibited on Sundays and holidays, since »*allermaßen besonders die Gemeinen und Dienst Leuthe das Spazierengehen in den Bratter dem Heil. Gottes Dienst vorziehen dörften*« (Staatsarchiv: Akten des Oberjägermeisteramtes. Fasz. 113, fol. 860-3).

The spectacular quality of these forms of entertainment is particularly noticeable in the most popular of all spectacular genres, the fireworks. Rather than being staged in connection with an aristocratic or upper bourgeois reception/soiree/ball/gathering, they were set off in the *Prater* for the first time on May 24, 1767 (Lotz 80). Although considered the most ›popular‹ form of entertainment, attending them still required the payment of a hefty entrance fee, which was actually higher than most theater tickets and effectively excluded the poorer population while ideologically creating a shared space. It is difficult for us to imagine what they looked like, but they certainly were not visible from far away; the term is misleading in itself, as *Feuerwerke* were rather forms of pyrotechnical displays also used inside, e.g. in theaters, functioning like giant birthday cake sparklers, as in the following description:

> *Das ganze Gebäude ward plötzlich auf das stärkste illuminirt und schiene gleichsam mit vielen 1000 Lampen besetzt zu sein, die alle weiß-gelblich brannten, wo dazwischen eine Art von recht gelb brennenden Feuerrädern sich befande.* (K. k. priv. Anzeiger aus den Erblanden. 2. Jg., 24. Heft. Wien 1772. 190f.)

The same principle can be found in the German-speaking commercial theater in Vienna at that time. Places like the *Kärntnertortheater* and later the *Theater an der Wien* established an eclectic tradition of vernacular theater based on pathos and mayhem-filled »blood and thunder« dramas (*Haupt- und Staatsaktionen*), on *commedia dell' arte*, on popular German material and on material derived from the Italian opera, all of which was mobilized by Enlightenment rulers Maria Theresia and Joseph II. in their attempts to establish a »national« theater, smoothing out the rough edges of the tradition while continuing to attract a diverse audience to a playhouse conveniently located within walking distance of the city center. This was done in a pre-enlightened manner through strict social control. Sonnenfels's *Briefe über die Wienerische Schaubühne* (1768) brought the controversy to a head. He demanded that the theater be cleansed of all vulgarities in order to establish a national German theater along the lines of the *comédie française*. He defined the function of theater as neither for the glorification of the ruler nor the amusement of the masses, but rather as an educational institution, a »school of manners, courtesy, and language.« Nothing shows more clearly the constant process of negotiation between an enlightened educational program that is extended to commercial entertainment and popular traditions of entertainment than the repertory of the *Theater an der Wien*. This popularity was by no means frowned upon officially. When bankruptcy of the *Theater an der Wien* was imminent in 1806, Emperor Franz prevented closure, as it provided, according to Yates, the »favorite entertainment of the upper and middle classes, and even the lower classes.« The longest lasting was a monumental melodrama called *Timur the Tartan Chan* (1822). The popularity of parodies in the commercial theaters corroborates the thoroughly mixed nature of the audience and their tastes (at least some of the spectators have to know an original story to appreciate the parody).

Plays written for these theaters relied heavily on illusionism (transformations of scenery and people), lavish sets with splashy fire- and water effects, stage tricks and stage-fights, crowd scenes with a strong emphasis on visual effects, etc. Plays were interspersed with music, gymnasts and dressage riders. These performance aspects remained closely related to other ›popular cultural‹ practices, such as the fireworks staged in the *Prater* and, above all, the circus (at that time basically a show of equestrian artistry). Putting artistic horsemen on the stage had a further equivalent in the equestrian spectacles performed in the *Prater* (de Bach's *Circus gymnasticus*), where artistry was often supplemented with pantomime and presented real competition to the theater. The line between sports and theater was (still) blurred at this point, and the stage spectacles clearly capitalized on this. Equally, fireworks recreated plots from the theater and even classical literature, which also substantiates the close connection between the genres. A firework show in 1796 recreated *Die Leiden des jungen Werthers* (*The Sorrows of Young Werther*) by Goethe, and in 1823, the *Zauberflöte* (*Magic Flute*) was recreated by using puppets and silhouettes.

The court and the official administration embraced and promoted this form of entertainment while at the same time policing and cleansing it – another instance of the (discursive) creation of shared spaces of entertainment at the end of the eighteenth century, spaces which were meant to produce, in the same movement, entertainment, standards of taste, and revenue. Still, this should not be romanticized as a rich unified culture in Williams's/Levine's sense – this discourse was counterbalanced by very real measures of stratification, control and exclusion that defined »shared« in an exclusionary class sense (or *tried to make everybody middle class* in appearance and behavior, but predominantly in taste patterns) while maintaining a social hierarchy.

This period of creating an *officially sanctioned and legitimated* public entertainment culture chronologically coincides with the (brief) emergence of a public culture of open discussion and reasoning towards the end of eighteenth century that bears all the hallmarks of Habermas's liberal public sphere. Widespread literacy and the emergence of a bourgeois reading public were achieved by the well-known reforms of Maria Theresia and Joseph II., reading clubs were formed (Martino 121), and pirate printers like Trattner and Kurzböck, encouraged by official privileges, started their (successful) campaigns to catch up with the north of Germany in regard to literary production. The free enterprise spirit of pirate printing was appreciated widely by travelers from Northern Germany:

> *Jetzt hält man in Oestreich die Buchdruckerey für das, was sie wirklich ist, für eine f r e y e K u n s t, welche durch keine Gebräuche und Förmlichkeiten eingeschränkt werden muß; und für eine höchst nützliche M a n u f a k t u r, welche ein jeder anlegen kann, welcher verstehet, was dazu gehöret, (...) und in der ein jeder arbeiten kann, welcher die dazu nöthige Geschicklichkeit hat. Es wäre sehr zu wünschen, daß es im übrigen Deutschlande auch bis dahin käme, wodurch diese edle Kunst geschwinder sich der weitern Vollkommenheit nähern würde.* (Nicola 461)

Karl von Zahlheim programmatically lays out what kind of institution he has in mind when he became the head of the first Viennese *Lesegesellschaft* in 1776:

> *Es giebt vielleicht keine Anstalt in Deutschland, die zur Verbreitung der Lectur, und zu Einführung eines gesellschaftlicheren Umganges, zwischen Gelehrten und Großen, soviel beytragen könnte als diese. Als ein Ort betrachtet, dessen Öffentlichkeit auf* alle Personen, von einer gewissen Lebensart und Erziehung, aber auch nur auf diese allein *sich erstreckt, der also, für Wien, der Mittelpunkt der guten Gesellschaft, und wegen der vielen Neuigkeiten, die da stäts zusammenfließen, zugleich der angenehmste und unterhaltendste Zusammenkunftsort für alle Stände und Geschlechter werden könnte, von dieser Seite betrachtet, muß das neue Lecturcabinet sich denjenigen vorzüglich empfehlen, die den Mangel eines dergleichen, in jeder großen Stadt, zumal wegen der Fremden so unentbehrliches Ortes, lange schon eingesehen haben.* (Einrichtung des neuen Lecturcabinets zu Wien im Jahr 1776. Nebst einem Angehängten Verzeichniß der vorhandenen Zeitungen, Brochüren und Bücher, Wien, auf Kosten der Impresa; und zu haben bey E.F. Bader, in der Bognergasse, IIIf.)

For a brief period, Vienna became – in the eyes of enlightened liberals, at least – something like a realization of Habermas's utopia. Centers of sociability, e.g. the *Kaffeehauskultur*, provided meeting grounds for the newly rising bourgeoisie and the aristocracy. This is particularly true for the amalgamation of the newly ennobled *Zweite Gesellschaft* (second society) and the upper echelons of the bourgeoisie, whose beginning amalgamation was also manifested by intermarriage and economic relations. However, the reading societies and libraries, as well as the newly dynamic book trade, were soon to become the victims of restrictions of censorship and the pressures of the new autocratic style of rule after 1789/90. Only a few years after the English ambassador had noted (in 1782) that the public culture of coffeeshop discussions in Vienna was equal to London, Ernst Moritz Arndt remarked in his travels in 1798:

> *Es ist unmöglich, daß kraftvolle und schöne Menschen in dem reichsten Lande, unter dem schönsten Himmel, in der Fülle der Vergnügungen und des Lebens, solche Stöcke sein könnten, wenn nicht eine Augenverkleisterung und Stirnbebretterung vorgenommen würde, die sie so weit nur sehen und laufen läßt, wie man gerade will. Hier wäre der Ort, etwas darüber zu sagen, inwiefern eine Regierung und wie weit sie berechtigt sei, in das Gebiet des Geistes einzugreifen und diesem Feuerelement ihr erkaltendes und löschendes Wasser zuzugießen. Es ist unangezweifelt, daß sie den Wiener so am Gängelband führt, daß er das Bewußtsein seiner Kraft verliert und endlich nicht mehr ahnt, daß der Mensch bessere Angelegenheiten habe als Essen und Trinken und Sichschlafenlegen (...) Was würde Wien sein, wenn zu allen seinen Vorzügen noch Geistesfreiheit und Freiheit des Geschmacks hinzukämen, die doch den Menschen erst zum Menschen machen?* (Arndt 228)

The institutions that constitute a public sphere in the Habermasian sense – the coffeehouses, literary circles, masonic lodges and clubs –

did not, as they supposedly did in Germany, erode in the 1860s and 70s. In Austria, they were forcefully, decisively and effectively suppressed immediately after the French Revolution. The case of the other (semi-) public spaces created by the enlightened emperors – the public entertainment culture in the theaters, amusement areas and spectacles – is worth pursuing because it showed a greater resilience at the institutional level.

In these (semi-)public spheres, a spatial separation of social classes occurred only very incompletely, and a sense of sharing space seems to have prevailed. The popularity of the *Prater* continued undiminished:

> *Hier ist eigentlich der Tummelplatz für die bürgerliche Welt und die unteren Volksclassen, welche an Sonntagen und Feyertagen scharenweise das Mittagsmal hier einnehmen, und dann den ganzen Nachmittag unter lautem Freudengefühl zubringen.*
>
> *Die vierte Allee, rechts, ist der Sammelplatz der vornehmen und schönen Welt. Was hierher kommt, kommt meistens in Wagen oder zu Pferde*
>
> (...)
>
> *Alles zusammen, finden sich an schönen Sommertagen immer gegen 12 bis 15.000 Menschen im Prater ein.* (Pezzl 236-7)

It was certainly neither a coincidence that it was the site of the *Weltausstellung* in 1873, nor that its flagship building, the *Rotunde*, actually supplanted the scaffolding used for the display of fireworks. The same discourse is very evident in the descriptions of the *Corso*, the promenading about the *Ringstrasse*, which was opened in 1857 and hailed as a place in which »every branch of society, from the great world, to the demi-monde, to the ›quarter world,‹ as well as the world of diplomacy and the court« was represented (Tissot 202-3, quoted in Olsen 237-8). This is definitely more a claim than reality: Even in this supposedly shared space, the aristocracy retained their privileges in a corner of the *Volksgarten* for which entrance fees had to be paid; and the lower strata of society would rather be found in *Hernals* and the outer suburbs than on the *Ringstrasse*. At this point, clearly, the bourgeoisie had set the tone and had become the normalized »everybody,« the citizenry.

How can this discourse of a public entertainment culture be conceptualized in terms of *Öffentlichkeit*? Is there a connection between the creation of a public entertainment sphere and the creation and/or suppression of a public sphere of rational, political discourse in the Habermasian sense?

The traditional interpretation and notion of the pre-March period in Austrian history actually establishes such a connection by arguing that the *Backhendlzeit* in some mysterious way channeled and morphed the political aspirations of the bourgeoisie into *Biedermeier Gemütlichkeit*, that a spectacular and popular entertainment culture provided a vicarious form of public existence under the conditions of political oppression while at the same time creating a sybaritic, Phaiákan-like image for the city – Vienna became known for the leisure space it provided, and for its »traditional« character. I have never found this smooth line of argumentation very convincing in view of the (apparently sudden and unforeseeable) outbreak of political sentiment in 1848, apart from its tendencies to essentialize mentalities.

The underlying assumptions of such interpretations exhibit a *narrow understanding of the public sphere vis-à-vis the political*, which impedes our understanding of the political implications of public entertainment culture, which was created by a paternalistic regime and which retained its character and appeal in the reactionary days of Metternich's influence. Habermas's public sphere is based on the literary culture of bourgeois associations and reading clubs, but what about, say, the theater? His *idealtypisch* distinction between a literate liberal and an illiterate plebeian public sphere (Habermas 8) can hardly accommodate the stage, which, as a public space, had a much more profound influence in Austria than its short-lived literary clubs. While it is less easy to tie the theater to a public sphere in Habermas's sense, it very clearly provided a meeting place and forum for discussion, definitely for the aristocracy and bourgeoisie, but reaching well into the lower middle classes, a place where space was shared and communication about values took place. Lawrence Levine's claim that »[t]he theater in the first half of the nineteenth century played the role that movies played in the first half of the twentieth: it was a kaleidoscopic, democratic institution presenting a widely varying bill of fare to all classes and socioeconomic groups« (21) draws attention to this characteristic feature while at the same time romanticizing its origin. It seems important to recognize the existence of such a public sphere in order to account for the negotiations of power and hegemony that occurred there.

If we consider the public entertainment sphere not as a complete denial and suppression of political discourse but rather as a forum in which questions of power/ hegemony/ exclusion could be articulated and negotiated, then this could be regarded as precisely the sphere where a political discourse could manifest itself under the conditions of overt repression by articulating itself through questions of taste and value, i.e. through culture.

This must not, however, be mistaken for a romanticized notion of an inherently subversive popular culture. The discourses around a publicly accessible entertainment culture that I have described – being partially paternalistic in origin and socially controlling in intention – are definitely not the organic continuation of a homogeneous and ›grassroots‹ popular culture characterized by resistance and spontaneity (the organic shared culture of Williams and Levine that supposedly became stratified only towards the end of the nineteenth century). Rather, they are discourses that were carefully orchestrated and manipulated in order to create a pseudo-public sphere characterized by a bourgeois (but not liberal) value system fully embraced by the dynasty. The probably clearest manifestation is a picture of Emperor Franz in the circle of his family in bourgeois garb (Fertbauer). But this did not completely block articulations of subversion. The (enlightened, urban) process that created the utopian discourse Habermas invokes when he speaks of the »normative values of rational-critical debate« (McGuigan 176), which he identifies with his vision of the public sphere, that is, a discourse of common accessibility, shared spaces and values, is the same one which also created *Biedermeier* society, negotiated questions of social prestige and hegemony while maintaining the (enlightened/paternalistic) discourse of a public forum for entertainment *and* taste creation – but these necessarily remained fundamentally contradictory negotiations of authority, behavior, taste and participation staged in a public forum.

In the theater, the potential of cultural resistance should not be underestimated despite the fact that censorship was pervasive and the most popular plays very strongly asserted the *status quo* on the content level and thus seem to provide straightforward, escapist entertainment (where good is rewarded, evil is punished and they always live happily ever after, preferably in Vienna, the best of all places in the world.) The *role of fantasy and the fantastic* has to be regarded as a possible key to symbolic forms of resistance in the theater. A world of myth, fairytale and superstition at least questions a unified, rational, and socially controllable subject position (as the Romantics had shown), and this seems to be precisely the form in which it was implemented in the popular theater: playfulness, juxtaposition, heterogeneity, parody, inversion, travesty, gross humor, and self-parody as the dominant formal elements of popular (and court) theater resisted enlightenment reason and the imposition of reflection and contemplation. A form of symbolic resistance can thus be attributed to the possibility of the theater to offer an ongoing challenge to the narrowly conceived forms of reason propagated by the Enlightenment, forms of reason desiring to legislate single standards for culture, and it continued, and continues, to challenge, destabilize, relativize and pluralize single notions of cultural hierarchy.

The plots of most plays of Viennese popular theater are characterized by what structuralists would call a para-tactical nature: the story lines are not linear, but often interrupted, full of reduplications of patterns, often referred to as unintelligible and confused. Inter-textual references to other plays or, indeed, trivial literature (as well as contemporary events) are frequent and transgress a coherent fictional stage universe. It is easy to dismiss such plays as simply badly written, but doubtless they also contain an element of subversion in against the conventions of enlightenment theater and literature. The signifying practice of the theatrical, organized around para-tactical principles, subverts the idea of a unified, disciplined and controllable/controlled spectator-subject and exposes the materiality of its signification as well as the physicality of the performer-spectator relationship (music, incongruities, etc.). The spectators were not allowed to insert themselves into an easily intelligible world created on stage, but were thrown into a universe of signifiers organized along para-tactical principles, a universe in which popular tradition, high culture and travesty all co-exist. This produces, in Roland Barthes's sense, pleasure (*jouissance*), not closure. This is not escapism in the sense of the sentimental novel; the mirages of motifs and plots signify the production of the subject itself. Coherent fictionality, as propagated by the Enlightenment, is the dominant mode of cultural hegemony, providing closure by restoring order to the signifiers mirroring the order of society. This is Althusser's well-known process of interpellation, safeguarding the consistency and continuity of the individual by providing harmony through transparency. Such closure does not need censorship; the coherent universe, not disrupted by comic interludes and parodied morality, is presented as unproblematic, transparent and universal. This is precisely what the theater reformers of the Enlightenment propagated, and this is precisely what failed to be established in Austrian theaters in this period.

The contents of the preferred plays confirm that no matter how commercialized popular theater was, its staple fare, consisting of melodrama, romance, vaudeville, pantomime, fantasy and magic resisted any easy insertion of the audience into ideological patterns ensuring cultural passivity, psychological subjection and social acceptance. It is a discourse that constantly draws attention to its own artificiality.

It takes up traditions from court culture mediated through counterreformation and enlightenment propaganda as well as the popularity of clowns, singers, storytellers and pantomimes (all of which had a commercial interest even in 1500) and blends it into a commercial leisure industry dominated by cartels (like the society of cavaliers) catering for different yet overlapping markets, something that has a tradition itself.

In this sense, commercial theaters in Vienna did not change a paradigm, but rather adapted a popular tradition of interaction with elite culture to a new environment, a new set of cultural, institutional and social contexts. The public entertainment culture and the *literati* reading clubs are both cultural spaces where questions of identity and belonging, as well as difference and hegemony, are negotiated in a cultural field, and their concomitant occurrence should not come as a surprise.

In the specific Austrian case, a (hegemonically imposed) definition of urban community founded on the discourse of a public entertainment sphere was arguably used as a hegemonic attempt to negate precisely those (formal) citizenship rights which have constituted Balibar's (legal) »citizen-subject« since 1789. The discourse of public entertainment created a middle-class audience and standards of taste in an enlightened, rational manner while containing the political implications of citizenship, but it left open a space for subversion in this *culturally* contested territory, for negotiating issues of morality, taste and entertainment in complex processes of cultural and social interaction. Of course, theater in its spectacular form can be seen as an instrument of dominance leading to the de-politization of the masses, in the same way any cultural policy can be traced back to issues of power; of course, it was meant to cover up existing social problems and preclude political unrest, a ritual relief of tension. But it was not exclusively such. It resisted the imposition of taste and education, but also impeded collective political action. It created a universe that censorship could not touch because its application to the sphere of politics was severely limited, but it resisted a socially and politically meaningful imposition of aesthetics as the preferred taste of the dominant classes. The constant presence of the Harlequin-*Kasperl* character acts very much like Groucho Marx in the film *A Night at the Opera*, interrupting the performance of *Il Trovatore* with a rendition of »Take me out to the ball game« – it is the same principle of symbolic resistance through parody and incongruity that does not allow for any closure of meaning and representation. One should, however, beware of overestimating the longevity of carnevalesque traditions in popular theater. The survival of forms of this early modern symbolic system of social utopia and ritualized yet limited topsy-turvy world does not automatically imply that in a quite different social setting its function was also perpetuated in exactly the same manner. It is not the resistance of a genuine, authentic, centuries-old folk tradition that we find in the popular theater, but rather a cultural strategy that lends itself to being employed by the subordinate. *Kasperl* is not *Hanswurst*, Harlequin is not Groucho Marx, and neither of them is a trickster or a court jester, but that does not mean they do not sometimes employ the same strategies of symbolic resistance. Any potential of symbolic resistance is directly linked with the symbolic and cultural forms available in any culture. I do not see an »independent cultural subversive logic of the subordinate« in Bakhtin's sense; neither do I see the full rich life of a pre-industrial culture, in Richard Hoggart's sense, being perverted in a culture written by morons for morons, by transposing a vital rural folk culture into a commercialized urban culture. What I see is a set of cultural symbols taken out of a variety of traditions being negotiated in a period of important social upheaval accompanied by a basically anachronistic regime of power relying mostly on pre-modern methods of domination. (It should not, of course, be implied that these negotiations do not have a political impact, an impact on the legal definitions, rather the opposite: their political component does precisely that. James Donald relates this to the fantasy structure of identification, cf. Donald 100ff.) This cultural tradition contributed to the establishment of the class location of the bourgeoisie in a tradition of de-differentiation which promoted a cultural middle ground outside the regime of cultural values, allowing difference while at the same time containing the dimensions of difference in a pastiche of ›safe,‹ controlled and accessible leisure time activity.

In this sense, I would argue with Robert Isherwood (161) for the existence of a common culture of entertainment, not, however, as a form of counterculture but rather as an *officially sanctioned site for negotiations of power and hegemony*. Imposed entertainment and enlightened reasoning can be seen as part of the same process of public negotiation that is informed by patterns of hegemony in the construction of dominance and exclusion and the containment of subversion. The public entertainment culture emerges as the flip side of (and necessary contribution to) the emergence of a (bourgeois) public sphere. This could be seen as the background of an *always-already established nexus between »public« and »entertainment«*; yet it also points to the necessity of addressing issues of hegemony in singling out the uneasy tensions existing in these public entertainment cultures between the discourse/rhetoric of ›common‹ culture (that makes it consumable), the desires articulated and the actual cultural practices that keep out the undesirables and make it accessible only to certain social strata. In this tension, we might also locate the subversive and emancipatory potential of such a shared culture.

I would venture the guess that Habermas cannot recognize this nexus because his utopian vision of a liberal public sphere conflates legal and cultural definitions that elide (or fundamentally misrecognize) the heterogeneity of a democratic public in the urban sphere – his artificial dichotomy between liberal and plebeian is indicative of his positioning himself as a liberal bourgeois. The revealing formula »Das sogenannte Freizeitverhalten ist apolitisch schon deshalb, weil es, in den Kreislauf von Produktion und Konsum einbezogen, eine vom unmittelbar Lebensnotwendigen emanzipierte Welt nicht zu konstituieren vermag« (194) epitomizes his approach. It's as simple as that for Habermas – politics in his sense are not constituted by cultural negotiations, but by pure *Geist*.

The rowdy, noisy and socially diverse theater and spectacle audiences are not the male liberal subjects of learned clubs, yet they are closer to a democratic public sphere that consists of negotiations between culturally diverse people in urban spaces, who make use of this space (among others) to negotiate their socially stratified and diverse identities and forms of living together *in difference*, difference that Habermas cannot, or does not want to, see. His rationally communicative liberal subjects are culturally as well as legally determined. »Habermas is still trying to give the legal *status* of citizenship a cultural *identity*. ... He knows that *Gesellschaft* is all there is or should be, but he still wants it to feel like *Gemeinschaft*« (Donald 98).

I would therefore suggest an alternative mode of thinking this public sphere through a cultural identity and legal status that *do not overlap*. This could be what James Donald calls, in his own utopia, »the *republican* city, the city which... has been supposed to provide the forum for debates about what constitutes the good life and the non-violent resolution of conflicts arising from the sheer difficulty of people living together in the shared space of the city« (96). The concept and rhetoric of a public entertainment sphere – and the apparent necessity of creating, promoting and policing it in an urban context – accommodates this notion of the necessity of negotiating diverse (socially determined) identities while acknowledging the existence of structures of hegemony and power.

Maybe we are not at the end of history, where corporations have finally taken over culture and produced the global hegemony that was always inherent in capitalism. If the idea of public culture has always been a highly contested discourse, it is important to describe the parameters of this discourse as implemented in specific historical moments and spaces. The post-industrial city as an entertainment hub could be connected to this public entertainment sphere that was, in a *bürgerliche Gesellschaft*, always part of identity formation and the communication process.

REFERENCES

Arndt, Ernst Moritz. *Sehnsucht nach der Ferne. Die Reise nach Wien und Venedig*. Berlin, 1988 (1798).

Balibar, Etienne. »Citizen-Subject.« *Who Comes after the Subject?* Eds. Eduardo Cadava, Peter Connor and Jean-Luc Nancy. London: Routledge, 1991.

Donald, James. *Imagining the Modern City*. Minneapolis: University of Minnesota Press, 1999.

Fertbauer, Leopold. *Familienbild des Kaiserhauses um den Herzog von Reichstadt*. Vienna: Museum der Stadt Wien, 1826.

Habermas, Jürgen. *Strukturwandel der Öffentlichkeit: Untersuchungen zu einer Kategorie der bürgerlichen Gesellschaft*. Sammlung Luchterhand; 25. [17., Aufl.] ed. Darmstadt: Luchterhand, 1987 (1962).

Hannigan, John. *Fantasy City: Pleasure and Profit in the Postmodern Metropolis*. New York: Routledge, 1998.

Horak, Roman et. al, eds. *Metropole Wien: Texturen der Moderne*. Vienna: wuv, 2000.

Isherwood, Robert. *Farce and Fantasy: Popular Entertainment in Eighteenth-Century Paris*. New York: Oxford University Press, 1986.

Leach, William R. *Land of Desire: Merchants, Power, and the Rise of a New American Culture*. New York: Pantheon Books, 1993.

Levine, Lawrence W. *Highbrow/Lowbrow: The Emergence of Cultural Hierarchy in America*. Cambridge, Mass.: Harvard University Press, 1988.

Lotz, Arthur. *Das Feuerwerk, seine Geschichte und Bibliographie*. Leipzig, 1940.

Martino, Alberto. »›Lekturkabinette‹« und Leihbibliotheken in Wien (1772-1848).« *Die Österreichische Literatur. Ihr Profil an der Wende vom 18. zum 19. Jahrhundert (1750-1830)*. Ed. Herbert Zeman. Vol. 1. Graz, 1979.

McGuigan, Jim. *Culture and the Public Sphere*. London: Routledge, 1996.

Müller, Britta. *Die beliebtesten und meistbesuchten Spektakelveranstaltungen Wiens im 18. und 19. Jahrhundert sowie Spektakelstücke am Theater an der Wien im 19. Jahrhundert*. MA Thesis. University of Vienna, 1992.

Nicola, Friedrich. *Beschreibung einer Reise durch Deutschland und die Schweiz, im Jahre 1781. Nebst Bemerkungen über Gelehrsamkeit, Industrie, Religion und Sitten*. Vol. 4. Berlin; Stettin, 1784.

Olsen, Donald J. *The City as a Work of Art: London, Paris, Vienna*. New Haven: Yale University Press, 1986.

Pezzl, Johann. *Beschreibung der Haupt- und Residenzstadt Wien*. Wien, 1820.

Schwartz, Vanessa R. *Spectacular Realities: Early Mass Culture in Fin-De-Siècle Paris*. Berkeley; Los Angeles; London: University of California Press, 1998.

Snyder, Robert W. *The Voice of the City: Vaudeville and Popular Culture in New York*. New York: Oxford University Press, 1989.

Tissot, Victor. *Vienne et la Viennoise*. 19th ed. E. Dentu, 1878.

Weinstein, R. M. »Disneyland and Coney Island: Reflections on the Evolution of the Modern Amusement Park.« *Journal of Popular Culture* 26 (1992): 131-64.

Yates, W. E. *Theatre in Vienna: A Critical History, 1776-1995*. New York: Cambridge University Press, 1996.

Public Entertainment in Nineteenth-Century London

SUSAN INGRAM

In May 1901, the following advertisement appeared in *The Era*:

> Stafford & CO. Theatrical Printers. Netherfield, Nottingham. Have a large and varied stock of Pictorials suitable for the following – Dramas. Comedies and Farcical Comedies. Burlesques and Comic Operas. Comic Scenes and Dancers. Ladies' Heads and Figures, Pierrots and Pierrettes, Circuses, Acrobats. Menageries. Music Halls. Cinematographs. War. Magicians. Ventriloquists. Dioramas. Ghosts. Minstrelsy. etc. Illustrated lists post-free. Courteous attention to all enquiries. Letterpress Posters and Window Bills effectively displayed and promptly executed. Write for estimates. (Haill 12)

Citing this list in the introduction to *Fun Without Vulgarity: Victorian and Edwardian Popular Entertainment Posters*, Catherine Haill finds that it »exhaustively covers all types of theatrical entertainment in demand in 1901, the year Queen Victoria died and Edward VII came to the throne« (13). In *Popular Culture: The Metropolitan Experience*, Iain Chambers charts the rise of British popular urban culture through the nineteenth and twentieth centuries by studying »popular culture's central role in the making of urban culture as a whole« (18). »Popular entertainment,« »theatrical entertainment,« »popular culture,« »urban culture,« »mass culture« – these categories have been mobilized in attempts to capture something about the very substantial changes which occurred in nineteenth-century British leisure practices and to articulate them to larger contexts of industrialization and urbanization.[1] Categories such as »popular culture« and »theatrical entertainment« set particular methodological trajectories which have tended to preclude the interrogation of cultural practices and venues in which meanings are contested and negotiated as to their possible public sphere functions. »Public sphere« discourse in the Habermasian tradition, on the other hand, as Reisenleitner details in the preceding article on the construction of a public entertainment sphere in nineteenth-century Vienna, is also inadequate to the complicated social, commercial, educational and political workings of specific public entertainments. How can we think a public entertainment sphere »through a cultural identity and legal status that do not overlap« (p. 29 in this volume)? How can »the concept and rhetoric of a public entertainment sphere – and the apparent necessity of creating, promoting and policing it in an urban context – accommodate this notion of the necessity of negotiating diverse (socially determined) identities while acknowledging the existence of structures of hegemony and power« (ibid.)? The following account will chart a terrain of public, as opposed to popular or theatrical, entertainment in nineteenth-century London and in doing so will draw attention to how such a concept allows one to attend to processes of identity construction in hegemonic fields.

Key to the developments in nineteenth-century London is the emergence of the working-class and working-class culture. E.P. Thompson has shown in *The Making of the Working Class* how »in the years between 1780 and 1832 most English working people came to feel an identity of interests as between themselves, and as against their rulers and employers« (11) and how the working-class presence came by 1832 to be »the most significant factor in British political life« (12). It is not, as Chambers spells out, that the Victorian upper and middle classes were not affected by urban change; however, they »remained largely protected from the direct impact of industrialism and the wrenching forces of city life« (30), whereas the working classes and urban poor had no such buffers:

> It was their culture that was forced to change, and often dramatically. It was they, in particular, who most keenly felt the full and novel impact of capitalism, industry, and urban living. Unprotected by wealth or property, and sucked in by economic forces and daily needs, these were ›the people‹ who had to make Britain's towns and cities ›habitable by their own efforts.‹ (Hobsbawn 1969, 87; quoted in Chambers, 30)

As a result, an important gap opened up between the more prosperous classes, who for the most part vacated the urban morass for the purity of the countryside, and the poor they left behind, and in their cultures:

> The limited overlap and reciprocity between the lives of the eighteenth-century gentry and plebeian culture at the markets, fêtes, festivals and village rites that had once punctuated the rural and pre-industrial urban calendar had now disappeared. A *sharp geographical and social separation* between different cultures was literally mapped out along the streets and districts of nineteenth-century urbanization. Official culture was publicly limited to the rhetoric of monuments in the centre of town: the university, the museum, the theatre, the concert hall; otherwise it was reserved for the private space of the Victorian resi-

> dence or the separate sports and pursuits of leafy suburbia. (Chambers 30, italics added)

Separation need not imply a lack of contact, as Chambers seems to suggest. Indeed, it is precisely the *Reibungspunkte* between these different cultures – the spaces and spheres of contact in which conflicts could be played out – the description and analysis of which can reveal the structures and identities Reisenleitner argues are integral to identifying the potential of a public entertainment sphere. It will behoove this study to detail the contexts of three sites in which nineteenth-century Londoners rubbed shoulders, or tried not to, and to show the types of conflicts that resulted from such contact, or the pains and procedures to which people went to avoid it. In the first section, the streets of London are examined and a conflict between prosperous property owners and itinerant, foreign street musicians explored to reveal the social and legal mechanisms by which class boundaries were regulated and reinforced; in the second, the concomitant decline of the pleasure garden tradition and rise of music hall is pursued in order to detail the processes by which increasingly privatized commercial entertainment practices helped to structure and segregate people in line with increasing economic discrepancies; and in the third, the Crystal Palace is approached as a site of public entertainment and arguments given as to why it could be considered the first theme park. In all three cases, in contrast to the situation in Vienna (or later New York), where the public entertainment sphere could claim a class-transcending function (however spurious), in London class never ceased to matter, and never ceased to structure, form, inform and deform the identificatory practices which increasingly impeded its citizens from seeing themselves as such.

TAKING IT TO THE STREETS

One was liable to come across the oddest of sights, sounds and smells in the crowded, chaotic streets of nineteenth-century London, but the one group found to be particularly objectionable and disturbing, and which caused for the greatest public furor, was not the elephants or dancing bears, the Punch & Judy shows, the little matchstick girls or the pickpockets. It was the street musicians of foreign origin.

The chapter on »›The transparent object of begging‹ on trial« in David Cohen's *The Buskers* offers a detailed account of such a conflict between a well-educated, literary-minded, English property-owner and a »violent« Italian organ-grinder:

> A barrister, J.F. Stanford, was at home in Langham Place, in Marylebone, engaged in literary occupation, when Capatali's organ disturbed him. Capatali left when Stanford asked him to, but reappeared on the other side of the house. Stanford asked a constable to arrest the Italian, who grew violent. The following day in court, the magistrate Mr. Know conceded that Stanford had given a reasonable cause to ask Capatali to go away, but ruled that, as the prisoner had been sitting on his organ, and not playing it, when the constable arrived, he had been wrongfully arrested. Mr. Knox said the correct procedure would have been for Stanford to have taken out a summons against Capatali. He discharged the prisoner, but granted a summons against him. When Capatali reappeared he was acquitted because he had been wrongfully arrested, and Stanford was persuaded to withdraw his charge, as he was himself liable to a charge of wrongfully giving into custody. Mr. Knox sympathized with Stanford's case, and actually wrote to Sir Richard Mayne [Chief Commissioner of Police], asking for a plainclothes policeman to be stationed in Langham Place, to get round the loophole of the offence's needing to be in view of a police officer. Despite this preferential treatment, Stanford gained little satisfaction from the whole affair. In May 1864 he wrote to Bass [Michael T. Bass MP, who was leading a campaign against street music at the time]:
>
> After Antonio Capatali's case, I had a little respite from these abominable organ grinders. They have begun again, however. On Monday, before twelve o'clock, I had three organ-men, besides a brass band of five German lads, whose instruments were all out of tune.
>
> Stanford subsequently obtained a warrant for the arrest of Carlo Congini, but he could not be traced. It was often the case that the padrone would send an organ grinder on the country tramp for a while if he had been in trouble. (145-7)

This passage reveals that there was at the time considerable sympathy in at least some quarters of English society for its lesser off members, and one need not search far for confirmation of this sentiment. Thomson and Smith's 1877 *Street Life in London with permanent photographic illustrations taken from life expressly for this publication* provides the context of the above incident from the organ-grinder's point of view:

> The Italian, therefore, migrates with the knowledge that he may rely on the generosity of the English and that, if he only receives as such as many of the English poor, he may hope to save enough to buy himself a farm in his own country. They arrive, therefore, in shoals, and seeing how their presence is appreciated, do not realize the somewhat humiliating character of their avocation. Many, on the contrary, proudly claim a right to be ranked above the mendicant class. They urge, and to a certain extent justly, that they are of use to the community; that, as a rule, their performance, whether with the barrel organ, the piano-organ, the harp, fiddle, or other instrument, gratifies the majority of their hearers, and propagates the love for music among the poor. The only difference, so far as the political economy of the case is concerned, between them and actors and professional singers is the fact that they impose themselves on

> the public by performing in the street, and have to solicit, cap in hand, their reward. Otherwise, they argue, that they simply cater for the public amusement; that if their performance is of a very inferior character to what may be heard in concert-rooms or theatres, they consequently receive very inferior pay. ... The wealthy prefer to hear Italian singers instead of English vocalists at the great opera houses; why should not the poor display a similar unpatriotic predilection for the merry Southerner who plays the harp or grinds an organ in the street? Just as in the higher class of art the Italians excel, so also in the more modest street performances do they attract more applause. (85)

While this passage might at first appear to substantiate Chamber's claim that the »sharp geographical and social separation between different cultures [was] literally mapped out along the streets and districts of nineteenth-century urbanization,« its nationalistic argument undercuts the separation by drawing a polemical parallel between performances »at the great opera houses« and those »in the street,« arguing that the Italians who perform in the streets are responding to the same type of demands and desires as those in higher class venues. Further, it turns attention to the nature of the musicians' audiences. While »the majority of their hearers« may have been poor, not all were. Forced to perform in the fluid, heterogeneous space of the streets, these musicians were also necessarily forced to »impose themselves« on at least some the public, as it was a heterogeneous public, a minority of whom undoubtedly felt imposed upon, preferring to consume such entertainment in the regulated, sanitized space of the opera houses and to view streets that could not be adequately regulated as a mere conduit between controlled enclaves of propriety.

At stake in this conflict is not only a form of class conflict but also the issue of how that conflict was policed. Who had jurisdiction of the streets? It is evident from the case of Stanford vs. Capatali that the latter enjoyed considerable »loopholes« in the English law governing such instances. The Metropolitan Police Act of 1839 stipulated the terms according to which street musicians were to be dealt:

> That it shall be lawful for any householder within the Metropolitan Police District personally, or by his servant, or by any police constable, to require any street musician to depart from the neighbourhood of the house of such householder on account of illness of any inmate of such house; or of other reasonable cause; and that every person who shall sound or play upon any musical instrument in any thoroughfare near any house, after being to required to depart, shall be liable to a penalty of not more than forty shillings, and in default of payment to be imprisoned for any period not exceeding one month.

As Cohen notes, there were several drawbacks to the wording of the Act:

> Firstly, the word ›thoroughfare‹ excluded such places as mews or cul-de-sacs from the protection of the law. Secondly, the phrase ›other reasonable cause‹ was in effect worthless. In 1859 Sir Richard Mayne, Chief Commissioner of Police, sent out an order to superintendents, by which constables were forbidden to act against a street musician if any other reason besides illness was given. If a householder had another ›reasonable cause,‹ the constable was to report to the police station, and take advice from an inspector or superintendent. By the time any decision could be taken, the busker could be miles away. A third drawback was that only a householder could make an objection against a busker. Finally, for an arrest to be made, a busker had to play within view of a policeman, after a householder had once asked him, for a reasonable cause, to stop. So all a musician had to do was to stop playing when a policeman was fetched, and nothing could be done to him. (145)

This law would appear to have been designed to provide protection for the weaker members of society and, indeed, Bass's campaign in the 1860s to change the law and make it tougher on the street musicians received the support of many eminent Victorians. One letter he received read:

> Your correspondents are, all, professors and practitioners of one or other of the arts or sciences. In their devotion to their pursuits – tending to the peace and comfort of mankind – they are daily interrupted, harassed, worried, wearied, driven nearly mad, by street musicians. They are even made especial objects of persecution by brazen performers on brazen instruments, beaters of drums, grinders of organs, bangers of banjos, clashers of cymbals, worriers of fiddles, and bellowers of ballads; for, no sooner does it become known to those producers of horrible sounds that any of your correspondents have particular need of quiet in their own houses, than the said houses are beleaguered by discordant hosts seeking to be bought off. (cited in Cohen, 148)

The letter was signed by Charles Dickens, Alfred Tennyson, John Everett Millais, W. Holman Hunt, and Wilkie Collins, among others. These protests went for all intents and purposes for naught. When Bass's street music bill passed in July 1864, to *Punch*'s great delight, all that was changed was the means of arrest:

> ... it shall be lawful for any constable belonging to the Metropolitan Police Force to take into custody without warrant any person who shall offend as aforesaid, provided that he shall be given into custody by the person making the charge and provided also that the person making a charge for an offence against the Act shall accompany the constable who shall take into custody any person offending as aforesaid to the nearest police station-house, and there sign the charge sheet kept for the purpose.

Cohen focuses on the class aspect of this battle and reads in the denouement a »real triumph... for democracy«: »Street music has been spared because enough people liked it to make a sufficient opposition to the self-important grandees« (153-4). While this is undoubtedly the case, the very fact of, and the location of, the battle go under-explored. This law also served to establish and legalize boundaries between private and public property by insisting on public (i.e. court) jurisdiction over public spaces, such as streets. Parliament proved unwilling to allow the privileged, property-owning classes untrammeled rule of the streets outside their property, taking action to guarantee that the streets remained an equal access *public* entertainment sphere.

The extent of that access is detailed in Henry Mayhew's influential *London Labour and the London Poor; A Cyclopaedia of the Condition and Earnings of Those that Will work, those that Cannot work, and those that Will not work.* On the basis of a bewilderingly elaborate series of personal interviews, Mayhew compiled »a cyclopaedia of the industry, the want, and the vice of the great Metropolis« (Preface 1), a Foucauldian classification scheme that details the tremendous range of diverse activities which took place in the streets of mid-nineteenth-century London. Section iv on Street-Performers, for example, is divided into seven sub-sections:

1. The Street-Performers, who admit of being classified into (a) mountebanks – or those who enact puppet-shows, as Punch and July, the fantoccini, and the Chinese shades. (b) The street-performers of feats of strength and dexterity – as ›acrobats‹ or posturers, ›equilibrists‹ or balancers, stiff and bending tumblers, jugglers, conjurors, sword-swallowers, ›salamanders‹ or fire-eaters, swordsmen, etc. (c) The street-performers with trained animals – as dancing dogs, performing monkeys, trained birds and mice, cats and hares, sapient pigs, dancing bears, and tame camels. (d) The street-actors – as clowns, ›Billy Barlows,‹ ›Jim Crows,‹ and others.
2. The Street Showmen, including shows of (a) extraordinary persons – as giants, dwarfs, Albinoes, spotted boys, and pig-faced ladies. (b) Extraordinary animals – as alligators, calves, horses and pigs with six legs or two heads, industrious fleas, and happy families. (c) Philosophic instruments – as the microscope, telescope, thaumascope. (d) Measuring-machines – as weighing, lifting, measuring, and striking machines; and (e) miscellaneous shows – such as peep-shows, glass ships, mechanical figures, wax-work shows, pugilistic shows, and fortune-telling apparatus.
3. The Street-Artists – as black profile-cutters, blind paper-cutters, ›screevers‹ or draughtsmen in coloured chalks on the pavement, writers without hands, and readers without eyes.

4. The Street Dancers – as street Scotch girls, sailors, slack and tight rope dancers, dancers on stilts, and comic dancers.
5. The Street Musicians – as the street bands (English and German), players of the guitar, harp, bagpipes, hurdy-gurdy, dulcimer, musical bells, cornet, tom-tom, etc.
6. The Street Singers, as the singers of glees, ballads, comic songs, nigger melodies, psalms, serenaders, reciters, and improvisatori.
7. The Proprietors of Street Games, as swings, highflyers, roundabouts, puff-and darts, rifle shooting, down the dolly, spin-'em-rounds, prick the garter, thimble rig, etc.

The conditions under which these performers lived, and their social status, can be gleaned from the manner in which Mayhew presents his interviewees and from the unique value he saw in his research:

> It [this book] is curious, moreover, as supplying information concerning a large body of persons, of whom the *public* had less knowledge than of the most distant tribes of the earth – the government population returns not even numbering them among the inhabitants of the kingdom; and as adducing facts so extraordinary, that the traveler in the undiscovered country of the poor must, like Bruce, until his stories are corroborated by after investigators, be content to lie under the imputation of telling such tales, as travelers are generally supposed to delight in. (Preface 1, italics added)

Street life was something exotic for Mayhew and his public, and as he makes clear, only rarely did this faraway land fall within the grasp of the long arm of the however well-intentioned law. Nonetheless, when it did, as we have seen in this section, the streets proved a site governed by fairness and humanitarianism, in which citizenship or even literacy had little place. For most of their inhabitants, the streets were to be survived; »Mayhew makes it clear that even in the best of times making a living on the streets was an uncertain and unrewarding business. ›It's only another way of starving,‹ says one of his informants‹« (Richards 41). Because of the enormity of the power discrepancies between »the majority« who sought and provided entertainment in the streets and those with property who could afford to seek it elsewhere, the danger of the streets becoming the kind of public entertainment sphere which enables political engagement was remote. If, as Gareth Stedman Jones argues and which will be discussed in the second part of the next section, music hall provided a »culture of consolation« (79), the law permitted the streets of nineteenth-century London to remain what we could consider in the same vein a »space of consolation.«

NEVER ON A SUNDAY: FROM PLEASURE GARDENS TO MUSIC HALL

In 1842, a citizen of London felt compelled to write a twenty-four page pamphlet to the Right Honourable Sir Robert Peel, Bart. &c&c&c. on the necessity of protecting places of public entertainment from persecution by restricting and defining the power of magistrates:

> Not only are musical and other performances, and exhibitions and spectacles of every description, strictly forbidden [on Sunday], but public libraries, museums, and other places which not only possess the negative merit of being perfectly harmless to morality and religion, but are also useful and instructive in a high degree, are also rigorously closed. How far such legislation as this may tend to uphold the dignity of the law, and incline the multitude to honour and revere the wisdom and goodness of their rulers, I do not pretend to determine, or to discuss: but, in the name of the great body of my fellow citizens, I do earnestly protest against any further encroachments upon that liberty which, as Englishmen, we have been taught to consider our birth-right. There are now, in the Metropolis – the very heart of the Empire – projects on foot, which, if carried into effect, would make us the laughing-stock, instead of the ›admiration,‹ of the world; and instead of being, as Napoleon designated us, ›a nation of shop keepers,‹ we should be degraded to the condition of a nation of Mawworms. Not contented with conspiring to deprive us of innocent, healthy, and cheap excursions in the Chelsea and other steamers, and putting their veto upon railways and all other public conveyances, the puritanical crusaders are now intriguing and tampering with the licencing Magistrates, to induce them to close all tea gardens and other respectable places of resort, to the hundreds of thousands who are in the habit of frequenting them; and it is with surprise, not unmixed with alarm, that I perceive they have already succeeded. (6-7)

As in the previous example in defense of the Italian street-musicians, a nationalistically formulated argument here draws revealing parallels, in this case among the varied forms of weekend leisure which provide a necessary respite for »the hundreds of thousands« of »fellow citizens,« who had come to regard such liberties their »birth-right.« On the basis of his eloquence, rhetorical strategies and long-windedness, the letter-writer might very well have a background in law. He argues persuasively, and at great length, on primarily two levels: one addressing the legal status of those to be deprived of public leisure space by the proposed legislation and one addressing their moral status:

> [D]iscontent should never be needlessly created in *the people*. The crowds that are conveyed in steamers, up and down the Thames, or traveling in various conveyances on the roads, or walking through the fields to taverns and tea gardens, on a Sunday, *are not the mob* or canaille of London – *they are our fellow citizens*, and the females are their wives and daughters: the very circumstance of their going out only on a Sunday is a satisfactory proof of their prudence

> and industrious habits. ... The Sunday promenaders and occasional visitors to taverns in and about London are more than a million in number; and if they are to be deprived of their liberty by the fiat of a clique of obscure individuals, the consequences must be general discontent, darkening into indignation, and preparing the mind to imbibe the poison of blasphemy and sedition which intrudes itself under a thousand aspects of all sides. ... You would have the glory of seeing inscribed over the gates of our taverns ›Deus nobis haec otia fecit.‹ (22-4, italics added)

The temperance movement's zealous attempts to regulate the public sphere of Sunday leisure are thus dismantled on their own terms:

> Pleasant taverns and gardens, and cheap conveyances on a Sunday are perfectly consistent with pure Christianity; and the public cannot be coercively excluded from them, without violating that spirit of tolerance and forbearance which adorns the Christian faith, and causing great discontent and discouragement among the well disposed of the industrious classes. The only restraint which it is necessary, or in any respect desirable to put upon places of public amusement, is the prohibition of all presentations and representations that are not strictly and unimpeachably moral. (18)

The anonymous letter-writer, who signs his epistle »Your humble, but very faithful servant, a Citizen of London,« goes on to quote St. Paul (Rom. C. xiv) and translates a passage from the Henriade, chant 2 on the St. Bartholomew massacre to show that: »History has recorded no instance of rampant bigots showing mercy to their subdued victims« (21). The temperance movement might shut down libraries, museums and steamers, but threaten the tea gardens, taverns and other refreshment facilities, and they become »rampant bigots« of the worst sort.

Nineteenth-century London tea gardens and taverns bear little resemblance to the establishments now graced with these labels. While one would be hard pressed to find a tavern today possessing of a bowling-green or »gardens where tea could be had,« these were once common features of such establishments (Chancellor 373):

> All over London, during the earlier half of the last century, were scattered a number of these pleasure gardens, all of which had more or less a resemblance to each other, in that they were places where people could lounge about, partake of refreshment, and often ›assist,‹ in the French sense of the word, at such entertainments as were provided by the proprietor; sometimes in the form of ballets, music, pantomimes on a restricted scale, balloon ascents, tight-rope dancing, conjuring, and so forth. They formed, indeed, open-air equivalents to the variety shows of to-day [1925]; but many of them were of so subsidiary a character as really to be little more than adjuncts to the taverns with which they were generally connected. (412)

Chancellor gives as examples of such places: the Sir Hugh Myddelton's Head, near Sadler's Wells; the Mermaid, at Hackney, which had a regular assembly room and where balloon ascents were a feature; the so-called Weston's Retreat, in Kentish Town, which posed as a miniature Cremorne, became a nuisance to the neighborhood, and was finally absorbed, in the 1860s, by the Midland Railway; Chalk Farm, where pony-racing and rifle-shooting took place, and whose original tavern was demolished in 1853; the Eel-Pie House, Highbury, noted for its wrestling-matches, dog-fights, and rat-killing matches, which differentiated it from many of its congeners, although people resorted there to eat the eel-pies for which it was, at least locally, famous; and the Panarmonion Gardens, at Battle Bridge, King's Cross, which contained a »Suspension Railway« (412).

These »pleasure gardens« or »pleasure haunts« were remnants of a form of recreation dating back to the Tudors, which peaked in the eighteenth century and coasted through the nineteenth. Such illustrious places as Paris Gardens, Ranelagh, Vauxhall and Sadler's Wells catered to »the varied permutations of the same instinct on the part of the Londoner to take his [sic] pleasure out of doors« (192). While pleasure gardens gravitated towards the city's outskirts due to the rapid increase in building development in London in the first half of the nineteenth century (the relocation of the Crystal Palace to Sydenham after the Great Exhibition is a later example of this trend), the century's most renowned one, Cremorne, remained in its original house and grounds in Chelsea »on the banks of the Thames, slightly to the west of Battersea Bridge« from its opening in 1832 until a renewal of its licence was refused on October 5, 1877 (Chancellor 397). Cremorne offers us an example of how such nineteenth-century spaces functioned as providers of public entertainment and how they were increasingly contested and taken over by a not-so-silent moral minority, which wanted them sanitized as part of its attempt to isolate itself from undesirable, threatening elements in society, a move similar to concomitant processes of suburbanization.

The anonymous letter-writer previously cited who peopled his leisure tableau with »fellow citizens« was accurate. This tradition of public entertainment was for the most part open to large cross-sections of Londoners. Of one such garden, Bagnigge Wells east of Gray's Inn Road, Chancellor writes:

> It need hardly be said that in a resort such as this, where all classes mixed together, and the dame from Cheapside brushed shoulders with the high-born lady from St. James's, the member of White's with the ›cit‹ from the Minories, the young girl fresh from the paternal acres in Shropshire with the sempstress and mantua-maker from Whitechapel and the Seven Dials, there mingled oth-

ers who came for purposes of their own, and the pickpocket of both sexes, and the lady of easy ethics from Whetstone Park were to be found plying their varied trades. The notorious ›Sixteen String‹ Jack Rann appeared here in a dress as audacious as his manner, and as he flaunted his scarlet coat, tambour-waistcoat and laced hat, he no doubt little thought that in the space of four months he would be hanging from Tyburn Tree. But even on this occasion he ran a risk of his life, for he is said to have behaved so badly that some outraged gentleman threw him out of one of the windows of the Great Room. (391)

BAGNIGGE WELLS
THE LONG ROOM

(*The Pleasure Haunts of London during Four Centuries*, 1925)

Aside from the frighteningly determinative nature of place and the insistently place-bound form of identification in this passage, it also indicates the way appropriate levels of behavior were negotiated by patrons. The appeal of pleasure gardens, as Neil Harris has also noted, lay to a definite extent in »the atmosphere of (controlled) risk they contained, the casual and unpredictable encounters they offered« (20). This was also true of Cremorne. One visitor described its crowd in 1857 as follows:

Cremorne was never able to parade in the newspapers that array of fashionable and distinguished personages who ›last night visited Vauxhall.‹ It was not, for one thing, a place that ladies (in the strict sense of the word) were in the habit of visiting, unless perhaps (as Mr. Sala puts it) ›in disguise and on the sly,‹ or, at any rate, under the safe conduct of a husband, or a brother. Ladies of some sort were, no doubt, considerably in evidence there, though we are not to think of Cremorne as so entirely given over to ›drink, dancing, and devilry,‹ as its sterner critics declared. If it was a place for the man about town, it also attracted a number of worthy citizens and country cousins who went there for an evening's pleasure with their wives and daughters, and were ›not particular.‹ A livelier element was imported by the medical student – a high-spirited race made responsible in those days for the sins of many non-medical

> youngsters – by Oxonians and Cantabs, by temporarily irresponsible clerks and shopmen, and ›flash‹ personages of various kinds. (cited in Chancellor, 402-3)

»Drink, dancing, and devilry« hardly does justice to the types of entertainment available at Cremorne; however, it does capture, in a kind of rallying cry, the nature of the threat it was perceived by temperance types to represent.

While dancing was indeed »the chief end and aim of the majority« of Cremorne's patrons, Chancellor reports: »I have been told by those who knew the place that it was ›the thing‹ not to indulge in this till after the fireworks had been let off« (400), hinting at a wide scope of pre-dance amusements. The grounds themselves covered some twelve acres »abutted on the river and on the King's Road« (399), allowing visitors to arrive by steamboat, coach or foot. There were tree-lined allées to stroll and a shooting butt for target practice:

> In the grounds was an immense orchestra, something on the lines of that at Vauxhall, and around it a vast circular dancing platform, on which gentlemen in frock-coats and top-hats, and ladies in crinolines and coal-scuttle bonnets, may be seen gyrating in a print published in 1847.
>
> On the left of the main entrance was a Pagoda of immense proportions, and elsewhere, dotted about among the trees, were buildings of a kind familiar to habitués of exhibitions of a later date, refreshment rooms, kiosks, bandstands, temples, Swiss châlets and such-like adjuncts. ...

CREMORNE
THE BANQUETING HALL
ABOUT 1845

(*The Pleasure Haunts of London during Four Centuries*, 1925)

> Among other attractions was a piece of water; and the more sophisticated found a circus and a theatre, and a miniature play-house where marionettes, introduced in 1852, disported themselves and were a favourite show. (399-400)

Cremorne usually opened around 3 or 4 pm, and suppers were available for two shillings and sixpence. While fireworks were a crowd favorite, special entertainments were constantly being arranged for the ever so modern pleasure-seeking attendees:

> Now it was an Aquatic Tournament, or a Naval Fête; anon ›the Italian Salamander,‹ as he was called, emulated Shadrech and his companions in passing through a fiery furnace unharmed; sometimes special balloon ascents were organized, and it was from that the veteran Green made his 365th ascent, on August 2, 1847; one, too, in 1852, a Madame Poitevin went up seated on a heifer, as Green had done, at Vauxhall, on a pony two years earlier; but in the latter instance the magistrates interfered and stopped future performances of a live character. ...
>
> For those who preferred theatrical entertainment the playhouse offered farces and vaudevilles and ballets; while in the concert-room popular singers, such as Samuel Cowell, Robert Glindon and Jack Sharp performed between 1846 and 1850; and the eccentric Herr von Joel ranged the gardens and turned up in unexpected places, giving his curious vocal imitations or yodelling, which at first produced a sensation, but from over-repetition finally only a sensation of boredom. (401-2)

This great range of activity continued through the 1860s when it was managed by a well-known impresario who:

> inaugurated his management by presenting to an astonished public the lady (Selina Young) known as ›the female Blondin,‹ who was billed to cross the Thames on a tight rope. She had partially done so, in the presence of a vast crowd, when it was found that some ruffian had cut the guy-ropes, and she was only saved from falling into the river by the presence of mind with which she caught hold of the rope and gradually lowered herself into a boat. ... Still other attractions, organized by the resourceful manager, were the Man Frog, and the Beckwith family in their natatory exhibitions; and the captive balloon in which anyone who was ready to pay ten shillings could ascend, and which, on one occasion, soared aloft bearing a female centenarian from the Fulham Workhouse, free of charge. (403-4)

In all of these instances, one will note the crowd-pleasing nature of the entertainments as well as the heterogeneity of the crowds they attracted.

This range was curtailed later in the century in much the same way as outlined by Lawrence Levine in *Highbrow/Lowbrow: The Emergence of Cultural Hierarchy in America*, and the splitting along class lines was announced in Cremorne's demise. By the 1870s, »it had become, if not habitually riotous, at least a sort of recognized centre for riotry on special occasions, and the storming and wrecking of the bars characterized one of these disturbances on the night of Oaks day. ... Race days, and Bank Holidays, the Boat Race and any special occasion were caught at as an excuse for unlimited drunkenness and shameful rowdyism, until the Chelsea Vestry and Canon Cromwell, the Principal of St. Marks Training College jointly took steps to put it down« (404-5). There had been previous attempts by the Vestry to have Cremorne's licence withdrawn, as early as 1857; however, it was only once the manager fell onto hard times, suffering from debt and poor health, that these attempts succeeded.

By the 1870s, then, the degree of tolerance required to coexist peacefully in public with one's »fellow citizens« no longer existed. Patrons of pleasure gardens separated along already well-established class (and to a certain extent also, of course, gender) lines, with the more refined classes remaining in their homes, clubs and theaters and the working-class migrating to the music halls:

> The queen's patronage of the theatre had a great effect upon changing the attitude of public opinion towards the stage. In 1848 professional actors and actresses appeared for the first time in the royal theatricals at Windsor castle during the Christmas festival. The queen and the royal family went to plays in London, and not merely to the opera; the upper and middle classes followed their example. One important result was an improvement in the comfort of theatres; the rowdier spectators went away to the music-halls and less reputable entertainments, while the theatres began to increase the number of seats of fair price for the well-to-do middle classes. The new type of theatre-goer wanted a quieter type of acting and greater realism. (Woodward 603)

In his history of Victorian theater, George Rowell refers to a »Return of Respectability,« and in a section on »The Crown and the Theatre« argues that »by spreading her theatrical patronage so widely in the 1850s, Victoria contributed materially to that transformation of theatrical taste which is usually assigned to the Bancrofts' management at the Prince of Wales's ten years later« (155), also noting that »her example was taken up by her children, particularly her heir (whose interest in the theatre, unlike his great-uncles', stretched further than the stage-door)« (155). Following the Royals' example in this regard, as in others, necessarily required a certain means, and thus cultural purchasing power served to inscribe and reinforce growing class differences. In »Working-Class Culture and Working-Class Politics in London, 1870-1900: Notes on the Remaking of a Working Class,« Gareth Stedman Jones addresses this emergence of a new working-class culture in London in the second half of the nineteenth century:

> Many of its institutions dated back to the middle of the century, but its general shape had first become visible in the 1870s, and dominant in the 1890s. ... This culture was clearly distinguished from the culture of the middle class and had remained largely impervious to middle-class attempts to dictate its character or direction. Its dominant cultural institutions were not the school, the evening class, the library, the friendly society, the church or the chapel, but the pub, the sporting paper, the race course and the music hall. (70)

Stedman Jones reads in this separation a form of political retrenchment resulting from a realization and acceptance on the part of the working class that the defeat of Chartism meant that capitalism was »an immovable horizon« and »the inevitable framework of action« (78-9). The rowdy vulgarity of music hall becomes in this view »a culture of consolation« (79), and a symptom of larger societal changes:

> Music hall highlighted the peculiarities of the working-class situation in London. But it also reflected the general development of the English working class after 1870. Fatalism, political scepticism, the evasion of tragedy or anger and a stance of comic stoicism were pre-eminently Cockney attitudes because the decline of artisan traditions, the tardiness of factory development, the prevalence of casual work and the shifting amorphous character of the new proletarian suburbs were particularly marked features of London life. (77)

Temperance morality thus capitalized on changing socio-economic realities to evict those from the pleasure gardens no longer willing or (more to the point) able to comport themselves as industrious fellow-citizens.

The decline of the pleasure gardens reflects not only the enhanced social stratification brought about as the capitalist economy became more entrenched, but also, as Richard Sennett has drawn attention to in *The Uses of Disorder: Personal Identity and City Life*, the intolerant, fear-motivated unwillingness of a particular stratum of society to mix with those below it for fear that their poverty and dirt would rub off on them and that, as the motoring maelstrom of modernity revved, they too would be knocked off their perches and ushered out of their comfortable cages. Sennett's analysis of the growth of American suburbs, which he locates in an adolescent psychological need for sameness, is equally applicable to nineteenth-century Londoners, with the qualification that their self-identificatory practices were primarily class and not nation-based:

> When the French writer Alexis de Tocqueville came to America a century and a half ago, he was struck by the grip this repressive myth had on American community life. The Americans he observed needed to be assured by each other that they were the same – that is, *equal in condition*. Tocqueville believed they felt this need because they felt insecure about their own dignity as men; the act of drawing together, in confirming to each other their sameness and their

> coherence in a common image, warded off the apprehension of threatened dignity. The issues so far explored could be expressed in Tocqueville's terms, as a way men counterfeit a feeling of dignity through an image of equality. There is born in adolescence, and subsequently reified in community life, a means of reassuring oneself that the process of learning about life has occurred even as the substance of learning is avoided. The result is a feeling of dignity in the image of sameness, of equality of condition, as Tocqueville put it, that men forge for themselves. (41)

Sennett goes on to identify three marked social consequences of this myth of dignity through communal solidarity, which are also relevant to the demise of the pleasure gardens and segregation of music hall: 1) the loss of actual participation in community life, the loss of situations of confrontation and exploration between individual groups of men; 2) the repression of deviants; and 3) violence – to escalate discord with other communities. Banishing the working class from respectable society proceeded to no small extent through their (secular) demonization and their being associated in the »public« (Mayhew's public is meant, of course) imagination precisely with violence and deviancy.

Instead of concentrating on the sharp geographical and social separation that the segregation of music hall no doubt represents, I would again like to point to the leakages. The impermeability and artificiality of the (class) barrier, with the transgressions of Victoria's heir exceptional only in the magnitude of the scandal they unleashed, encourage a probing of what precisely was being held apart and why. For all their resolute working-class-ness, music halls also signify a decisive break with the tradition of outdoor public entertainment. Music halls were, as Peter Bailey has noted in *Popular Culture and Performance in the Victorian City*, »a laboratory of style whose patrons went there to learn how to conduct themselves as competent moderns« (8), and as such, one of the parts of popular culture to be:

> increasingly colonised by emergent culture industries, a rogue branch of liberal capitalism whose operations may at one and the same time match or surpass the Fordist or Taylorist aspirations of manufacturing industry, while retaining a populist address akin to the pseudo-gemeinschaft of the republican and the prostitute. These industries – the new pub, the music hall, the theatre and the popular press – compete with each other, territorially and rhetorically, as also with the state and other respectable fractions of the social order. (10)

Pleasure gardens were immune from such colonization because there was nothing »pseudo« about them, not least because of the diversity of their patrons, who located themselves in terms of citizenship rather than along a scale of morality. A noteworthy example in this regard is Vauxhall Gardens, which, some historians have suggested, had an important political dimension: »A cockpit of antigovernment feelings for part of the eighteenth century, it was a place where those out of sympathy with the Crown and its ministries gathered to exchange their grievances« (Harris 20). Music halls, on the other hand, as well as theaters, opera houses and the cinemas which followed them, were public entertainment spaces in which patrons were encouraged to behave strictly as consumers, of cultural products as well as of food and drink, and to allow their class identity to be fixed by the nature of the products they imbibed. The issue is, as Chambers rightly identifies, the choices available to Londoners as their leisure time increased over the course of the nineteenth century due to the introduction of such legislation as the ten-hour working day in 1847 and the practice of leaving Saturday afternoon free for sports (32). However, how are these choices to be contextualized? Chambers's valorization of popular culture leads him to contrast it with »the self-righteous paraphernalia of Victorian respectability« and to read »important transgressions« in »the growth of an urban commercial culture of pleasure around drink and song, gambling and professional sport, [which] created a new recreational nexus that frequently existed outside the workplace and paternalistic control« (32):

> Beyond the immediate reach of the moral economy of religion and responsibility there was now a culture that ›never demanded complete sobriety, self-restrain or other personal virtues recommended by working-class political and trade-union leaders or the middle classes.‹ (Storch 1982, 7, quoted in Chambers, 32)

Viewing the problem solely through the lens of morality, without at the same time keeping in mind the citizenship issues so important to our letter-writing citizen, results in a loss of focus on the public-sphere function which public entertainment spaces can also provide. In glorifying the adolescent freedom allowed in this »new recreational nexus that frequently existed outside the workplace and paternalistic control,« Chambers is oblivious to its problematic consequences in the urban context, as identified in Sennett's analysis, as well as doing injustice to the complexity of the previous nexus and its context. Behind the temperance movement's objections to the pleasure gardens, as we have seen, lay far more powerful forces than mere middle-class morality.

Why did music hall prove to be more amenable to modernizing capitalist impulses than the pleasure gardens? In *The Melodies Linger On: The Story of Music Hall*, W. MacQueen-Pope captures some key elements in the character of this phenomenon. First, unlike the theater, it was an affair of individuals, not troupes (2). Each act was separate:

> They were always distinct and separate units within themselves, never fusing into a whole for one moment, seldom even traveling together in a mass like members of a theatrical touring company, never mingling on the stage or anywhere at all, no, not even on the bills announcing their appearance.
>
> There, they were as individual as upon the actual stage when performing. Each had his, her or their separate compartment on the bills, cut off from their fellow-performers by ruled lines, ›boxes‹ and space. There was very strict precedence in such matters, all the jargon of ›Top,‹ ›Bottom‹ or ›Middle.‹ The main act ›Topped,‹ ›Bottomed‹ or ›Middled‹ the bill, according to importance. (2)

Music hall was thus governed by the strict rules of competition and hierarchy so integral to capitalist structures, the very structures in which it came into existence and in which it thrived. Music hall was born, as McQueen-Pope puts it, »on the wave of prosperity which came into being on the accession of the young Queen Victoria, it belonged to an era of prosperity and the people who welcomed it and supported it were the sons and daughters of an age of Beef, Beer and Peace« (4). It was for a class »that believed that by working hard it could get on and share the prosperity which was abundant in the nation. There was plenty of work and good jobs for skilled men. So it did them« (5). Not only did music hall work to foster the capitalist sensibilities of its patrons, it also encouraged their nationalist proclivities. The audience:

> ... was proud of its country, it was proud to be British, it believed in the figure of John Bull, a plump sturdy man, rubicund and well fed, with no nonsense about him and a bulldog at his heels. It believed that as a race it was superior to all the rest of the world. It pitied and even despised foreigners, although it could be very hospitable to them, and its innate love of freedom made its land the safe harbour for all those unfortunate beings who were oppressed by tyrants. It had won freedom for itself when the rest of Europe endured slavery and it would stand no nonsense in respect of any tampering with what it regarded as its rights. It had an Empire of which it was sensible in general, but of which, in particular, it knew very little about. But it had an intense patriotism of which it was entirely unashamed and it was equally unashamed of showing its own feelings. It wallowed in sentimentality, and it cheered the Union Jack. It was a proud race, but a very law-abiding one, with tremendous loyalty to the throne and a respect for those of high rank which, in its unenlightened way, it still regarded as its ›betters.‹ It was not an educated mass of people, illiteracy was quite a usual thing, but it was strong and virile. (5)

While this highly generalizing passage requires the concrete substantiation a study of the texts of popular music hall songs or of the posters of music hall acts would provide (cf. Haill), what it nonetheless sketches is a type admirably well-suited for integration in an increasingly industrialized and nationalized society (cf. Hobsbawm), one not encouraged to explore or even be curious about the rest of the world, let alone its own, one not encouraged to inform itself about legislation and industry standards, and certainly not one to demand universal suffrage. Rather, musical hall audiences were invited to sit back, relax, and have another gin, to pack up their troubles in their old kit-bags and smile, smile, smile. Rebellious tendencies were thus contained by being channeled into moral, and not political, formations, by a form of public space being provided for behavior that was explicitly immoral – vulgarity and naughtiness were, after all, music hall's pride and calling card. This space, as well as its more moral counterparts, replaced heterogeneous ones in which the increasing disparity between social classes would have been visible and possibly exacerbated, and in which political consciousness and cross-class solidarity would have at least had a chance to emerge. This is the shift John McKean finds embodied in the Crystal Palace's delicate sheathing, beneath which »[t]he public realm of the mid-19th century, *a world of the spectacle and promenade rather than of the social*, is fleetingly captured« (n.p., italics added). In positioning the Crystal Palace as a precursor, indeed the progenitor, of the theme park tradition, the next section shows not only the emergence but also the expansion and increasingly hegemonic entrenchment of a pseudo-public, corporatist entertainment sphere in which cultural and social distinction prevails.

THE CRYSTAL PALACE: THE MAKING OF A MODERN THEME PARK

There were not one but two Crystal Palaces. The first was erected with great efficiency in Hyde Park between September 1850 and January 1851 for little more than £150,000 in time to house the Great Exhibition of the Works of the Industry of All Nations between May 1 and October 11, 1851. Due to the »immense success« of the Exhibition – 6,201,856 paying visitors, 4,237,240 visitors to London (Altick 457)[2] – and the Exhibition Committee's early promise to remove the building from its site at the end of the Exhibition, its architect, who was by this time »Sir« Joseph Paxton, found himself with a budget of half a million pounds to dismantle the original structure, have it transported to the top of Sydenham Hill, on the southern outskirts of London in Kent, rebuilt and furnished as a Winter Park and Garden (Beaver 79). This second, considerably larger structure opened with great fanfare on June 10, 1854, and burned downed in obscurity on a cold November evening in 1936.

> As a kind of surrogate Parliament, it was perhaps the most influential representative body of the nineteenth century. For not only did it erect a monument to the commodity that lasted eighty-five years, but it also prescribed the rituals by which consumers venerated the commodity for the rest of the century. It was the first world's fair, the first department store, the first shopping mall. (Richards 17)

Not only was it the first department store and shopping mall, others followed directly from it:

> [A]mong the six million who visited the Great Exhibition was a Yorkshire lad of farming stock, William Whiteley, whom people came to call ›the universal provider.‹ It was his twentieth year and his first holiday. As a draper's apprentice he inspected with peculiar interest the silks, lines, damasks and other textiles so beautifully displayed. Why should not London have great shops of this type, bright and open, through which, and outside which, customers might pass in parade? Gas-light and plate-glass were in abundant supply; and since there was then no restriction on shop assistants' hours of work it would be possible to shop till midnight in well-lit streets with well-lit window fronts. [Whiteley], therefore, migrated to London to master the wholesale side of the business in the employ of Bradbury Greatorex, and after eight years of intense application opened his shop in Westbourne Grove, by Paddington, on 11 March 1863, timing it to the day after the marriage of the Prince of Wales to the Princess Alexandra, when all London would be in a festive mood. Whiteley was the father of the department store. His premises grew, like the early factories, by adding shop to shop, till the time was ripe for rebuilding the cluster in a great and orderly emporium. ... Whiteley's... followed the fashion of the Great Exhibition in seeking to attract every range of purse. It is a matter of history that the head of his provisions department, Richard Burbidge, left him to build up Harrods and that he also supplied the men who put John Barker and the Army and Navy Stores on the shopping map. (Fay 91)

> Being inside the Crystal Palace was an almost hallucinatory experience: you felt overpowered by sweetness and light. Paxton's design had liberated the enclosure from seasonal fluctuations in temperature, and the result was a landscape of perpetual spring (a result not lost on Jules Jaluzot, who some years later named his Parisian department store ›Printemps‹). (Richards 31)

I begin this section by linking the Crystal Palace together with the shopping center tradition it helped spawn in order to point to a key indicator of the reconfiguration of London's public entertainment sphere in the second half of the nineteenth-century, as well as to highlight the ties between modern theming and the identificatory practices inherent in commodified consumption I will further lay out in this section.

What most prominently distinguishes the Crystal Palace from the nineteenth-century London streets and pleasure gardens is a lack of conflict. Coming as it did on the heels of the failed Chartist uprising of 1848, many expected the Great Exhibition to be marred by violence:

> To the skeptics, it was at once grandiose, hare-brained, and downright dangerous. The perils possibly attending the concentration of large numbers of people in a limited space had been a recurrent theme in the testimony before the select committees on the management of the British Museum and other national monuments. The Crystal Palace would be such an enclosed space, on a mammoth scale; so also, by extrapolation, might be an entire metropolis congested with throngs of unpredictable visitors. All too recently – on 10 April 1848 – Londoners had known the experience of living in a city considering itself in imminent danger of seditious takeover, when hundreds of thousands of workingmen gathered to march under the Chartist banner. Like all other public buildings, the British Museum, which still had its sentries at the gate, was fortified and its employees armed. (Altick 457)

However, no small part of the Exhibition's success was its peaceful course:

> The story, as everyone knows, had a fairy-tale ending appropriate to the fairy-tale atmosphere generated by the very appearance of the Crystal Palace. ... The potential for disturbance was there, but nothing happened. Neither the 1,000 extra constables nor the 10,000 troops that Wellington kept in discreetly hidden reserve were needed... [and] an article called ›The Grand Hatching Year,‹ based on a visit to Cantelo's incubator, now restored to the London show scene in Leicester Square, enumerated all the dreaded eggs – Chartism, Socialism, Red Republicanism, and so on – which had failed to hatch. (457)

In reporting on the final attendance figures on the Monday following the closing ceremonies (13 October 1851), *The Times* commented:

> When it is remembered that these extraordinary figures, which can be thoroughly relied on for accuracy, illustrate popular movements that only a few years ago would have been pronounced on the highest authority most dangerous to the safety of the State, we have the more reason to wonder that they should have taken place not only without disorder, but also almost without crime. The total number of charges made at the police-station at the Prince of Wales' Gate relating to offences within the building is, we are informed, 25, of which nine were for picking pockets, six for attempts to do so, and ten for petty larcenies at stalls. Such facts speak for themselves, and certainly constitute it as one of the proudest boasts connected with the Exhibition that property worth millions of money should have been inspected during nearly half-a-year by millions of people belonging to every class and grade of society, with only a few trifling crimes, involving no article of any value. (cited in Fay, 131-2)

Figures are similarly negligible for the average two million people who attended the Crystal Palace each day during its first thirty years; far graver risks and dangers were posed by ballooning than by rabid revolutionaries or pickpockets:

> Some performed spectacular aerial displays about the Palace grounds. One balloon showman was Signor Eduardo Spelterini who flew his balloon while a certain Miss Leona Dare hung on with her teeth to a trapeze dangling below.

> Another young lady, Viola Spencer, made parachute jumps from her uncle's balloon. On the first occasion she was so afraid that she had to be pushed on her way. After that her courage seemed to grow and she made 146 jumps in six years (Reeves 36-7).

Thus, while the types of entertainment the Crystal Palace offered resembled those of the pleasure gardens – there were Italian terraces and English Landscape Gardens to stroll about in; courts arranged for exhibitions, flower shows, dog shows and the like; a concert room with a capacity of 4,000, and its own orchestra, which was the site of the first »Great Handel Festival« in July 1857 and numerous festivals after that; dozens of meeting rooms, in one of which a showing of moving pictures was presented in 1868 on a gas-powered »Zoetrope« projector; regular Thursday evening firework displays; facilities for boating, cycling and soccer (the F.A. Cup final was often played there), and much, much more to be discussed in the second half of this section (cf. Reeves 31ff) – it was a safe space, a curious hybrid between the traditional type of gardens it was modeled on and the shopping palaces to come:

> Strolling in the urban jungle, all bourgeois fears and fantasies are concentrated. But of course it is a safe jungle; just as *Punch* had talked of Paxton's earlier Great Stove: ›The Glass Garden of Eden at Chatsworth where flourish palms without rattlesnakes, and sugar-cane with no yellow fever.‹ Thus we have the thrill of the terror of nature, at once safe but also sharpened by a building offering us no promise of refuge, no hiding place, being itself formless, shadowless. Here is the mid-century expression of the sublime. (McKean n.p.)

What dampened the conflict potential in the Crystal Palace was the changing identificatory practices of its patrons. While the pleasure gardens were peopled by citizens not intimidated by the public aspects of the gardens, the Crystal Palace's patrons confronted each other as, in the first instance, paying customers:

> Although there had been some mingling of the classes at certain exhibitions in the past – at the panoramas, for example, and the Polytechnic – it was at the Great Exhibition that social distinctions were, for the moment, most widely disregarded. A full-page *Punch* drawing captioned ›The Pound and the Shilling »Whoever Thought of Meeting You Here?«‹ celebrated the novel fellowship of the gentry and the laboring class inside the Hyde Park enclosure. (Altick 457)

Social distinctions were not so much temporarjly disregarded as resignified in currency: the pound and the shilling. Even during its speedy construction, visitors had to pay an admission fee (of five shillings, which went towards the workmen's accident fund) to enter the Crystal Palace. »Then sightseers were excluded until the opening day. For the first three weeks that the completed Crystal Palace was open to the public (1-22 May) the same five-shilling fee was charged, after which it was reduced to a single shilling for the first four days of the week (these were overwhelmingly the most populous) and half a crown on Fridays, the full charge being retained only on Saturday afternoons« (460). The decision to charge admission fees resulted in no little controversy and was of no little consequence:

> Shortly after the opening, the Executive Committee had the question of admitting charitable institutions gratuitously pressed upon their notice, and they decided not to do so, upon grounds which perhaps at the time were thought hard and unfeeling. – What was the result? An immense spring of private benevolence, which has not been confined to the metropolis or its neighbourhood, but has extended to every part of England, and the influence of which, passing from the very poor to the struggling independence of the country, has induced masters to send their servants, manufacturers their hands, bankers and merchants their clerks, tradesmen their apprentices, railway companies their men, and last, most wanted and most common of all, induced the owners and occupiers of the soil to send up, by subscription among them, their labourers. (cited in Fay, 132)

Charging admission fees across the board without exception, then, served to establish industrial standards of identity, encouraging patrons to view both themselves and others by the size of their wallets. Purchasing power, and not elocution, was the bottom line under the glass sheets and iron girders of the Crystal Palace. As Richards notes, »In the Crystal Palace the working class no longer looked like the indigenous ally of the class that rocked Europe in 1848. It was now just another segment of the market; it had become a customer« (37). However, understanding class in this context requires careful demarcation and specification. When Marshall Berman contends in *All That Is Solid Melts Into Air* that »[t]he Crystal Palace would probably not have been built at all, and would surely not have been rebuilt and allowed to stand for eight decades..., had it not been acclaimed enthusiastically both by the English common people and by foreigners from all over the world« (238), he would seem to be operating on the basis of romanticized wishful thinking rather than on the basis of widely available facts. The percentage of visitors from even England's neighboring countries was paltry; to talk of any international influx is as misguided as it is to assume that all of »the English common people« could afford even the lowest-priced 1 shilling entry fee. Greenhalgh underscores the fact that »by contemporary standards, admission was by no means cheap, the shilling fee being fixed so as to guarantee that the lower reaches of the working class would be absent. The audience for the Great Exhibition began at the lowest end with the more prosperous artisan and tradespeople, these being treated by contemporary commentators as though they were a reflection of the condition of the whole of the labouring classes« (30). Having some means, however limited, also meant that visitors to the Crystal Palace would later be able to put the consumer-oriented activities their visit encouraged into practice:

> Because so many people visited the Exhibition during the summer of 1851..., and because the Crystal Palace's police force... liked to keep traffic going at a good clip, visitors were virtually forced to acquire a limited attention span. Like it or not, they had to adjust themselves to the serial rhythm of the place; being set loose in the Crystal Palace was the Victorian equivalent of flipping the TV channel and sorting through various kinds of programmed information. Like today's television viewer, the Exhibition spectator was free to pick and choose from a limited spectrum of prefabricated choices. Allowed a certain amount of mobility within a confined space of exhibition, the spectator could formulate what were essentially consumer preferences... (Richards 35)

Flowing through the Crystal Palace left no opportunity for jostling or exchanging controversial opinions on social or political issues of the day; rather, visiting the Crystal Palace meant, however unwittingly, being initiated into the gamut of consumer behaviors.

The purpose of visiting the Crystal Palace was thus not predominantly social, to visit with other patrons, but rather to consume, to take in as much as possible and to thereby increase one's symbolic capital. The Dickinson brothers reported in their *Comprehensive Pictures of the Great Exhibition of 1851:*

> [E]veryone had experienced great personal pleasure and profit during an examination of the collections of machines, manufactures or fine art, and felt deeply how useful and interesting, and at the same time, how elevating the spectacle had been to the multitudes who came to study or to admire: everybody had felt it so obligatory to go and see for himself, to gain a knowledge of things of which he was ignorant, to admire in all their perfection, productions with which he was well acquainted, and to compare them with those of other nations, and then to feel that experience had given him a right to praise their excellent points and to decry their deficiencies, and so universal was the affirmative answer to the great question of the day ›Have you been to the Exhibition?‹ that it became almost possible to point to the solitary individual who would remain blind to the advantages of the undertaking, however patent they might be made to him, and who refused to look upon the whole enterprise in any other light but that of a ›vast humbug.‹ (cited in Fay, 90)

Stigmatizing those who did not attend the Exhibition coincided with the »elevating« of those who did. Social status began to be reassigned on the basis of knowledge about things that in many cases only a few years ago had not so much as existed:

> The United States sent McCormick's reaper and prodigious quantities of ore; the French sent sculpture and artificial arms, hands, feet, legs and eyes; the Germans sent musical instruments and stuffed frogs; the British contributed machines. These things – tens of thousands of them packed into fourteen thousand booths – were the featured attraction... (Richards 17)

Things suddenly began to matter a very great deal. However, the things on display in the Crystal Palace over the course of its 86-year history provided not only knowledge about the objects on display, they also made available secondhand knowledge about faraway places and times to those without the purchasing power to experience them firsthand:

> The show was all very instructive if taken in moderate doses, and it unquestionably broadened, if only for the moment, the mental horizons of the millions of men, women, and children who passed through the turnstiles. To countless numbers it was the unforgettable high point of their constricted lives. And the fact that so many of the exhibits came from abroad, often accompanied by natives of the countries represented, was an effective through hardly complete antidote to the tight insularity of the period. The Crystal Palace was a better vehicle for vicarious travel than any number of panoramas. (Altick 457)

This palliative, substitutive, vicarious quality of the exhibits, which would later morph into simulacra, was the opening through which theming was introduced to the consuming public. In effect, in addition to being »the first world's fair, the first department store, the first shopping mall,« it was also the first time that these phenomena were brought together on the level of mass culture, creating what could thus be regarded as the first theme park. It is not a question of novelty or innovation *per se,* as Richards stresses:

> No single element of the Crystal Palace was new; the Victorian taste for luxury, ostentation, and outward show had long been reflected on the stage as well as on the street and inside the home. What the Crystal Palace did was to synthesize and systematize these elements of spectacle by putting them all together under one roof in the service of manufactured objects. (21) ... The Crystal Palace combined museum, laboratory, factory, railway station, workshop, theater, auditorium, restaurant, and greenhouse, but in a crucial sense it was also something quite different from any of these. For not only did it assemble thousands of manufactured objects under one roof, but it amalgamated them and created a coherent representational universe for commodities. (30)

The Crystal Palace, then, brought together enlightenment and entertainment, spectacle and speculation under the rubric of all-purpose consumption. Its very name served to enact the kind of sublation which enables theming.

If theming served clear commercial, social and political interests in the case of the Ramona-ization of Los Angeles (see pp. 223-40 in this volume), it is no less difficult to enumerate whose advantages the Crystal Palace served. The connection between Crystal Palace and industry is evident even in the official name of the exhibition it was first built to house, the Great Exhibition of the Works of the Industry of All Nations. The way the Exhibition »assembled the dominant institutions and vested interests of mid-Victorian England to pay homage to the way commodities were produced« has been amply elucidated by Richards (3), who has also detailed the way its organization underscored and pandered to the same nationalistic sentiments as music hall, with the west end of the building reserved for English products and the east for foreign ones:

> At the west end of the building, which was reserved for English articles, you began with mirrors that recalled Versailles. Above there was a basilica-sized organ surrounded by daguerreotypes, clocks, firearms, and hanging globes. Moving eastward, you followed the path of locomotives set on railroad tracks and passed dioramas of cities, models of churches, and booths displaying fabrics, furs, and tools of every size and description. To the north of the Grand Aisle, you generally saw machinery; to the south, raw materials and produce. Before leaving the English half of the building, you passed sculpture and furniture and entered a little enclosure called the ›Mediaeval Court,‹ the handiwork of A. W. N. Pugin. ... If visitors expected the foreign half of the Crystal Palace to measure up to the English half, they must have been sorely disappointed. Because the planning commission had decided to let each participating country do whatever it liked with its allotted space, there was not even a pretense of order on the east side. Next to the virtual encyclopedia of manufactured objects crammed into the English half, the foreign half looked like a disheveled cabinet of curiosities. In rapid succession strollers along the Grand Aisle passed the characteristic national products of thirty-two nations: Egyptian carpets, Turkish embroidery, Roman mosaics, German porcelain, Russian furs, and India rubber. But for every foreign item on display there were a dozen comparable items in the English section, and even the *Official Catalogue* of the Exhibition had to admit that the foreign half of the building was at best a mutilated copy of the English half. (25)

As Richards concludes, »The exhibition layout essentially balkanized the rest of the world, projecting a kind of geopolitical map of a world half occupied by English, half occupied by a collection of principalities vying for the leftover space... prov[ing] once and for all that the best way to sell things to the English was to sell them the culture and ideology of England, its plans for commercial dominance, its dreams of Empire, its social standards, and its codes of conduct« (25, 40). The longevity of the Crystal Palace confirms this assertion, just as it points to what it was that the Palace, like the other world exhibitions which followed it, was really peddling. Designed as a monument to capitalist industry, the Crystal Palace worked as an anti-polis to turn its public into consumers, knowledgeable about and interested in all kinds of inventive contraptions and spectacles and far-away places, and uninterested in the nuts and bolts of their own society.

The distinction that this paper has worked to establish between corporatist and non-corporatist forms of a public entertainment sphere is similar to the direction Marshall Berman seems to be gesturing towards in playing Dostoevsky's and Chernyshevsky's visions of the Crystal Palace off against each other in *All That Is Solid Melts Into Air*. Concluding with Berman highlights what has been thus far lurking in the shadows in this paper: the question of the modern. »In a sense, Crystal Palace epitomizes the project of modernity,« McKean notes in his follow-up on Berman's follow-up on Marx.[3] Since Habermas, it has been common currency to note that modernity is a not only incomplete but paradoxical project, a project based on intractable contradictions and aporias, and McKean describes the Crystal Palace in just these terms: »This paradox – the trembling insubstantiality of such a powerful image, so immaterial that even as an idea it cannot be grasped, but becomes a multi-faceted mirror, reflecting whatever looks at it – remains a catalytic metaphor long after all trace of it has gone« (n.p.). Berman was also bothered by just such a disjuncture, the almost Orwellian description of the ethereal, magical Crystal Palace in *Notes from Underground* (Book One, Chapters 8-10): »Readers who try to visualize the Crystal Palace on the basis of Dostoevsky's language are apt to imagine an immense Ozymandian slab« (237). As part of a larger argument which situates the shift from Russian to Soviet artistic practice in the context of European modernism, Berman quite rightly identifies Dostoevsky as responding not to Paxton's Crystal Palace but to the utopian vision of crystal palaces in the epochal *What is to be Done?*, which Chernyshevsky wrote in the Peter and Paul Fortress in St. Petersburg before being sentenced in 1864 to life imprisonment in Siberia. From the point of view of a society which abolished serfdom in 1861, one can imagine the modern longings and desires the Sydenham Crystal Palace set off in its Russian visitors – Berman notes that Chernyshevsky had seen it in 1859 and Dostoevsky in 1862 (236). However, the building represents much different fictional fantasies for the two authors:

> For Chernyshevsky and his vanguard of ›new people,‹ the Crystal Palace is a symbol of the new modes of freedom and happiness that Russians can enjoy if they make the great historical leap into modernity. For Dostoevsky and his anti-hero, too, the Crystal Palace stands for modernity; only here it symbolizes everything that is ominous and threatening about modern life, everything against which modern man must stand *en garde*. (Berman 220)

These two tendencies, embodied in the massive yet fragile and fleeting iron and glass structure, are what McKean calls the two strands of the modern:

> Utopian ideals, the purity of ›nakedness,‹ doesn't take long to become oppressive. Life exposed under a bell-jar soon runs out of oxygen. As penal reformers of the romantic period were well aware, light in the panopticon allows control. ... On the one hand we see a modernization of calming routines, where browsing makes passivity the norm. On the other is a modernization of frightening, dangerous, dynamic adventure; open ended and melting. ... Crystal Palace does both: it thrills by its disorientation, its sensual disintegration, its seeming insubstantiality. But also, it calms by its ghostly evenness of light, its endlessness of space, its shadowless homogenizing. (n.p.)

Berman's predilection is to glorify the romantic pole and back Dostoevsky's vision of Petersburg, and the Nevsky Prospect in particular, for its »public space« qualities, for being a place where Dostoevsky's Underground Man could stick his tongue out or thumb his nose. In a Zarathustrian moment, the Underground Man criticizes a crowd:

> You, you believe in a crystal edifice that can never be destroyed, an edifice at which one would not be able to stick one's tongue out, or to thumb one's nose, even on the sly. And I am afraid of this edifice just because it is of crystal and can never by destroyed, and because one could not stick out one's tongue at it on the sly. (cited in Berman, 236)

Leaving aside, as Berman does, the question of the narrator's notorious unreliability (he introduces himself to the reader as sick, evil and dishonest), Berman waxes nostalgic for the nineteenth-century Nevsky:

> the Nevsky was the one place in Petersburg (and perhaps in all Russia) where all the existing classes came together, from the nobility whose palaces and town houses graced the street at its starting point near the Admiralty and the Winter Palace, to the poor artisans, prostitutes, derelicts and bohemians who huddled in the wretched fleabags and taverns near the railroad station in Znamiemsky Square where the Prospect came to an end. The Nevsky brought them all together, whirled them around in a vortex, and left them to make of their experiences and encounters what they could. (194-5).

However, there were no dancing bears in the streets of 1860s Petersburg. A far cry from those of London and much more akin to the Crystal Palace (and to West Edmonton Mall, as other papers in this volume make clear), they were marked by the enforcement of hegemonic bourgeois decorum, by a lack of conflict and of spontaneous public entertainment. Berman must inevitably confront exactly what kind of space this nineteenth-century Russian city was:

> In generations to come, Petersburg's common people would gradually find ways to make their presence felt, to make the city's great spaces and structures

> their own [one will note he never specifies in which years this great occurrence took place as his condemnation of the real, existing USSR is unequivocal]. For the time being, however, they would slink away or stay out of sight – underground, in Dostoevsky's image of the 1860s [one will note that the Underground Man is not a ›1860s man‹ as Chernyshevsky was but rather ›the very embodiment of a man of the 1840s, a highly articulate representative of the educated class who has lost the ideals of that decade and is now fast losing faith in the new ideals of scientific rationalism he espoused at the beginning of the 1860s‹ (Humphreys xii)] – and Petersburg would continue to incarnate *the paradox of public space without public life.* (189, italics added)

Of course, the Russian example is only a fleeting moment on a very different modernizing track. Nonetheless, Berman's romantic reading of it usefully isolates a quality central to the comparisons in this volume – the different qualities of public life possible in different public spaces.

ENDNOTES

1 Including »mass culture« in this list draws attention to the kind of shift in conceptual vocabulary that I am referring to here. Adorno and Horkheimer started out using mass culture »to refer to the way in which a standardized and meretricious culture was imposed on the masses by modern technological media and entertainment businesses. However, they came to believe that the term could too easily be misconstrued as referring to an authentic cultural emanation of the active masses rather than something passively consumed by them. To put the word ›culture‹ together with ›industry‹ seemed much more unambiguously damning« (McGuigan 76).

2 This is the figure given in *The Times* of Monday, 13 October 1851. Although much is generally made of the introduction of grandiose ticket-counting technology, which theoretically allowed for the recording of exact numbers, one encounters different final tallies in the scholarship. Neither Greenhalgh nor Altick, for example, give the sources of their respective 6,039,195 and 6,093,896. McKean notes at the beginning of his Notes: »More than anything I have ever studied, Crystal Palace secondary sources provide a screen to confuse and divert. Almost every modern and many contemporary sources, from reviews in 1851 to Thomas Richards's most impressive *The Commodity Culture of Victorian England*, are riddled with tiny errors of date, magnitude, working, fact, fact, and fact. It is all very Crystalpalatial.«

3 Carver's recent retranslation »all that is fixed and feudal goes up in smoke« also captures this ephemerality, while having the added advantage of being much more in line with the historical resonances of Marx's writings.

REFERENCES

Altick, Richard D. *The Shows of London*. Cambridge, Massachusetts and London, England: The Belknap Press of Harvard University Press, 1978.

Bailey, Peter. *Popular Culture and Performance in the Victorian City*. Cambridge: Cambridge University Press, 1997.

Beaver, Patrick. *The Crystal Palace: 1851-1936. A Portrait of Victorian Enterprise.* London: Hugh Evelyn, 1970.

Berman, Marshall. *All That Is Solid Melts Into Air: The Experience of Modernity.* With a new preface. Harmondsworth: Penguin, 1988.

Carver, Terrell. *The Postmodern Marx.* Manchester and University Park, PA: Manchester University Press and Pennsylvania State University Press, 1998.

Chambers, Iain. *Popular Culture: The Metropolitan Experience.* London and New York: Routledge, 1986.

Chancellor, E. Beresford. *The Pleasure Haunts of London during Four Centuries.* London: Constable & Company Ltd; Boston & New York: Houghton Mifflin Company, 1925.

Citizen of London. *A letter from a citizen of London to the Right Honourable Sir Robert Peel, Bart. &c&c&c: on the necessity of restricting and defining the power of magistrates, and protecting places of public entertainment from persecution.* University of London, Senate House – Special Coll (Gold) G.L. 1837.

Cohen, David. *The Buskers.* North Pomfret, Vermont: David & Charles Inc., 1981.

Fay, C. R. *Palace of Industry, 1851: A Study of the Great Exhibition and its Fruits.* Cambridge: Cambridge University Press, 1951.

Greenhalgh, Paul. *Ephemeral Vistas: The Expositions Universelles, Great Exhibitions and World's Fairs, 1851-1939.* Manchester: Manchester University Press, 1988.

Gottdiener, Mark. *The Theming of America: Dreams, Visions, and Commercial Spaces.* Boulder, Colo.: Westview Press, 1997.

Haill, Catherine. *Fun without Vulgarity: Victorian and Edwardian Popular Entertainment Posters.* Published in association with the Public Record Office. London: The Stationery Office, 1996.

Harris, Neil. »Expository Expositions: Preparing for the Theme Parks.« *Designing Disney's Theme Parks: The Architecture of Reassurance.* Ed. Karal Ann Marling. Montreal: Centre Canadien d'Architecture; Paris – New York: Flammarion, 1997. 19-28.

Hobsbawm, E. *Industry and Empire.* Harmondsworth: Penguin, 1969.

Humphreys, Gordon, ed. *Notes from Underground.* F. M. Dostoevsky. With an Introduction, Notes and Vocabulary. London: Bristol Classical Press, 1994.

Levine, Lawrence W. *Highbrow/Lowbrow: The Emergence of Cultural Hierarchy in America.* Cambridge, Mass; London: Harvard University Press, 1988.

MacQueen-Pope, W. *The Melodies Linger On: The Story of Music Hall.* London: W. H. Allen, 1950.

Mayhew, Henry. *London Labour and the London Poor; A Cyclopaedia of the Condition and Earnings of Those that **Will** work, those that **Cannot** work, and those that **Will not** work. The London Street-folk; comprising, street sellers, street buyers, street finders, street performers, street artizans, street labourers. With numerous illustrations from photographs.* London: Griffin, Bohn, and Company, Stationers' Hall Court, 1861.

McClung, William Alexander. *Landscapes of Desire. Anglo Mythologies of Los Angeles.* Berkeley; Los Angeles; London: University of California Press, 2000.

McGuigan, Jim. *Culture and the Public Sphere.* London and New York: Routledge, 1996.

McKean, John. »Joseph Paxton. Crystal Palace.« *Lost Masterpieces.* Architecture 3. London: Phaidon, 1999.

Reeves, Graham. *Palace of the People.* Kent: Bromley Library Service, 1986.

Richards, Thomas. *The Commodity Culture of Victorian England: Advertising and Spectacle, 1851-1914*. Stanford, California: Stanford University Press, 1990.

Rowell, George. *The Victorian Theatre, 1792-1914: A Survey.* 2nd ed. Cambridge et al: Cambridge University Press, 1978.

Sennett, Richard. *The Uses of Disorder: Personal Identity and City Life*. New York: Alfred A. Knopf, Inc., 1970.

Stedman Jones, Gareth. »Working-Class Culture and Working-Class Politics in London, 1870-1900: Notes on the Remaking of a Working Class.« *Cultural Theory and Popular Culture: A Reader*. 2nd ed. Ed. John Storey. London: Prentice Hall, 1998. 68-79.

Storch, R. D., ed. *Popular Culture and Custom in Nineteenth-Century England*. London: Croom Helm, 1982.

Thompson, E. P. *The Making of the English Working Class*. London: Victor Gollancz, 1963.

Thomson, J., F.R.G.S., and Adolphe Smith. *Street Life in London with permanent photographic illustrations taken from life expressly for this publication*. London: Sampson Low, Marston, Searle, & Rivington, 1877.

Woodward, E. L. *The Oxford History of England: The Age of Reform, 1815-1870*. Oxford: At the Clarendon Press, 1938.

Once upon a Time: The Commodification of the Middle Ages in German *Trivialromane* around 1800

MARKUS REISENLEITNER

In 1800 Heinrich Kleist issued the following complaint about the holdings of German libraries: »Rittergeschichten, lauter Rittergeschichten, rechts die Rittergeschichten m i t Gespenstern, links o h n e Gespenster, nach Belieben« (563).[1] Kleist was talking about a genre that usually does not receive much mention in literary histories, where a ›rediscovery‹ of the Middle Ages in German literature around 1800 is generally attributed to the Romantics, who created a whole poetic universe called the Middle Ages at precisely the time when Kleist was so appalled by the aforementioned »Rittergeschichten.« And indeed literary productions like Wackenroder's *Herzergießungen eines kunstliebenden Klosterbruders* (1797), Tieck's *Franz Sternbalds Wanderungen, eine altdeutsche Geschichte* (1798) and, above all, Novalis's *Die Christenheit oder Europa* (1799) show evidence of their authors' boundless fascination with this period of time, which resulted in a poetic appropriation for political as well as escapist agendas characterized by an often reactionary and apologetic glorification of medieval institutions and power relations (cf. Krogoll). Novalis's manifesto *Die Christenheit oder Europa* (*Christendom or Europe*), which has been described as the »new testament of political romanticism« (Krogoll), sums up the political agendas of this utopian, literary creation:

> Es waren schöne glänzende Zeiten, wo Europa ein christliches Land war, wo Eine Christenheit diesen menschlich gestalteten Erdteil bewohnte; Ein großes gemeinschaftliches Interesse verband die entlegensten Provinzen dieses weiten geistlichen Reichs. – Ohne große weltliche Besitztümer lenkte und vereinigte Ein Oberhaupt, [sic!] die großen politischen Kräfte. – Eine zahlreiche Zunft zu der jedermann den Zutritt hatte, stand unmittelbar unter demselben und vollführte seine Winke und strebte mit Eifer seine wohltätige Macht zu befestigen. Jedes Glied dieser Gesellschaft wurde allenthalben geehrt, und wenn die gemeinen Leute Trost oder Hülfe, Schutz oder Rat bei ihm suchten, und gerne

> dafür seine mannigfaltigen Bedürfnisse reichlich versorgten, so fand es auch bei den Mächtigeren Schutz, Ansehn und Gehör, und alle pflegten diese auserwählten, mit wunderbaren Kräften ausgerüsteten Männer, wie Kinder des Himmels, deren Gegenwart und Zuneigung mannigfachen Segen verbreitete.[2]

This passage is often quoted to stress the Romantic movement's pronounced opposition to enlightened thinking about the state and its institutions, and often used as evidence of the reactionary character of German Romantic literature: the state is presented by Novalis (in an anticipation of Hegelian concepts) as a realization of divine will (as opposed to the idea of natural law and a social contract); the quasi-organic nature of a social hierarchy and the idea of a unifying ›Holy Empire‹ negate the class antagonisms that were so clearly manifested in the events after the French Revolution (which was supported by most of the Romantics) – thus a specific view of history is very obviously employed to promote a conservative social agenda. This is made possible by the aesthetisizing of history (the writing of which was presented as a poetic act of creation), which provided an escapist moment just as Napoleon's empire was casting its shadow over Europe and the neo-feudalist reality of the German states was shutting down opportunities for petty bourgeois intellectuals to promote their political and/or aesthetic interests.

The Middle Ages that the Romantics created was thus a very specific construction which was meant to respond to the immediate political and social situation of a group of uprooted artists who appropriated a specific period in history as a tool to accommodate art, literature, historiography, anti-rationality and untamed subjectivity. While classical antiquity had already been appropriated by the Enlightenment, a reconceptualized feudal age, redeemed from the stigma of the ›Dark Ages‹ but poetically altered beyond recognition and stripped of any continuity with the absolutist state that re-asserted itself after the Napoleonic wars, provided the Romantics with a counter-foil that idealized the society of estates in the same moment that it glorified its poetic appropriation. The historian and the poet were conflated, and the Middle Ages were mediated through layers of a (poetic/artistic) subjectivity that left room, indeed even encouraged, an imaginative, dreamlike, fairytale vision of the era. By combining history, literature and fantasy, the Middle Ages became the projection screen for desires of origin, wholeness and a perfect society (easily adaptable to a nationalist re-interpretation), in short a nostalgic vision of a particular period of the past in which belonging (as something always already lost) could be located.

This coherent (re-)interpretation of a historical period influenced generations to come. However, the immediate influence of the Romantic vision of the Middle Ages should not be overestimated: thus only passages of Novalis's manifesto, written for the *Athenaeum* (edited by Friedrich Schlegel and Ludwig Tieck), the main journal of the Romantics, were printed in the first through third editions (1802, 1805, 1815); only in 1826 was it published in its entirety. This suggests that the particular image of the Middle Ages born at this moment is not entirely a creation of a socially, politically and intellectually quite isolated group of artists. Such an interpretation would disregard an already well-established tradition of interest in the Middle Ages initiated by enlightened encyclopedists; the Romantics were not the first to discover the Middle Ages; editions of medieval literature (especially of the High Middle Ages), particularly of Minnelieder and the Nibelungenlied, are actually more a product of enlightened efforts than of Romantic rediscovery – those efforts were just framed differently.

What the Romantics were also able to tap into – worlds apart from the learned encyclopedists and neglected by scholarship – was an unbroken tradition of appropriating (particularly literary) medieval tales, motifs and images of the Middle Ages in popular culture, which by 1800 had established a narrative genre that appropriated history for popular fiction – the *Rittergeschichten* that Kleist felt the need to complain about.

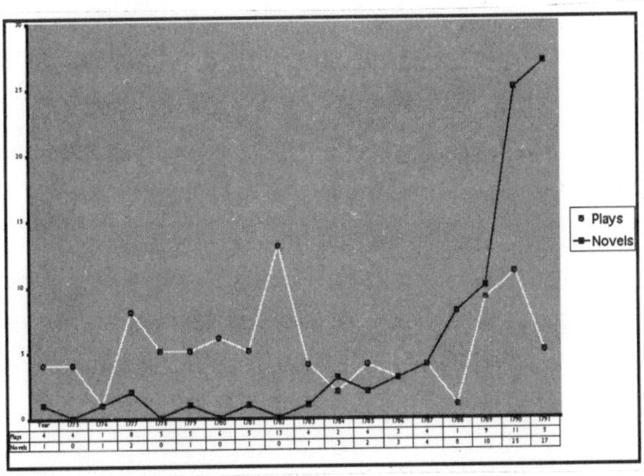

Ill. 1: Journal von und für Deutschland (1792)

In 1792 we find concrete evidence for a remarkable increase in historical fiction, which led the enlightenment journal *Journal von und für Deutschland* (edited by the Freiherr von Bibra) to provide a bibliography of this growing genre (*Ill. 1*).[3] The editor draws attention to its proliferation and its combined attraction as entertainment and history, while also identifying the main themes of these historical novels and plays:

> Aus obigem chronologischen Verzeichniß kann man sehen, wie sehr die Begierde unsrer Dichter, vaterländische Gegenstände zu behandeln, neuerlich zugenommen hat... Im Jahr 1767 eiferte noch der selige Sturz in dem Briefe über das Theater, dem er seinem Trauerspiel *Julie* voransetzte, über die Saumseligkeit unsrer Dichter, die deutsche Geschichte mittlerer Zeiten zu benutzen, und schlug als Stoffe zu Nationalschauspielen folgenden Gegenstände vor: Karl der Große..., Kaiser Heinrich der Vierte, Konradin von Schwaben, die Eifersucht Karl des Dritten und Heinrich des Zweyten gegen ihre Gemahlinnen, Otto der Dritte von der Witwe des Crescentius vergiftet. Bey allem Überfluß, den wir jetzt an Schauspielen und Romanen haben, welche sich auf die alte deutsche Geschichte gründen, sind doch noch nicht alle Wünsche von Sturz in Erfüllung gegangen. Manche altdeutsche Begebenheiten (z.B. Konradin›s Schicksal, der sächsische Prinzenraub) sind vielfach bearbeitet, indessen daß die Geschichte Heinrich des Zweyten und Otto des Dritten noch keinen Dichter gefunden hat, der sie benutzt hätte. (570)[4]

What is also remarkable about this particular bibliography is the pronounced shift from plays to novels during this period (*Ill. 2*).

Jahr	Dramen	Romane
1775	4	1
1776	4	0
1777	1	1
1778	8	2
1779	5	0
1780	5	1
1781	6	0
1782	5	1
1783	13	0
1784	4	1
1785	2	3
1786	4	2
1787	3	3
1788	4	4
1789	1	8
1790	9	10
1791	11	25
1792	5	27

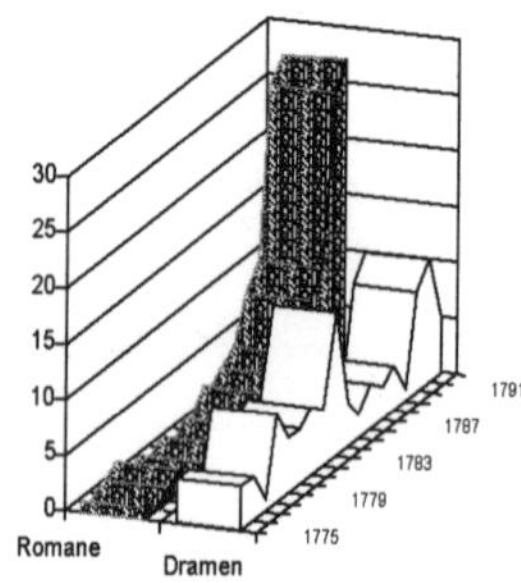

Ill. 2: Distribution novels/plays in Bibra's bibliography

While historical plays remain at an even level, it is mostly novels which are responsible for the increase in historical topics in the period Bibra investigates.

Evidently historical novels became increasingly popular in the last decade of the eighteenth century, and medieval themes were prominent in this development (*Ill. 3*). The genre maintained its popularity in the first decade of the nineteenth century (despite the Napoleonic wars)

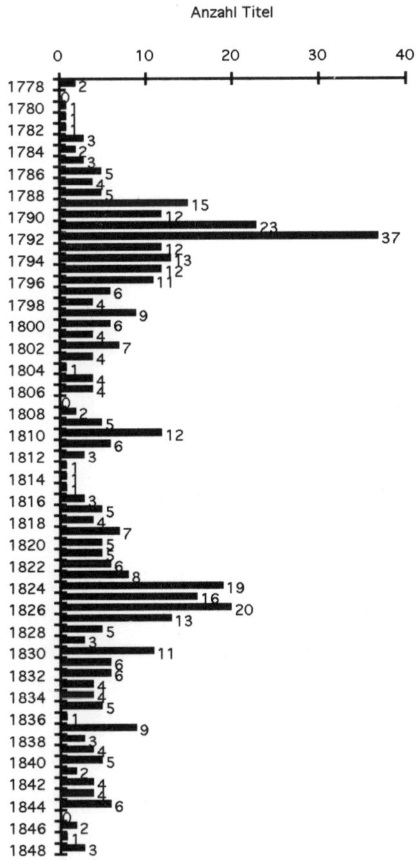

Ill. 3: Development of historical novels that deal with medieval themes

Zeitraum	Titel
5. Jht.	11
6. Jht.	2
7. Jht.	3
8. Jht.	3
9. Jht.	8
10. Jht.	11
11. Jht.	25
12. Jht.	64
13. Jht.	66
14. Jht.	45
15. Jht.	64

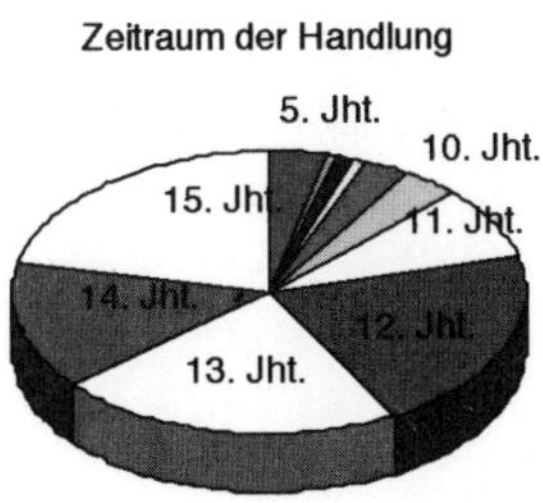

and saw a new boost with the reception of Walter Scott's *Ivanhoe* (published 1819, translated 1820) before finally declining in the 1830s.

Which particular period was appropriated in these novels? There are very clear preferences (*Ill. 4*): the High Middle Ages (the splendid period of knighthood, tournaments and courtly festivities, and the Crusades), but also the fifteenth century (especially the Hussite wars) captured the popular imagination more than earlier centuries. (The relatively high proportion of the fifth century is due to the popularity of Arthurian legends, which might arguably be included with the High Middle Ages because of their reliance on the literature of the high Middle Ages, particularly the courtly novel, rather than their actual setting). This is a clear indication in regard to the function of the Middle Ages: the era is not the realm of fantasy, a completely empty signifier randomly to be filled by the authors' imaginations (which would have been more easily framed by the Twilight of the Gods). This particular type of fiction relied on a frame of historical knowledge available to its (bourgeois) readers, particularly in regard to the social framework into which the narratives were inserted. The pre-feudal era could not provide that.

The novels clearly relied on the reading public and the new forms of private reading that had emerged in the second half of the eighteenth century. (While difficult to prove, it can also be assumed that a large percentage of the readers were female.) The average length of the novels is quite substantial (2 to 3 volumes with 300 to 400 pages each). Most of them focus on fictional protagonists placed in the vicinity of prominent historical figures (mostly emperors and princes); the names of the protagonists themselves are almost always fictional. Most of the novels were published anonymously, but with important additional information in their titles: a historical reference is usually made by either mentioning a century, a well-known figure or a battle. Additional information pertains to an area, with a clear preference for the classical settings of medieval literature, history or legends – such as Bohemia and Thuringia, one thinks of the Kyffhäuser legend, in which Frederick I. (in some retellings it is the II.) returns to save Germany, or of the *Sängerkrieg* on the Wartburg. Additional information in the title leaves no doubt as to the nature of the fiction – *romantische Geschichte aus dem Mittelalter* / a romantic story from the Middle Ages; *ein Gemälde aus der Vorzeit* / a painting from the Dark Ages; *ein Ritter- und Geistergesang aus der Zeit der Kreuzzüge* / a song of knights and ghosts from the time of the crusades – and provides some connection to other novels of the same genre – either by including the author in the title or, more interestingly, providing an intertextual connection to another novel –

Gottlob Heinrich Heinse's *Ludwig der Eiserne, Landgraf von Thüringen* (1792) is introduced as the grandson of »Ludwig der Springer,« the protagonist in another of his other novels (which was published in the same year). This form of cross-referencing is not limited to works by the same author: while Friedrich Christian Schlenkert uses a supporting character from his novel *Heinrich IV* (1789) for his novel *Graf Wiprecht von Groizsch* (1792), the above-mentioned Ludwig der Springer in Heinse's novel also makes his first appearance in Schlenkert's voluminous tale.

LOCATION

The characters of the plot thus move in a space defined clearly in time and space; their existence is legitimized by historical figures and events. The era itself functions as a safeguard for the possibility of adventure and is characterized most fundamentally by a certain (not clearly defined) instability – those were »stürmische, unruhevolle Zeiten.« Take this fairly typical introduction:

> Es war vor Alters einmal eine Zeit, wo ein gedrücktes Volk plötzlich seine Fesseln zu fühlen begann, und in der Bemühung sie abzuschütteln, sich und einem verkannten Fürsten nahmloses Elend bereitete. Lange tappte es, von kleinen und großen Verführern irre geleitet, die nichts suchten als eigenen Nutzen, ungeachtet sie dem betrogenen Haufen viel von Freiheitssinn und Patriotismus vorschwatzten; lange tappte es in dicker Dunkelheit, und verblutete sich an selbst geschlagenen Wunden, bis endlich der Zauber der Verblendung wich, die Feinde der wahren Freiheit fielen, und Ruhe und Ordnung wiederkehrten. Aus jenen stürmischen unruhvollen Zeiten, aus jenem Gewirr von Schreckensbildern, wo erst das Auge der Nachwelt besondere Züge zu unterscheiden, und Schicksale einzelner Personen mit Ursach und Folgen von andern zu sondern vermag, aus ihnen – es waren die Zeiten Kaiser Friedrich des Dritten – wollen wir einige Scenen ausheben, und Euch, liebe Leser, zur Unterhaltung vorlegen. (Naubert, Bd. I, 3)[5]

This is the first paragraph of Benedicte Naubert's *Ulrich Holzer, Bürgermeister von Wien*, published anonymously in 1793. The tone is clearly moralizing, patterns of good and bad are readily identifiable, and the whole historical frame is laid out right at the beginning of the novel. Reader and author are placed in a privileged position to judge the events of the past, unintelligible to its contemporaries (»Those looking back were first able to discern specific characteristics and the fates of specific persons«) – historicity creates distance and superior insight. Another example:

> Es war gerade damahls, als ein schönes Licht sich von Süden aus zu verbreiten anfing. Die Kreuzfahrer hatten schon früher die Künste, die Kenntnisse, die blumenreichen Gesänge des Aufgangs in ihre Heimath zurück gebracht; glücklich verschmolzen mit der Kraft und Tiefe des Abendlandes und des ernsten Norden ging ein schöneres Daseyn, ein frisches Leben aus dieser Vereinigung hervor. Die heiligen Funken der Dichtkunst waren erwacht, an den Höfen der Fürsten hatten Dichter gesungen, die Fürsten selbst, die ersten Helden ihrer Zeit waren Sänger der Liebe (Minnesänger) gewesen; aber eben jetzt entfaltete sich eine noch schönere Blüthe der Kunst und Wissenschaft unter dem milden Himmel von Italien. Petrarca wurde gegen den Anfang dieses Jahrhunderts geboren, und seine Gesänge, seine zarte hohe Liebe entzündeten in verwandten Seelen ähnliche Gefühle, und äußerten ihre sympathetische Gewalt jenseits der Alpen und des trennenden Meeres. (ibid., Bd. II, 46f)[6]

Locating these plots in the Middle Ages allows their authors to exploit a wide range of traditions/signifiers that would have been well-known to their readers, creating a frame of reference for the stories:

> Je herrlicher die geschichtliche Gestalt eines Volks oder Geschlechts sich ausgebildet hat, um so mehr pflegen im Hintergrunde seiner Vorzeit sich wunderbare Gebilde der Sage zu bewegen, die, als reine Erzeugnisse der Natur, dem Boden, auf dem sie gewachsen, durchaus verwandt sind. So ist die griechische Fabelwelt heiter wie jener Himmel und das sanft lächelnde Meer, in dem die blühenden Küsten sich bespiegeln; die ossianischen Gestalten der Vorzeit dagegen sind riesenhafte Nebelgebilde, die im Sturm über die öden Heiden dahinsausen. Und noch wunderbarer durchzieht die abenteuerliche Gestalt der Sage den im Eis erstarrten Norden. Dort folgen ihr grausenhafte Züge von Riesen und Ungeheuern, und sie selbst, mit wildem, kriegerischem Auge und blutigem Schwert, blickt uns so furchtbar an, daß wir die phantastisch reizende Gestalt, der wir im Süden zuerst zu begegnen gewohnt waren, kaum wiedererkennen. Und doch ist sie eine und dieselbe, gebiert aus ihrem fruchtbaren Schos, hier wie dort, im Laufe der Zeiten die schönsten Früchte für die kommenden Geschlechter. Wie aber das deutsche Vaterland eine schöne Mitte hält zwischen der allzu rasch entflammten Glut des Südens und der fast erstarrt festen Kraft des Nordens, so zeigt uns auch hier die Sage, dieser wunderbare Hohlspiegel der Geschichte, in dem sich die Völker in ihren ersten kräftiggroßen, kühnern Grundzügen erblicken, zeigt uns, meine ich, auch hier die bedeutsamsten Gemälde, die einen gleichen Reiz von freundlicher Anmuth des Südens und ernster Wehmuth des Nordens haben. (Rellstab 47f)[7]

The specific imaginary of the Middle Ages conjured up by these passages has the capability to signify as a real *and* as an imaginary place simultaneously; placing the Middle Ages as the point of origin and authenticity establishes truth claims that frame the narrative.

PLOT STRUCTURES

Once this setting is established, however, the main emphasis of the novels shifts to the destinies of individuals. The novels are intricate and confused/-ing, with convoluted plots around fictional protagonists (male and female) which follow certain formulaic patterns: we usually encounter a virtuous but dowdy heroine; an equally dowdy suitor who is prone to being seduced by women and vice; another suitor who is adventurous and mysterious; a villain who manipulates and spins elaborate pattern of intrigues; a noble bandit; and a distant yet humane despot who is generally misjudged by his people. None of these characters are described in great detail; they are part of a stock repertoire immediately recognizable to readers and mostly characterized through their actions (which are full of anachronisms). None of the novels follow a single protagonist or have a first person narrator. The characters act against a highly simplified societal structure (feudalism) dominated by knights and peasants, set in rural areas and at courts rather than in medieval cities. While artisans and guilds do appear, they are clearly integrated into an organic vision of medieval society that is free from social tension or struggle. Indeed, the social structure is not challenged; it is rather the quest of individuals to find their specific place within this social structure that is the basis for tension and plot complications.

THE MERRY-GO-ROUND OF IDENTITIES

This is clearly expressed in one of the major motifs in these novels: an abandoned infant (usually of noble birth, as often female as male) grows up among *Köhler* (coal-pickers) and has to go through a number of adventures in order to find his/her soulmate, family, and rightful place. In a merry-go-round of identities, these plot patterns of abandonment, (mis-)recognition and resolution are repeated in similar, only slightly different constellations with a whole arsenal of characters who are sometimes quite difficult to keep track of. Thus, in Caroline Pichler's *Die Grafen von Hohenberg*, the protagonist Herrmann has to save the day not once but repeatedly and in disguise (which is revealed to the reader at the latest possible moment – the reader is not allowed to follow the protagonist or even know when he will make his next spectacular appearance to rescue yet another damsel in distress). The basic character constellation of the plot – the story of Herrmann and his sister Agnes, of noble descent but abandoned as infants, raised in the same orphanage with hints of a possibly incestuous relationship – is repeated in subplots with different couples. Although completely predictable to the reader of the genre, the true relationship of the couple is not revealed for the longest time; the true »identity« of the characters – i.e. their relationship to each other – is constantly presented as precarious. The (often reduplicated) encounters are only partially revealing; the discovery of sexual desire is only the first step on this journey:

> So hatte sie ihn noch nie gesehen. Das geistliche Gewand hatte ihr so wesentlich zu ihm zu gehören geschienen, daß sie es in ihren Gedanken nie von ihm trennte, daß ihr keine Möglichkeit eines andern Verhältnisses, als das treuer Schwesternliebe zwischen dem Gott geweihten Jünglinge und der künftigen Nonne, erschien. Jetzt, da sie ihn in weltlichen Kleidern erblickte, fühlte sie eine plötzliche Verwandlung in sich vorgehen. Eine zarte Scheu entfernte sie von dem fremd gewordenen Jüngling, indeß ein geheimer Zug sie fester an ihn zog. Auch er schien diese Veränderung zu theilen. Kühner, als je, schlang er zum ersten Mahle den Arm um ihren schlanken Leib, er führte sie zu der Bank vor der Hütte, er setzte sich Arm in Arm mit ihr nieder, sein Blick ruhte mit nie gefühltem Wohlgefallen auf ihrer Gestalt. Es war beyden, als sähen sie sich heute zum ersten Mahle; sie hatten sich so viel zu sagen, so viel zu entdecken, und dennoch war beyder Seele zu sehr mit dem Anblicke des geliebten Gegenstandes beschäftigt, um irgend ein Gespräch anhaltend fortzusetzen. (Pichler, Bd. I, 114)[8]

Incest is, of course, another main motif, not only in a great number of novels, but in the literature of the period in general.[9] Yet it seems to me there is more to the particular plot structures of these novels than an obsession with incest transposed into playful titillation. The mis-recognition of people in regard to their most prominent identity markers, which are constantly in jeopardy (social status, family relationships, male or female, ghost or human, dead or alive), provides the fuel, which constantly sparks the readers' interest by providing more and more intricate constellations that resist a final self-recognition on the part of the subjects. In Ludwig Rellstab's tale *Elsbeth*, two couples are on the brink of incestuous relationships until it turns out that not only the girls, but also the boys were mixed up as infants. Yet the results are not always so accommodating; in the short novel *Waldhulde* by the same author, father and son fall for the same woman, who also happens to be their sister/daughter, and after their relations are consummated, they all end up dying.

The constant intrusion of the supernatural (in the form of ghosts rather than the medieval motifs of giants, dwarves and dragons) seems to operate in a similar mode. It is remarkable that a literature that relies so heavily on its literary predecessors performs such a substitution, but ghosts are singularly more apt to straddle the line between madness, mistaken identity and supernatural intervention than dragons, which quite obviously existed in (or for?) the medieval mind. (This seems to be borne out by the fact that in all the novels I looked at, which is more than I care to admit to, about half of those which feature ghosts provide »natural« explanations for them while the other half acknowledge supernatural intervention.) Yet this remains a fine line when authors deal with the Middle Ages, which is after all a »real« place and time that readers know from their history books. More arcane and bizarre plots have to be set elsewhere, and for this genre, this elsewhere is called the »Orient,« a complete utopia and dreamland/-time. Whenever plot structures step over an imaginary border of believability, they have to be located in a magical east where no historically confirmed person or place inhibits fantasy. The orient is the land of fairytales, of shapeshifting and magic, a place and time that cannot abide fixture along a space/time axis. Such episodes are often introduced in lengthy digressions that break up coherent narratives by displacement and disruption: in *Ulrich Holzer*, a 30-page story leads us back to the place and times of the Egyptian Pharaoh Necho. Sometimes, however, it is enough to introduce an earlier event »at the dawn of time,« rather than a different location; in Ludwig Rellstab's *Elsbeth*, set during the struggles for the empire between Rudolf of Habsburg and Ottokar Przemysl, such a digression traces the origin of a mysterious fairy to the times of Otto I.

CONCLUSION

I suggest that we regard the establishment of historical distance through a shared frame of historical knowledge, the convoluted, divergent plot structures that constantly recycle each other in a circle of incremental repetition, the intertextual allusions and the basic formulas that construct the narratives as manifestations of a coherent signifying practice within this particular form of appropriation of the image of the Middle Ages, a signifying practice which deliberately prevents any form of realist closure that would allow for easy identification and immersion into a fantasy of the past. Rather, this genre manages to create different forms of pleasure which transcend yet contain the unified subject position of the reader characteristic of bourgeois realism, which arguably accounts for its (literally) popular nature (its *Volkstümlichkeit*). These signifying practices – on a formal level as well as at the level of plot construction – constantly subvert the idea of a unified, finite subject as the origin of meaning while maintaining enough elements of closure to accommodate the bourgeois reader-subject. It is the double movement of containment and challenge that provides the basis for pleasure and entertainment.

Let's take a look at the treatment of history itself. It was obviously not the aim of the authors of this particular form of popular literature to provide a »realistic« depiction of a historical period. Historical background is fairly accurate when it concerns dates, battles, emperors and councilors (the stuff that traditional history is made of) but completely anachronistic in regard to mentalities, social structures and even institutions. So while there is an obvious attempt by most of the authors to get their »facts« right, they pay not the slightest attention to historical probability. Motives and characters are strictly eighteenth century, and the more obvious anachronisms provide a bridge between the readers and the historical frame of reference, such as the following description in *Ulrich Holzer* of an emperor who is more like a father in a Waldmüller painting than a premodern ruler:

> Unruhig und gedankenvoll kam der Kaiser vom Rathhause. Erholung in den Armen seiner Familie war ihm nöthig! Heute wäre ihm Maximilians Abwesenheit night länger zu verbergen gewesen. Er sehnte sich, den geliebten, und über sein Alter verständigen Knaben an seine Brust zu drücken, aber so süß ihm diese Umarmung war, so tief, so bitter fühlte er, was er aus dem Munde seiner Schwester, die oft mehr über ihn vermochte als die Gemahlinn, nun erst erfuhr. (265)[10]

Escapist identification is made possible by making the Middle Ages familiar and interpellating the readers in a movement of closure that is at the same time anachronistic and realistic. At first sight, this would seem to be the classic definition of realism: »Through the presentation of an intelligible history which effaces its own status as discourse, classic realism proposes a model in which author and reader are subjects who are the source of shared meanings, the origin of which is mysteriously extra-discursive« (Belsey 72). Internal textual strategies allow the reader an escape into the past that those texts construct.

But the appropriation of the past cannot be complete: as important as this self-identification on the part of the reader through the closure achieved by realist textual strategies is the alterity produced by distancing the fiction in time, the nostalgic motif that constitutes the basis for escapism. The symbolic universe called »the Middle Ages« thus produced is profoundly ambivalent; history and its markers (dates, kings etc.) make it familiar yet distance it precisely because it is only intelligible from the present; this process of creating historical distance resists closure.

This has crucial effects on the way the reader-subject is constructed in the text. These historical novels simultaneously produce and transcend the transcendental ego, the precondition for the identificatory reading practice created by the Enlightenment. The structure of these texts serves to mirage the individual subject created in the process of enlightened reading by closure, by the classic realist mode; a stable (bourgeois) identity is thus only very incompletely produced and at the same time critiqued – pleasurably critiqued.

The formal peculiarities of the genre seem to bear out this observation. The narrative strategies themselves transcend closure by constantly foregrounding their constructed nature, the materiality of the signifiers and their surplus production of meaning. Each digression, each sub-plot is equally meaning-full, the processes of producing meaning are repeated and create precisely the unity that is denied to the subject as the origin of meaning-production. On the content level, the themes – abandoned infant, mistaken identities, anonymous knight etc. – similarly refer to their origin of meaning. The reading subject is thus not inserted into a completely intelligible world as the origin of the production of meaning (as in the realist novel), but is thrown into a universe of para-tactically constituted signifiers that construct this particular reality – a universe which is called the Middle Ages here, but is actually the subconscious that simultaneously relies on and rejects unreflected enlightened reason as the *ultima ratio* of the production of meaning. The multiple mirages of the plots constantly throw into jeopardy this process of identification; the reader does not find herself but rather finds reflections of the similar, a speculum rather than a mirror held up by form and content in a movement of double jeopardy. These are short glimpses into the realm of fantasy, dream, madness and the constant shift and transcendence of the (symbolic) boundaries that keep them apart.

This is the basis of the gratifying effects of the genre: pleasure is created by dissolving the homogeneous, unified subject position of the rational subject of the Enlightenment while at the same time conjuring up a nostalgic vision of an organic community – the nostalgic vision of origin operates on top of, but only in the context of, a historical frame of reference for the bourgeois reader-subject. The de-centered reader thus escapes his role as a monad through the process of appropriating and being appropriated by the (fictional) past (however incompletely); a coherent, rational subjectivity is substituted by a relative position of similarity that leaves room for desire and indeterminacy, the latent operation of the unconscious.

The popular literature of the period thus offered the possibility of symbolic pleasure and resistance to the narrowly conceived forms of reason propagated by the Enlightenment while adopting some of their conventions and truth claims. In this sense the genre was able to work against a hegemonic interpellation that could safeguard harmony and universality through transparency. Locating these stories in the Middle Ages accommodates the imaginary quality of this literary operation while also exploiting the literature of the Middle Ages itself that had been handed down by a hybrid learned and poetic reception (on which the Romantic appropriation of the Middle Ages was based). Moreover, the Middle Ages as a period of a »super-natural economy« (a period when belief in supernatural forces was a determinant of everyday life) facilitated the move to portraying them as a projection of the human psyche while perpetuating tradition as an antidote to unreflected enlightened reason. The Middle Ages were thus superbly suitable for critiquing closure by combining a literary reception with a turn toward the unconscious, thus in a way both resisting realism in a reactionary way while simultaneously reaching beyond it – the miraculous is transformed into the uncanny.

Ultimately I would argue that it is this particular image, vision, and treatment of the Middle Ages in popular genres and in a popular tradition that the Romantics drew on – by appropriating a truly popular tradition, a tradition that produced pleasure by transporting its readers to a time long, long ago and an era far, far away.

ENDNOTES

1 »Knights' tales wherever you look. To the right, tales without ghosts; to the left, tales with ghosts, whatever kind you want.« (Unless otherwise noted, translations are by the editors.)

2 »Once there were fine, resplendent times when Europe was a Christian land, when one Christendom occupied this humanly constituted continent. One great common interest united the remotest provinces of this broad spiritual realm. Without great worldly possessions, one Head guided and unified the great political forces. A numerous guild, to which everyone had access, stood directly beneath him and carried out his behests and strove with zeal to confirm his beneficent power. Every member of this organization was universally honored, and if the common people sought comfort or help, protection or counsel from this member, and in return were happy to provide generously for his manifold needs, he also found protection, respect, and hearing among the more powerful, and everyone cared for these chosen men, equipped with miraculous powers, as for children of Heaven whose presence and favor spread manifold blessing abroad.« (trans. Charles E. Passage)

3 All illustrations are from Reisenleitner.

4 »One can see from the above, chronologically arranged list how our poets' desire to deal with subjects related to the fatherland has increased of late... In 1767 in his letter about the theater, the preface to his tragic play *Julie*, the late Sturz was still interested in the dilatoriness of our poets in drawing on the German history of the Middle Ages, und suggested the following as material: Charlemagne,... Emperor Heinrich the 4th, Konradin of Schwaben, the jealousies Karl the 3rd and Heinrich the 2nd felt on account of their spouses, and Otto the 3rd, who was poisoned by Crescentius's widow. Despite the stupendous excess of plays and novels based on Germany's past history that we now enjoy, Sturz's wishes still haven't been fulfilled. Many ›old German‹ events have often been used, but the story of Heinrich the 2nd and Otto the 3rd has yet to find its poet.«

5 »There was, a long time ago, a time when a subjugated people suddenly began to feel their chains and, in the attempt to shake them off, brought much suffering upon both themselves and an undistinguished prince. How they blundered along, led astray time and again by self-serving tempters on both a large and small scale who blathered a lot of nonsense about freedom and patriotism to the betrayed downtrodden masses; how they blundered along in the thickest of darknesses and how their self-inflicted wounds bled dry until finally the enchanted spell wore off, the enemies of freedom fell, and peace and order returned. From those tempestuous and treacherous times, from that confusion of horror, where those looking back were first able to discern specific characteristics and the fates of specific persons from the causes and consequences of others, it is from these times – the times of Emperor Friederich the 3rd – that we want to lift some scenes and lay them down for your entertainment, dear reader.«

6 »It was just then that a wondrous light began to spread its way from the south. The crusaders had already brought the arts, the knowledge, the sweet-scented songs of the orient back home; happily melded with the power and depth of the East and the serious North, a more bounteous way of being, a new life emerged from this union. The holy sparks of poetry had been lit, poets had sung in princely courts, the princes themselves, the first heroes of their times, had been bards of love. But now, precisely now, an even more beautiful blossoming of art and science unfolded under the mild Italian skies. Near the beginning of the century, Petrarch was born, and his poems, his delicate, lofty love enflamed similar sentiments in similarly inclined souls, and spread its sympathetic power beyond the Alps and the divisive sea.«

7 »The more impressive the historical frame of reference that a people or clan has amassed for itself, the more amazing the structures of sagas that float about in the background, which, as pure products of nature, are intimately related to the earth. That's why the Greek world of myths is as light as the sky and the soft, smiling sea, in which the soothing coastline is reflected; the Ossian-like figures of the Dark Ages, on the other hand, are massive structures of fog, which rush in to smother the bleak moors during a storm. And still more amazing is the adventurous shape of the saga from the ice-encrusted north. In the north, giants and monsters parade after the saga, and the saga itself, with its wild, warrior gaze and bloody sword, looks at us in such a terrifying way that we barely recognize the fantastically appealing figure we first met in the south. Und yet it's one and the same, born of fertile womb, here as there, the most beautiful

fruits for the coming generations. The way our German fatherland maintains a perfect balance between the all too quick to enflame south and the almost frozen power of the north, here too the saga shows us, this wonderful speculum of history, in which peoples catch sight of the first daring flexing of their characteristics, shows us, I think, also here the most important paintings, which contain the south's friendly disposition and the north's solemn melancholy in equal measure.«

8 »She'd never seen him like that before. His priestly robes had seemed to be such an integral part of him that she had never separated him from them, even in her thoughts, no other type of relationship had occurred to her besides that of the pure sibling love of a young man whose life was devoted to God and a future nun. Now that she'd seen him in street clothes, she felt a sudden change inside her. With a tender shyness, she drew away from the youth who was now a stranger to her, while a secret sensation pulled her closer to him. He too seemed to share in this change. More forward than ever, he for the first time put his arm around her slender form, he led her to the bench in front of the cabin, arm in arm they sat down together, his look rested on her figure with never before experienced satisfaction. It seemed to both of them as though they saw each other today for the first time, they had so much to say to each other, so much to discover and yet, both souls were too preoccupied looking at their beloved object to be able to continue with any kind of conversation.«

9 As Praz notes: »Incest itself also... became a theme dear to the Romantics... who invested incestuous love between brother and sister with poetic charm and sentimental dignity... [Chateaubriand] makes the lovers' passion culminate in the discovery of bonds of spiritual brotherhood... Chateaubriand is also full of longing for the état de nature idolised by the Encyclopédistes, in which he imagined it possible to realise his sensual ideal... the relationship of lovers between brother and sister fascinated him inasmuch as he felt it through the consciousness of sin; and since the possibility of the latter is lacking in the primitive natural state, that particular relationship could have no different savor from the relationship between strangers« (111f.).

10 »Restless and pensive, the emperor returned from the courthouse. How he needed to be in the regenerative bosom of his family! Today it was no longer possible to hide Maximilian's absence from him. He longed to press the cherished boy, who was wiser than his years, to his breast, but as sweet as this embrace was to him, he felt as deeply, as bitterly what he only now learned from the lips of his sister, who often had more influence on him than his wife.«

REFERENCES

Belsey, Catherine. *Critical Practice*. London/New York, 1980.

Kleist, Heinrich von. *Sämtliche Werke und Briefe*, vol. 2. Munich, 1977.

Krogoll, Johannes. »Geschichte im Drama und im Roman der Romantik.« *Europäische Romantik* 2. Ed. Klaus Heitmann. Wiesbaden, 1985. 319ff.

Naubert, Benedicte. *Ulrich Holzer, Bürgermeister von Wien*. Leipzig, 1793.

Novalis. *Fragmente und Studien. Die Christenheit oder Europa*. Stuttgart, 1984 (1799).

—. *Christendom or Europe*. Trans. Charles E. Passage. Indianapolis, 1960.

Pichler, Caroline. *Die Grafen von Hohenberg*. Wien, 1820.

Praz, Mario. *The Romantic Agony*. Oxford, 1988.

Reisenleitner, Markus. *Die Produktion historischen Sinnes: Mittelalterrezeption im deutschsprachigen historischen Trivialroman vor 1848*. Frankfurt am Main, 1992.

Rellstab, *Ludwig. Sagen und romantische Erzählungen*. Leipzig, 1860.

Meet Me in Vienna (*Alt-Wien*), Meet Me at the Fair

SUSAN INGRAM

The 1904 Louisiana Purchase Exhibition in St. Louis was the last world exhibition in which the Austro-Hungarian (a.k.a. k&k) monarchy participated before being thrown from its car on the dizzying roller-coaster of capitalist-driven (inter)nationalist desire it rode for almost half a century before the derailment of the First World War (Felber, Krasny and Rapp 109). The 1904 fair marked the first appearance of a »modern« Austrian pavilion at such an exhibition – the exterior was designed by Ludwig Baumann and the interior by Josef Hoffmann –, and it was the first time that the entirety of Austria's exhibited material was housed in one building, and not scattered among Machinery, Agricultural, Fine Arts and other Halls (111). This pavilion was not the only »Austrian« presence in St. Louis, however. On the midway-type amusement area known as the Pike was a Tirolean Village, at which »German« folksongs and dances were performed by singing associations from the Tyrol, and an Oberammergauer passion play was accompanied by a spectacular light show. Sponsored by an American brewery, it proved to be one of the fair's most popular and most visited attractions (114).

These two competing visions of Austria – folksy vs. modern – did not originate with the St. Louis fair, but were rather, by 1904, an established part of the complex of exhibitionary traditions. Nor was this splitting particular to Austria. Rather it is akin to what Homi Bhahba refers to in his essay »Dissemination: Time, Narrative and the Margins of the Modern Nation« as the »›double and split‹ time of national representation« (144), and it was a key factor in, and symptom of, the development of nationalist-inflected corporatist discourse towards the end of the nineteenth century, a process I examine in this paper by drawing on the example of Austrian participation at the world exhibitions before the First World War, and more specifically on the slippage between Austrian and k&k participation, between the monarchy and »the nation.« I want to take advantage of »Austria's« dual nature in this regard to show how it disrupts the customary national and imperial narratives constructed about the world exhibitions and how it underscores Bhabha's call »to question the homogeneous and horizontal view associated with the nation's imagined community,« to identify »the emergence of a national perspective – of an élite or subaltern nature – within a culture of social contestation,« and to specify which groups are behind »the nation,« mobilizing it as a homogenizing, »representative« mask for their own purposes and benefit (144). Such questioning is also helpful in isolating a particular historical period – the Middle Ages – the representation of which links the world exhibition tradition to the best known of the themed exhibitionary complexes it spawned.

The motivation for this paper is a set of postcards in the collection of world's fair memorabilia at the Wolfsonian–FIU in Miami Beach. These ten cards are of »Old Vienna/Alt Wien« on the Midmay [sic] Plaisance at the World's Fair. They feature:

1. The Austrian Band, C.M. Ziehrer Conductor (Musikkapelle des Hoch- und Deutschmeister Regiments – C.M. Ziehrer, Hofkapellmeister)
2. Hotel and German Restaurant, City of Vienna (Hotel und Garten-Restauration zur Stadt Wien)
3. Hazai Natzi's Hungarian Band (Hazai Natzi's Ungarische Kapelle)
4. Seidl's Garden (Höchster Heuriger)
5. The City Hall, built 1693 (Das Rathhaus, erbaut im Jahre 1693)
6. The Austrian Laender-Bank (Die Oesterreichische Laender-Bank)
7. View Toward the Gate (Ansicht dem Stadtthore zu)
8. At the Salvator (Zum Salvator)
9. The Eastern Court (Der östliche Hof), which features a Wiener Café
10. The Church (Die Kirche)

A final, uncaptioned view of the street completes the collection. Aside from the intriguing issue of how the captions were translated, as well as the expected presence of music (cf. Szabó-Knotik) and establishments for fine wining and dining, what is striking about the collection is how little it represents either the contemporary Vienna of 1893 – the city gates were long gone by then, and there was a new city hall on the Ringstrasse, reference to which is conspicuously absent in these images – or even the Vienna of 1693. There are no traces to be found in the collection of the baroque splendor now commonly associated with Vienna (such as in *Before Sunrise* (1995, dir. Richard Linklater)). One

(Ill. 1 – Courtesy of the Mitchell Wolfson, Jr. Collection, The Wolfsonian-Florida International University, Miami Beach, Florida)

would hardly date the city hall depicted on the postcard as anywhere close to the seventeenth or eighteenth century (*Ill. 1*). If pressed, its architectural style, and the general style of Old Vienna as a whole, would rather appear to be somewhere between the Romanesque and the Gothic. This Old Vienna is clearly generically old, recreated to evoke a past as distant and as misleading as the passion-play spectacle at the Tirolean Village in St. Louis. Why? Why at the world exhibitions, gatherings that celebrated industrial progress – »the works of industry of all nations« – did Vienna so ironically take on this particular form, a Vienna considerably before the Vienna of musical »days gone by« (cf. Saffle)?

The reading given the appearance of »Old Europe« at the world's fairs, a phenomenon which has not gone unnoted in the scholarship, seems to depend on which of the Old European nations is taken as the subject. Focusing on »the English national profile fabricated in the closing decades of the nineteenth century,« Paul Greenhalgh accounts for the popularity of the Tudor and Elizabethan era as »due to their historical location at the start of English imperial history. The establishment of the Church of England, the maturing of the arts, the growth of the navy, of overseas trade and conquest, made them the perfect periods to hark back to for nationalists« (122). Such an explanation is obviously not applicable to the phenomenon of Old Vienna. Going beyond England to include the other two major hosts of nineteenth-century world exhibitions, Aram A. Yengogan finds the growing trend of nationalism mainly responsible for how the leading nations represented themselves at the world's fairs, arguing that:

> In various expressions, the dominant exhibitions in France, England and the United States up to WWI all reflected ideological themes that were part of nationalism, the dominance of the State, and global imperialism. Each nation/state was concerned with creating its historical traditions from the past to the present and possibly the future. ... The past was understood as a major concern which could not be relegated to a distant time in a meaningless way. Historical continuity was essential in legitimizing the State, and the exhibitions generally played a vital role in conveying this position. Thus for example, in each of the French exhibitions of 1867, 1878, 1889, and 1900, images of medieval Paris were displayed alongside those of a putative rural bucolic France. In addition to the imposing grandeur of these portrayals, one also notes an intrusive disjunction, for certain of the displayed images bore little or no relation to actual historical documentation. Images of Paris in the past were recast in terms of 19th century Paris, and once established, took on a reality of their own which in turn was recast onto the past. Each succeeding exhibition then portrayed what had been constructed in previous exhibitions. As each particular projection took hold, it became assumed truth, and was reworked back into an impression of how medieval Paris might have been envisaged. Thus each case not only established ›another reality,‹ but over time itself became historical evidence. (77-8)

There is certainly something to the influence that exhibition displays had on the creation of historical evidence as well as to the question of invented traditions with little or no relation to historical documentation (cf. Hobsbawn and Ranger). However, while his argument would appear to hold for Old Paris in Paris, Old Antwerp in Antwerp (1885, 1894, 1930), Old Brussels in Brussels (1897, 1935), Old Edinburgh in Edinburgh (1886), Old London at Wembley (1924-25), and even the Spanish restaurant in Barcelona which gradually expanded to a Quarter (1888, 1929-30, 1992), can one equally maintain that it held in the same way for Old Vienna in *Chicago*? One would then have to account for the absence of an Old Vienna at the Vienna World Exhibition of 1873 as well as the presence of the notably and stylishly *modern* Parisian display on the Chicago and St. Louis midways.

More problematic, however, is Yengogan's unproblematic, homogenizing »imagined community« approach to nation. This focus on the »leading« nations excludes others, like Austria-Hungary, which call into question over-easy generalizations. As I alluded to at the outset, to write even of »the French« (let alone, as Katherine Arens has very forcefully argued, »the Austrians«) is to ignore »the *emergence* of a national perspective – of an élite or subaltern nature – within a culture of social contestation,« a trajectory which Homi Bhahba develops from Bakhtin's:

> wonderful description of a national *vision of emergence* in Goethe's *Italian Journey*, which represents the triumph of the Realistic component over the Romantic. Goethe's realist narrative produces a national-historical time that

> makes visible a specifically Italian day in the detail of its passing time: ›The bells ring, the rosary is said, the maid enters the room with a lighted lamp and says: *Felicissima notte!... If one were to force a German clockhand on them, they would be at a loss.*‹ For Bakhtin, it is Goethe's vision of the microscopic, elementary, perhaps random, tolling of everyday life in Italy that reveals the profound history of its locality (*Lokalität*), the spatialization of historical time. (143, italics in original)

And for Bhabha, the failure of the Realistic to completely triumph over the Romantic reveals that there is »always the distracting presence of another temporality that disturbs the contemporaneity of the national present« (143), a present which must constantly surmount the ghostly, the terrifying and the unaccountable. Freud, he reminds us, »associates surmounting with the repressions of a ›cultural‹ unconscious; a liminal, uncertain state of cultural belief when the archaic emerges in the midst of margins of modernity as a result of some psychic ambivalence or intellectual uncertainty« (143). When archaic representations of nation – of all nations, not merely the leading ones[1] or the European ones[2] – emerged at the world exhibitions towards the end of the nineteenth century, they actually did emerge on the margins – the midways – in a process detailed in the next section.

THE MIDWAY

> From the scattered and disconnected amusement and pleasure offerings in the city of London in 1851 to the carefully positioned and controlled settings of Paris in 1889, Chicago in 1893, and St. Louis in 1904, the Midway has moved closer to the center – and central purposes – of the exposition. And when detached to develop on its own right in theme amusement parks after World War II, the Midway stood almost by itself, a monstrous child greater and more vigorous than its parent. (Gilbert 16-17)

> The Midway Plaisance... bears the same relation to the Exposition that the sideshows have to the circus. [Here are] German, Irish, Austrian, Turkish, Javanese, and Egyptian villages, mosques, kiosks, and pagodas, menageries, panoramas, casinos, cliff-dwellers, snake-charmers, Esquimaux... It is ... a vivacous, cosmopolitan medley. (*Chicago Tribune*, April 30, 1893, cited in Çelik, 50)

Chicago's Midway Plaisance was the first amusement area of its kind at a world exhibition. While amusements were to be found on the grounds around the main buildings, the display halls and pavilions beginning with the 1867 Paris universal exposition, Chicago marked the first time paying concessions were allotted their own separate area, something Burton Benedict attributes to cultural difference:

> The French did not make the sharp distinction between the amusement zone and the main fair that characterized British and American expositions. Perhaps the Protestant ethic does not run so strongly in France. In the Paris expositions of 1867, 1889, 1900, 1931, and 1937, ethnic exhibits and performances were not placed among Ferris wheels and carousels but formed an integral part of the main fair. Moreover visitors were free to mingle with the inhabitants of the exposition villages, which militates against their being seen as human curiosities on a par with physiological monsters. In the 1889 Paris fair there were processions of all the indigenous people through the exposition grounds, which were virtual parades of colonized peoples. The nightly procession was so popular that it was imported to Chicago in 1893, where it was more of a fun fair attraction and lacked the overt colonialization there. (52)

In the case of that ultimate nation-state, France, what mattered was not amusement but rather giving material expression to ideas of nation; in 1878, they came up with the idea of a so-called »Rue des Nations« and required that pavilions along it be provided with a »façade typique« (Felber, Krasny and Rapp 75). The WASP work-ethic, on the other hand, would seem to have required that the corrupting influence of play be isolated from the spaces set aside for more serious, instructive matters. In further contrast to nationally motivated continental mingling, the segregation of »fun fair attractions« at the American fairs coincided with their depoliticization. Whereas the theme of the Parisian 1867 and 1878 fairs was »labor,« with San Simonian attention paid to the plight of the working class (cf. Greenhalgh 145-6), the purpose of the WASP amusement zones was clearly, and solely, commercial. Lenox Lohr, the legendary manager of the 1933 Chicago Century of Progress fair, emphasized in his autobiographical directives to future fair managers how critical these areas were to a fair's overall success:

> Concessions, including food, drinks, souvenirs, rides, shows, spectacles, and transportation, present some of the most important problems for which the fair management must find satisfactory solutions. They produce the bulk of the operating income, they attract large numbers of care-free visitors, but they are the source of many headaches. The financial responsibility of all concessionaires should be carefully checked by management, as previously successful operators may be forced to seek outside financial aid under disadvantageous conditions. (274)

The question then becomes – was it commercial or nationalist pressures that led to the emergence of archaic representations of nation? Or possibly some intriguing combination thereof?

This returns us to the argument about nationalism as the force driving nations to represent themselves as such at the world exhibitions. Both Yengogan and Greenhalgh ascribe to an understanding of nationalism, which locates motivation in a state-induced desire for unity. Greenhalgh writes:

> In the turmoil of the first industrial age, nationalism became the principal means whereby government could ensure a unity amongst people who might otherwise have had little or no cohesion. In part replacing loyalty to monarchy or local overlord, love of nation was not in the first instance an emotion easily instilled into the masses. ... Nationalism, *as encouraged by state-machines throughout Europe*, entailed the convincing of a population that it should be proud – aggressively so – of the country it lived in, and that the country somehow had a life of its own to be acknowledged and supported. (112-13, italics added)

In a similar vein, Yengogan continues the argument outlined above:

> If the nation/state may be said to have established a past that would converge into the present, it was still the present, however, which would be most significant in *forming a citizenry* as a means of *creating state hegemony* through cultural and technological enterprise. Almost all of the exhibitions stressed the present in terms of science, technology, production, aesthetics and knowledge. (78, italics added)

While his emphasis on the present is doubtless on target, one must question the significance of Austria-Hungary's representation in Chicago and St. Louis in regard to the formation of a citizenry – there were, after all, far more Austro-, Hungarian-, Czech- et al.- *Americans* than Austrian-Hungarians there to be influenced, not to mention those who were coming to understand themselves as just »plain« Americans. Such an assertion, like Greenhalgh's, would appear to conflate state with commerce. The increasing dominance of the midway zones would lead one to believe that the world exhibitions seem to have been less about forming citizenries than they were about opening up new markets and finding or forming new customers. It is hard to believe that Old Vienna appeared in the form and location it did because some government officials back in Vienna thought it could productively be used to mold k&k visitors, who were hardly numerous; rather more convincing is the line of reasoning that its immigrant concessionaires chose this form because they thought it most likely to attract mostly indigenous visitors not likely to venture beyond the confines of their state, let alone beyond the sea, to stop at their concession for a beer or a glass of wine, and not further down at the Algerians or the Javanese or the Irish or the Germans or the Chinese or the Brazilians or... This is not to deny the influence of nationalism in soliciting or interpellating a particular form of identificatory practice, but rather to attend to the ways that consumption and consumerdom complicate what are usually taken to be rather straightforward political mechanisms.[3] In order to get behind the apparition that was Old Vienna and the question of why we find specifically pre-industrial forms of nation on the midways and not in the official displays or vice versa, in the next section I will take a closer, comparative look at these two forms of nationally coded display.

TOURING THE AUSTRIAN ATTRACTIONS AT THE 1893 CHICAGO COLUMBIAN

To get a feel for the basis of Old Vienna's attraction and the impression both it and the official Austria display made on American visitors, this section looks at the way two such visitors reported on the two areas of the fair associated with Austrians. The first account is from *Shepp's World's Fair photographed: being a collection of original copyrighted photographs authorized and permitted by the management of the World's Columbian Exposition*. The Shepps attempt in the text accompanying their photos to paint a scene for their readers and to transport them to the midway in the same way the photos do:

> Out of the glare and rush of the Plaisance, we pass between the two *quaint* towers, under the massive arch, which forms the entrance to ›Old Vienna.‹ At the portal, we are confronted by a tall, motionless figure, clad in the uniform of the municipal guards of *ancient* days, and holding a halberd in his hand. After passing this, it seems that the hands on the dial of time had been turned *backward*; around us are the *picturesque* structures such as stood in Vienna *150 years ago*; *quaint* gables and projecting balconies, with *odd little* windows, and, in some cases, *old* German mottoes painted on the buildings make up, with the people crowding the square, a *fascinating* and *unusual* sight. There are about seventy buildings in all, facing on a sort of curved street, that widens greatly toward the center, and, in the middle of the open space, the grand stand is seen. Visitors sit at *little* tables in the open air, and while partaking of the delicacies served in *dainty* style by young Vienna girls, listen to the music discoursed by the band, under the leadership of the Hofcapelmeister, who is musical director of the Royal Fourth Austrian Infantry Regiment. He is a great composer, and is permitted to remain here by the Emperor of Austria. Thirty-four stores are filled with *rare goods from Vienna*, and the principal towns of Austro-Hungary; and the courteous and engaging Viennese, nearly all of whom, by the way, speak French [?!], seem to drive a brisk and profitable trade. In the center of this village, we see the Rathhaus, or *old* town Hall, a *faithful copy* of that in the ›Graben‹ [?!] of *old* Vienna. We must not overlook the *museum* here; it is filled with Grecian pictures, taken from the tombs of Farjum, in Egypt; they are *about 2000 years old*. Farjum was made a military colony by Alexander the Great; the soldiers here did not marry the Egyptians, but sent for wives to Macedonia and Greece. The result was that the Greek speech and culture remained among them. Other *curiosities*, such as face mummies and very ancient papyri, may be seen. To have missed Old Vienna in

> our rambles, would have been to lose one of the pleasantest memories in our lives. Over 500 Austrians are engaged in the Fair, and they are quite as courteous as Frenchmen, as brave as Germans, as proud as Magyars, and as clever in trade as any Yankee that we can produce on this continent. (518, italics added)

A second account of Old Vienna is to be found in Major Ben C. Truman's *History of the World's Fair: being a complete and authentic description of the Columbian Exposition from its inception*:

> A center of attraction for all passers-by on the Midway Plaisance is the beautiful Vienna café, or Old Vienna, with its 40 shops, which reproduces not alone the fine architecture but the delightful cookery of the imperial city of Austria. And it is the cookery which appeals most strongly to the wayfarer. Charles Earnest, the manager of the café, who came from Delmonico's of New York to take charge of this enterprise, is known to gourmets the world over as a past master of the art of dining. Equipped with unlimited means and gifted with a genius for catering, Mr. Earnest brings a cosmopolitan experience to a cosmopolitan task. He has managed restaurants in Paris and Vienna, as well as in Rome and London, and he can sympathize in half a dozen languages with the artistic appetite that has been educated on the Boulevard des Italiens and given its doctor's degree on the Ringstrasse.
>
> Messrs. Koenig and Griesser, the proprietors of the café, deserve the congratulations of Chicago for the admirable manner in which they have carried out every detail of their excellent idea. Mr. Koenig came to America with the prestige of having successfully conducted one of the largest cafés in Vienna. The café is one of the most attractive parts of the whole World's Fair and neither money nor brains has been spared in completing it. A magnificent orchestra under the direction of Prof. Julius Schiller is a component part of the attractions provided, and the quick and experienced service, the elegant cookery, and yet thoroughly Viennese, economical scale of prices, and *the whole foreign, old world flavor* of the café bring to it the success it so well deserves.
>
> There have been as many as 4,000 people at one time in Old Vienna. The village occupies a large space in the Plaisance. Its charm lies in its *antiquity*. The reproductions are of Garben [sic] and Bogner streets, Vienna. These are the *oldest* and best-preserved streets of the Austrian capital. They were built *200 years ago* under the protection of the Archduke Ludwig Victor and the Imperial and Royal Lander Bank of Vienna. The buildings, which form a large court, are *exact reproductions* of the *old* streets. Even the cracks in the *ancient* walls are facsimile.
>
> The design creates the impression of a part of an *ancient* city built up with great irregularity, and presents *old*, gable-end houses with frescoes and shields, and these open up a prospective to *small*, narrow streets. The council house, with outside staircase and covered way, stretches along the entire distance of the square, in the middle of which stands an *ancient* well. The shops are built after the fashion of *former times*, and there *only special Viennese products* are sold.

> It is not necessary to draw on the imagination in the Vienna village to become imbued with a *foreign* influence. There is *nothing modern* to meet the eye except the Columbian Guards. The first floors of all the buildings are fitted up as shops. Viennese women are on guard in nearly all of them, and the bank, under whose assistance the street was built, has a branch in the village, and the office is fitted up in the same style as the original institution, founded *300 years ago*.
>
> In the center of the court is the bandstand, where the emperor's own orchestra gives daily concerts. In the garden the tables are *ancient* and the barmaids are dressed in the black and yellow of Austria. All were brought over from Vienna. The village cost $125,000. Early in June the managers gave a banquet to the Columbian officials and others. The guests were given many an Austrian toast, which in plain English was ›Drink and be merry.‹ (575-7)

In these two accounts, Old Vienna is clearly coded »foreign« through adjectives relating to its old, quaint, picturesque, dainty, tiny and, most importantly, *authentic* appearance; it is valued for being a »faithful« copy, an »exact« reproduction. If it were not »young Vienna girls« (and one will note that it is only the barmaids/waitresses who are young) who served the delicacies and »rare goods from Vienna« that were in the shops, Old Vienna would surely have been a less pleasant memory for the Shepp Brothers; if the tables in the courtyard and the barmaids had not been »brought over from Vienna« at a cost of $125,000, Truman would surely have been less impressed. Indeed the parallelisms of the two passages – references to the orchestra's conductor, to the Graben, etc. – lead one to surmise that both were initially based on the same press release, information package and/or set of postcards.

Truman's passage points to the fact that Old Vienna was not intended to officially represent Austria at the fair but rather was run by entrepreneurial immigrants with strong connections to Austrian commerce and culture. What neither Truman nor the Shepps seem to have been aware of was that Chicago 1893 did not mark the debut of Old Vienna: it was originally conceived in 1888 on the occasion of a trade fair celebrating the fortieth anniversary of Franz Joseph's accession and then built for the 1892 *Musik- und Theaterausstellung* held in Vienna's Prater:

> Since 1888 such a project had already been the dream of exhibition architect Emil Bressler. In the summer of 1892, he was approached by the young architect Oscar Marmorek, who built such a reconstruction for the great Music and Theater Exhibition on the Viennese Prater. With the aid of seventeenth-century miniatures, a row of houses from the Hoher Markt was reconstructed in front of the Rotunde, with restaurants, cafés and pubs. Viennese society was enthused, and Archduke Karl Ludwig suggested that the idea be exported to America. Under contract with the Austrian Länderbank, Emil Bressler was

> supposed to built an ›Old Vienna‹ for Chicago. Shops were set up in the buildings, some of which were permanent, and then rented out to Austrian industrialists as well as American concessionaires. (Felber, Krasny and Rapp 90)[4]

What we have here, then, is a slightly different version of the story, between the lines of which the forceful and influential spirit of enterprise is perceptible. Recognizing and responding to a possible opening/niche in the market, Austrian entrepreneurs first tried out »Altwien« in Vienna, where it proved profitable enough that they cast a greedy eye to the larger international market, which, with a royal stamp of approval in the form of Archduke Karl Ludwig's support, and the cooperation of American colleagues, they conquered with equal ease.

While the Shepps may not have known the details of Old Vienna's proprietorship and the machinations which brought it to Chicago, the influence of the »amusement area« on them is registered in their description of the other – official – Austria in Chicago. Like Truman, they detail the »palaces and temples filled with laces, rich chinaware, porcelain, statuary, silverware, textile fabrics, etc.« on display in the mammoth Manufactures Building; however, unlike Truman, they succumb to the same type of historical dissonance they experienced on the Midway. Not knowing how else to describe or locate the Austrian display, the Shepps note that: »There is a queer mixture of the *mediaeval* and the *modern*, as our picture well shows. In the foreground, two lofty pillars support the arms, and are crowned by the eagles of Austro-Hungary, and between them stretches a long vista of glittering glass and china, with numerous other exhibits« (78, italics added).

The internal tensions and conflicts which the Shepps attribute to the realm with which they are most familiar, that of temporality (the mediaeval vs. the modern), were not limited to the Austrian displays in Chicago. However, they receive perhaps their most striking depiction in the *Festschrift* published on the occasion of »Austria Day« at the fair, which was celebrated on the Kaiser's birthday: 18th August 1893 (*Ill. 2*). Against a regal background appropriately shaded Habsburg yellow-ochre, the *Festschrift* features two figures: one male and one female. The female, clad in a gauzy, rosy robe of antiquity and sporting enormous gauzy wings, stands in an erect yet serene posture, one foot delicately resting on a display of fruit, occupying the left half of the picture. She gazes vacantly with a doll-like expression into the space above an undressed male figure, reclining back to the viewer on a bearskin in the lower right quarter of the picture. Jauntily holding a large urn erect in his lap, he does not look up at her and the large gold plate embossed with Franciscus Josephus I. Rex Imperator's likeness and title she is

(*Ill. 2 – Wirtschaftskammer Wien*)

holding as a shield; his head is not thrown back but sits straight on his well-formed shoulders so that his gaze falls calmly just below the plate to where her equally well-formed thigh is exposed by one of the slits in her robe. Here the tension is revealed not to be simply between the old and the new, but rather between an ethereal feminine monarchy and an up-and-coming (almost literally and certainly figuratively) masculinity of indeterminate social origins. As embodied in the *Festschrift* illustration, it was played out in the spirit of the liberal principles governing the exhibition as a whole. The two figures are friendly rivals; with their youthful, white-skinned good looks they would make ideal Olympic athletes. Further it is supposed that they are equivalent if not equal competitors. While the male figure is down, he is hardly out, particularly given the patriarchal norms evidenced in the virile, mustachioed presence of Franz Joseph. The unclad, new-born and very nouveau, young entrepreneur is shown in this illustration to be on his way up, with the phallic order of naturalized biological supremacy clearly on his side. One would not need either of the two indications provided – the stamp of the *Handelskammer in Wien* (Chamber of Commerce in Vienna) or the *Oesterreichisch-Ungarische Zeitung* (Austrian-Hungarian Newspaper) crest – to realize that this illustration was not a product of the palace.

THE OLD AND THE NEW

We can now appreciate the old-new/folksy-modern split as a manifestation of societal reordering, a challenge to a weakened, feminised second (aristocratic) estate on the part of a rising third. It would be a mistake, however, to facilely link the folksy old with the nobles and the new modern with commerce. Rather, as evident in the story behind the appearance of Old Vienna in Chicago, both old and new forms of representation were mobilized by the entrepreneurial class and not without monarchical support; they thus have to be read as part of the larger re-imagining, realigning and reconfiguring of socio-economic and cultural (super)structures, which accompanied the realignment of (for the most part still monarchical) nation-states in the larger and, yes, distinctly imperial context of burgeoning globalism.[5]

Before 1893, Austrian displays at the world exhibitions do not seem to have set off any historical anxiety in North Americans, no matter on which side of the Atlantic they took place. Reviewers of the first world's fair to be held in the U.S., the 1853 New York Crystal Palace Exhibition (see Richards), and of the Universal Exposition in Paris in 1855 (see *Canada at the Universal Exhibition of 1855*), to take very early examples, uniformly describe the Austrian riches on display in great, worshipful detail, without finding anything historically off-putting about them. Their accounts very much follow the lead of contemporary French journalistic pieces in taking a highly evaluative approach to reviewing exhibition displays. The Austrian display in Philadelphia in 1876 was found to be equally impressive, though faulted not as a French journalist might on aesthetic grounds, but rather for its lack of practicality:

> There was hardly any department of the Exhibition more attractive than that of the Bohemian glass, characterized as it was by great beauty and variety of

> design, and richness of decoration and color. Most of the finer specimens of Bohemian ware, however, must be regarded as designed for ornament on the side board cabinet-shelf, and mantel-piece, rather than for actual table-use. (*Gems of the Centennial Exhibition* 65-6)

In 1893, however, the next world's fair Austria attended in the U.S. after Philadelphia, a display of the same sort of goods suddenly registers as »a queer mixture of the medieval and the modern.«[6] This shift in perception is linked, I would maintain, in no small part to the appearance of Old Vienna on the Midway. As we saw earlier in Bhabha's reading of the double time of national representation, a ghostly, terrifying, unaccountable (Romantic) presence is precisely what (avowedly Realist) nationalist presents must constantly surmount. That this presence should first make itself felt on the Midway, a space dedicated to commercialism, fits nicely with Colin Campbell's locating the beginnings of modern consumerism in the Romantic theory of artistic creation. If we understand Romanticism as Campbell does, to provide »that philosophy of ›recreation‹ necessary for a dynamic consumerism: a philosophy that legitimates the search for pleasure as good in itself« (201), then what else would we expect to find on the Midway but recreated archaic (at least from a Romantic point of view) sites of pleasure-oriented consumerist recreation?[7]

What remains to be discussed, then, is the specific attraction of the particular Romantic guise in which the archaic appeared and then reappeared at sites dedicated to consumptive pleasures. The source of the »medieval,« i.e. generically old, reproductions on the Midway, lies in a particularly Romantic understanding and recreation of the Middle Ages, as outlined by Reisenleitner in his reading of early nineteenth-century *Trivialromane* in the preceding article. In the final section of the paper, I consider how the Romantics' poetic appropriation of their particular version of the Middle Ages »for political as well as escapist agendas characterized by an often reactionary and apologetic glorification of medieval institutions and power relations« (p. 65 in this volume) returned at intervals of slightly over a half-century.

DISNEY: THE NOT-SO-MISSING LINK

Just as each of the world exhibitions aimed to have a »clou,« a monumental modern structure such as the Eiffel Tower or the Ferris Wheel which would come to signify the exhibition and its accomplishments in the public imagination, so too were each of the Disney theme parks conceptualized around a central structure, not a modern one but rather a fantasized late nineteenth-century recreation of something vaguely medieval. As every child soon comes to realize: »Each of the Disney theme parks has a castle as its central landmark, from the Cinderella Castle at Walt Disney World in Orlando (which was copied at Toyko Disneyland) to Le Château de la Belle au Bois Dormant at Disneyland Paris« (Doss 182). While Disney lore would have it that these castles were »inspired by the pinnacled Neuschwanstein castle in Bavaria« (cited in Doss, 183), they resemble more closely not the monumental *early*-Gothic château Ludwig II »built atop the ruins of several older castles on a mountain slope in Hohenschwangau« (183); rather, as Doss has shown, they are:

> far more like the last of ›Mad King Ludwig's‹ grandiose architectural schemes, a projected castle at Falkenstein near Fussen. Insistent on building an eagle's nest retreat atop sheer cliffs, a hideaway where he might completely *escape* the goings-on of the Second German Reich (to which he had essentially *abdicated* Bavarian sovereignty in 1871), Ludwig II contracted with Prince Thurn-und-Taxis's chief architect, Max Schultze, to draw up plans for a new castle in Falkenstein. Schultze's 1884 model of a three-story *late*-Gothic edifice with numerous turrets, a front balcony, and a five-story watch tower, enclosed by a rock wall with low towers, and entered through a uniaxial gatehouse, is remarkably similar to Ryman's 1951 conception of the Sleeping Beauty Castle. (183-4, italics added)

The similarities with the »Old Europe« midway concessions are also remarkable, as are the circumstances to which Doss attributes Disney's developing an attraction for neo-Gothic castles:

> Schultz's clay maquette of Falkenstein, along with numerous watercolor sketches he made of the castle's ground plan and interior rooms, have been on display since the 1920s in the König-Ludwig II Museum in Herrenchiemsee. During the 1950s, hordes of Americans trekked to Germany, from occupying forces and their dependents to *tourists aiming to get a taste of the cultural standards to which the United States*, the postwar globe's economic and military leader, *might also aspire*. Ludwig's castles were landmark ›must-sees‹ among the standard tourist packages assembled for tens of thousands of GIs stationed at bases from Bad Tölz to Baumholder, and for Americans from all over the States. Disney himself was certainly familiar with these examples of fantasy architecture from *his extensive travels in Europe* in earlier decades; apparently, a favorite spot was Tivoli Gardens, in Copenhagen. (184, italics added)

Should this be read as a case of *plus ça change*, an indication that American cultural insecurity (and not only European aristocratic abdication and escapism) continued to reverberate through the late-nineteenth century and well on into the twentieth? The phases Jim Collins identifies in sketching out the historical trajectory along which European high culture à la Shakespeare was transformed into popular entertainment offer a different point of departure. Of the four phases Collins identifies – from the development of new forms of popular culture in the first half of the nineteenth century to the appearance of hybrid »high-pop« forms in the 1990s – the Midway and Disneyland sprang into existence at the cusp of the second and third, that is, during periods of great cultural upheaval (Collins 3-6). The institutionalization of midway-type amusement zones can thus be read as part of a larger phenomenon: the sacralization of culture, i.e. »the bifurcation of [more general mass] culture into popular and elite arenas« (4), a hierarchy of tastes which »remained relatively stable until the late 1950s, when a third phase emerged in this evolving relationship between high and popular culture – the Pop Art era – which signaled a profound dissatisfaction with that great bifurcation as well as a growing contempt for the sacralization of culture« (5). If the attractions along the Midway and at Disneyland can thus be read as spatial equivalents of comfort food, it is not their common confectionary that begs for explanation, but rather their common architectural invocation of the same historical trope.

How much the Romantics' coherent (re-)interpretation of the Middle Ages influenced generations to come can be seen by comparing Reisenleitner's description of the unsettling historical circumstances and the conservative social agenda which characterize the development of Romantic literature (p. 65ff. in this volume). The following passage in particular highlights the reactionary spirit that such an artistic imagination has in common with those hired by both liberal Austro-American entrepreneurs and Disney:

> the state is presented by Novalis (in an anticipation of Hegelian concepts) as a realization of divine will (as opposed to the idea of natural law and a social contract); the quasi-organic nature of a social hierarchy and the idea of a unifying ›Holy Empire‹ negate the class antagonisms that were so clearly manifested in the events after the French Revolution (which was supported by most of the Romantics) – thus a specific view of history is very obviously employed to promote a conservative social agenda. This is made possible by the aesthetisizing of history (the writing of which was presented as a poetic act of creation), which provided an escapist moment just as Napoleon's empire was casting its shadow over Europe and the neo-feudalist reality of the German states was shutting down opportunities for petty bourgeois intellectuals to promote their political and/or aesthetic interests.
>
> The Middle Ages that the Romantics created was thus a very specific construction which was meant to respond to the immediate political and social situation of a group of uprooted artists who appropriated a specific period in history as a tool to accommodate art, literature, historiography, anti-rationality and untamed subjectivity. While classical antiquity had already been appro-

> priated by the Enlightenment, a reconceptualized feudal age, redeemed from the stigma of the ›Dark Ages‹ but poetically altered beyond recognition and stripped of any continuity with the absolutist state that re-asserted itself after the Napoleonic wars, provided the Romantics with a counter-foil that idealized the society of estates in the same moment that it glorified its poetic appropriation. The historian and the poet were conflated, and the Middle Ages were mediated through layers of a (poetic/artistic) subjectivity that left room, indeed even encouraged, an imaginative, dream-like, fairytale vision of the era. By combining history, literature and fantasy, the Middle Ages became the projection screen for desires of origin, wholeness and a perfect society (easily adaptable to a nationalist re-interpretation), in short a nostalgic vision of a particular period of the past in which belonging (as something always already lost) could be located. (66, in this volume)

If during the early nineteenth century, it fell to the poets to create soothingly historical creative works, that task has increasingly modulated from the literary to the material/ visual, becoming the domain of architects, designers and graphic artists, with the commodified and nationalist nature of the cultural products and the desires with which they are in substratal dialogue remaining provocatively constant. Each of these uncannily similar reiterations of archaic expressions of nation is an opportunity to identify the destabilizing forces summoning them up. The distracting conflict between the Realist and the Romantic continues?

HAPPY, CIVILLY EVER AFTER?

The dislocating cultural collisions and volatile economic conditions brought about by increasingly international trading practices have received a particularly historical material expression at both the world exhibitions and the theme parks into which they have mutated. The separation and disjunction brought about by the introduction of midways at the world exhibitions between medieval and modern representations of »Austria« needs, I have argued, to be located socio-economically as well as historically. By 1893, the financial fiasco of the 1873 World Exhibition was but a faintly bitter remnant of Viennese memory, much sweetened by the hymns of praise for the spectacle the city had provided and for the Austrian displays in Philadelphia in 1876, Paris 1878, Amsterdam 1883, and Antwerp 1885. Having officially refused to participate in the 1889 Paris celebration of revolution (as had all of the still intact European monarchies[8]), Chicago 1893 and St. Louis 1904 were further stepping stones along that well-lit liberal path of progress, the display of which was the raison d'être of those traveling shows that were the world exhibitions. Drawing on the Austrian example shows the role at the world exhibitions that increasing entrepreneurial influence (which has subsequently been resignified in the global imaginary as American in no small part thanks to Disney) played in relocating places like Vienna on a new global map, effectively removing them not in space but in time. Consideration of Disney's fantasy kingdom serves to highlight the processes already at work in the creation of Old Vienna. That cotton-candy substitutes for Proust's madeleine in both these neo-medieval settings is not accidental. Not so much for the maintenance of citizenry and civil society (cf. Yengogan 81-2), they were rather in the transportation and re-creation business: whisking visitors away for a day to a magical place where they could fancifully imagine daring encounters – slaying dragons in dungeons, freeing ravishing maidens with long dangling golden braids – and then enjoy a good cup of coffee or glass of wine afterwards.

ENDNOTES

1 See Bigler and Mudrey for a description of the Norway pavilion at the Columbian Exhibition, which was built as a model of a 12th-century stave church: »Bigler documents the design and construction of the building, from its prefabrication and display in Norway, its tenure at the fair, its use as a summer home and its current siting as part of a Norwegian historical village in Mt. Horeb, Wisc.« (Burke 220).

2 See Çelik for a discussion of the mythologizing tendencies evident in the architectural representations of Cairo and Istanbul at the Parisian exhibitions in particular.

3 Examples of more nuanced approaches to nationalism in the Habsburg context that go beyond the »new absolutism« model include Arens, Cohen and Judson.

4 »Ein solches Projekt war schon seit 1888 anläßlich der Jubiläumsgewerbeausstellung ein Wunschtraum des Ausstellungsarchitekten Emil Bressler. Im Sommer des Jahres 1892 kam ihm der junge Architekt Oskar Marmorek zuvor, der im Rahmen der großen Musik- und Theaterausstellung im Wiener Prater eine solche Rekonstruktion realisierte. Anhand von Veduten aus dem 17. Jahrhundert wurde vor der Rotunde eine Häuserzeile des Hohen Marktes rekonstruiert, in der Restaurants, Cafés und Bierlokale untergebracht waren. Die Wiener Gesellschaft war begeistert und Erzherzog Karl Ludwig schlug vor, die Idee nach Amerika zu exportieren. Für Chicago sollte nun Emil Bressler im Auftrag der österreichische Länderbank ein solches ›Alt-Wien‹ errichten. In den teilweise fest gebauten Häusern wurden Läden eingerichtet, die an Industrielle aus Österreich sowie an amerikanische Konzessionäre vermieten wurden.«

5 In that most prominent republican nation-state, the United States, the contestation between the second and third estates naturally took on a different form due to the lack of an indigenous aristocracy and also due to tricky issues of cultural inferiority vis-à-vis an Old World imagined as fundamentally aristocratic (hence the fixation on castles). Of particular interest is the fact that the American iconography at the Chicago Columbian appears to have been gendered in a fashion similar to the Austrian *Festschrift* with a clear linkage made between

women and the monarchy, on the one hand, and men and the middle-class, on the other. For a detailed account of the difficulties the elite yet middle-class female fair organizers in Chicago faced in negotiating the complicated figure of the »white queen,« see Boisseau.

6 The full description of the Shepps' visit to the Austrian pavilion reads as follows: »The great Austrian Empire has no special building in the Foreign Group, but has made ample amends by the splendor of her pavilion and the richness of her exhibits in this building. The main portal is a beautiful arch, supported by pillars and caryatides. The panels on the wings are ornamented with colored shields. Entering, we seem to gaze upon a bed of diamonds. The eyes are almost blinded by the many-colored lights that flash and sparkle from the abundant variety of Bohemian glass before us. Not only is each piece exquisite in itself, but the whole mass is entrancingly beautiful. There is a magnificent exhibit of china, gold and silver medallions, bronze and enameled tiles, from Vienna. Against the walls, candelabra, lamps and braziers of silver iron and bronze, are grouped in great profusion. Some of the handsomest curtains to be found in the whole exhibition are here. They are made of surah silk, richly brocaded in floral patterns. The ground tone of one especially fine pair is a delicate slaty gray, others are brown. One particularly attractive pair is of velvet. In the porcelain exhibit, we find some beautiful vases valued at $2000. The Royal Museum of Art and Industry, of Vienna, is a large contributor. Its display consists of cabinets inlaid with mother-of-pearl, cut glass, gold and silver jewelry, painting on metal, with copies of the frieze of the Parthenon and other ancient Greek temples. Looking very beautiful in their satin and velvet cases, a tempting display of cleverly carved meerschaum pipes, with large glowing amber mouth-pieces, arrests the eye. A complete line of shopping bags, porte-monnaies and cigar-cases, of seal and antelope skin, attract by their excellent finish and apparent soundness of manufacture« (76).

7 The Collins's collection demonstrates how pervasive this »fusion of Romantic sensibility and consumer desire« (27) has become.

8 The entry for the Paris 1889 universal exposition in the *Historical Dictionary of World's Fairs* reveals that: »when awards were distributed to exhibitors in September 1889, only the flag of the German empire was missing. The refusals, as France had hoped, were merely official, with no restrictions upon private exhibits. Special committees were formed in nearly every country to coordinate exhibits from private parties both with and without government support (only Germany, Montenegro, Sweden and Turkey had no committees, and exhibitors eventually came from all these except Montenegro). Thus, the world of business paid little heed to the political implications of the exposition or to the official or unofficial support of their govern« (110).

REFERENCES

Arens, Katherine. »Central Europe and the Nationalist Paradigm.« Working Paper 96-1. Center for Austrian Studies, 1997.

Benedict, Burton. »Rituals of Representation: Ethnic Stereotypes and Colonized Peoples at World's Fairs.« *Fair Representations*. 28-61.

Bhabha, Homi K. *The Location of Culture*. London and New York: Routledge, 1994.

Bigler, Brian J. and Lynn Martinson Mudrey. *The Norway Building of the 1893 Chi-*

cago World's Fair: A Building's Journey from Norway to America, An Architectural Legacy. Blue Mounds, Wisc.: Little Norway, 1992.

Boisseau, T.J. »White Queens at the Chicago World's Fair, 1893: New Womanhood in the Service of Class, Race, and Nation.« *Gender and History* 12.1 (April 2000): 33-81.

Burke, Bridget J. »World's Fairs and International Expositions: Selected References 1987-1993.« *Fair Representations*. 218-47.

Campbell, Colin. *The Romantic Ethic and the Spirit of Modern Consumerism*. Oxford: Blackwell Publishers, 1987.

Canada at the Universal Exhibition of 1855. Toronto: John Lovell, 1856.

Çelik, Zeynep. *Displaying the Orient: Architecture of Islam at Nineteenth-Century World's Fairs*. Berkeley, Los Angeles, Oxford: University of California Press, 1992.

Cohen, Gary B. »Neither Absolutism nor Anarchy: New Narratives on Society and Government in Late Imperial Austria.« *Austrian History Yearbook* 29.1 (1998).

Collins, Jim. »High-Pop: An Introduction.« *High-Pop: Making Culture into Popular Entertainment*. Malden, Mass. and Oxford: Blackwell, 2002. 1-31.

Designing Disney's Theme Parks: The Architecture of Reassurance. Ed. Karal Ann Marling. Montreal; Paris - New York: Centre Canadien d'Arhitecture/Canadian Centre for Architecture; Flammarion, 1997.

Doss, Erika. »Making Imagination Safe in the 1950s: Disneyland's Fantasy Art and Architecture.« *Designing Disney's Theme Parks*. 179-89.

Fair Representations: World's Fairs and the Modern World. Eds. Robert W. Rydell and Nancy Gwinn. Amsterdam: VU University Press, 1994.

Felber, Ulrike, Elke Krasny, and Christian Rapp. *Smart Exports: Österreich auf den Weltausstellungen 1851-2000*. Vienna: Verlag Christian Brandstätter, 2000.

Gems of the Centennial Exhibition: Consisting of Illustrated Descriptions of Objects of an Artistic Character in the Exhibits of the US, Great Britain, France, Spain, Italy, Germany, Belgium, Norway, Sweden, Denmark, Hungary, Russia, Japan, China, Egypt, Turkey, India, Etc., Etc., at the Philadelphia International Exhibition of 1876. New York: D. Appleton & Company, Publishers, 1877.

Gilbert, James. »World's Fairs as Historical Events.« *Fair Representations*. 13-27.

Greenhalgh, Paul. *Ephemeral Vistas: The Expositions Universelles, Great Exhibitions and World's Fairs, 1851-1939*. Manchester: Manchester University Press, 1988.

Historical Dictionary of World's Fairs and Expositions, 1851-1988. Eds. John E. Findling and Kimberly D. Pelle. New York: Greenwood Publishing Group, 1990.

Hobsbawn, Eric, and Terence Ranger, eds. *The Invention of Tradition*. Cambridge: Cambridge University Press, 1983.

Identität, Kultur, Raum: Kulturelle Praktiken und die Ausbildung von Imagined Communities in Nordamerika und Zentraleuropa. Eds. Susan Ingram, Markus Reisenleitner, and Cornelia Szabó-Knotik. Vienna: Turia+Kant, 2001.

Judson, Pieter. »›Every German Visitor has a *Voelkisch* Obligation He Must Fulfill‹: Nationalist Tourism in the Austrian Empire, 1880-1918.« *Histories of Leisure*. Ed. Rudy Koshar. Oxford, New York: Berg, 2002. 147-68.

Lohr, Lenox R. *Fair Management: The Story of a Century of Progress. A Guide for Future Fairs*. Chicago: The Cuneo Press, Inc., 1952.

Richards, William C. *A Day in the New York Crystal Palace and How to Make the Most of It: being a popular companion to the ›Official Catalogue‹ and a guide to all the objects of special interest in the New York Exhibition of the Industry of all Nations.* New York: G.P. Putnam & Co., M.DCCC.LIII.

Saffle, Michael. »›Do You Ever Dream of Vienna?‹ America's Glorification of Musical Central Europe, 1865-1965.« *Identität, Kultur, Raum.* 59-76.

Shepp, James W., and Daniel B. Shepp. *Shepp's World's Fair photographed: being a collection of original copyrighted photographs authorized and permitted by the management of the World's Columbian Exposition... All described in crisp and beautiful language.* Chicago: Globe Bible Publishing Co., 1893.

Szabó-Knotik, Cornelia. »Musikalische Elite in Wien um 1900: Praktiken, Prägungen und Repräsentationen.« *Identität, Kultur, Raum.* 41-58.

Truman, Ben C. *History of the World's Fair: being a complete and authentic description of the Columbian Exposition from its inception; with special articles by Geo. R. Davis ... [et al.].* Philadelphia, Pa.: Syndicate Publishing Co., 1893.

Yengogan, Aram A. »Culture, Ideology and World's Fairs: Colonizer and Colonized in Comparative Perspectives.« *Fair Representations.* 62-83.

Vom Vergnügungspark zum Entertainmentcenter: Wienerische Inszenierungen der Fremde kontextualisiert als Massenvergnügen einst und heute

EVA SCHWARZMANN

DER PRATER UND SEINE BESUCHER

Mit dem aufgeklärten Absolutismus wurden viele der großen repräsentativen Garten- und Parkanlagen der Herrscherhäuser auch dem Volk zugänglich gemacht. Die Öffnung des Wiener Praters war die erste ausdrückliche Widmung eines fürstlichen Grünareals für die Allgemeinheit.[1] Am 7. April 1766 machte Joseph II. den Prater allen Wienern zugänglich, und schon nach einer Woche kam die Anfrage, ob auch Kaffee, Tee und Gefrorenes verkauft werden dürfe. Kurz nach der kaiserlichen Zustimmung meldeten sich 66 »Wein-Würthe«, 46 »Bier-Würthe«, »allerhand Coffee-Sieder, Lebzelter, Fleischselcher, Bradelpratter, Kaßstecher«, ein »Limonihandler«, eine »Krapfenbacherin«, ein »Chocolattenmacher«, sowie ein Salami- und mehrere Obsthändler.[2] Auch wenn nicht alle, die ansuchten, von ihrem Verkaufsrecht Gebrauch machten, so verwandelte sich der Prater doch innerhalb kürzester Zeit zu einem der zentralen Orte populären Vergnügens. Zu den Greislereien, Bier- und Metschenken, Kaffee-und Gasthäusern kamen bald auch Ringelspiele, Kegelbahnen, mechanische Kunsthütten, Wachsfigurenkabinette, Panoramen, Camera obscura und Theatergebäude für mechanische Lustspiele. 1824 schreibt Leopold Matthias Weschel über den Wurstelprater:

> *Neben diesen Schenken bestehen mancherley Unterhaltungsplätze; man sieht hier Schaukeln aller Art, Ringelspiele, Gaukler, zahlreiche Vorstellungen mechanischer Künste usw, welche besonders an Sonn-und Feyertagen von einer großen Volksmenge umschwärmt werden.*[3]

Diese große Anziehungskraft des Praters beunruhigte den Statthalter Franz Ferdinand Graf von Schrattenbach und veranlasste ihn zur Überreichung eines Ansuchens mit dem Wunsch, den Prater an Sonntagen bis zehn Uhr gesperrt zu halten, da »allermaßen besonders die Gemeinen und Dienst Leuthe das Spazierengehen in den Bratter dem Heil. Gottes Dienst vorziehen dörften.«[4] Der Wurstelprater war innerhalb kürzester Zeit zum Treffpunkt des Volks geworden. Während in der Hauptallee der von tausenden Schaulustigen bestaunte Corso der Aristokratie und Neureichen stattfand, vergnügten sich die unteren Schichten im angrenzenden Wurstelprater. Ein Zeitgenosse beschreibt es so:

> Nur wenige aus der glänzenden oder der vom Glanz angezogenen Schaar verirren sich alsdann in den benachbarten Wurstelprater; ja Hunderte und aber Hunderte der feinen Leute, welche mit religiöser Gewissenhaftigkeit keinen Corso versäumen, haben von dem poetischen Wurstelprater nicht mehr Kenntniss, als wir vom Inneren Madagaskars.[5]

Für Wolfgang Maderthaner und Lutz Musner ist der Wurstelprater auch ein »Ort des ›Karnevalesken‹ und Grotesken, der Hanswurstereien und der ironischen Verkehrung der Wirklichkeit.«[6] Trotz ständiger Bemühungen gelang es der Polizeizensur nicht, den Praterwurstel zum Schweigen zu bringen. Zwischen Anpassung und Widerstand manövrierte er sich durchs Leben und wusste, die rationale Handlungsstruktur der gezeigten Stücke durch Komik zu brechen. Affirmative Aussagen wurden von ihm hinterfragt und damit dem Zuseher ein Blick auf alternative Sichtweisen ermöglicht. Aber der Wurstel war nicht nur eine Figur, die das populare Subversionspotential aktivieren konnte, sondern er spiegelte auch die Ängste der Wiener vor dem Fremden und Anderen. Was gerne vergessen wird, ist der mitunter militante Antisemitismus und Fremdenhass, die der beliebte Volksstückprotagonist artikulierte.

Als ein wichtiges »Ventil« bezeichnet Marcello La Speranza urbane Vergnügungseinrichtungen, die für das seelische Wohlergehen der Einwohner einer Großstadt ebenso wichtig wären wie kulturelle Einrichtungen.[7] Mit dem Prater hatte Wien schon sehr bald ein großes Vergnügungs- und Erholungsareal für seine Bewohner. Zeitgenössische Schilderungen und Reiseberichte vermitteln einen Eindruck davon, wie beliebt der Prater war. Die überlieferten Besucherzahlen sind beeindruckend. Stellvertretend soll eine Beschreibung aus dem Jahr 1820 zitiert werden, die einen schönen Eindruck vom sonntäglichen Pratertreiben vermittelt:

Zwischen allen diesen Häusern und Tischen sind eine Menge von Kegelbahnen, auch verschiedene jugendliche Spiele, als: Ringelspiel, Vogelschießen, Scheibenspiel, Schaukeln usw. Hier ist eigentlich der Tummelplatz für die bürgerliche Welt und die untere Volksclassen, welche an Sonntagen und Feyertagen scharenweise das Mittagsmahl hier einnehmen, und dann den ganzen Nachmittag unter lautem Freudengefühl zubringen.

Die vierte Allee, rechts, ist der Sammelplatz der vornehmen und schönen Welt. Was hierher kommt, kommt meistens in Wagen oder zu Pferde (...)

Neben diesen Alleen sind drey Kaffehhäuser und ein Traiteur; eine Menge Tische sind unter freyem Himmel aufgeschlagen; und an Sonntagen werden einige hundert Stühle längs dem Weg hingesetzt, auf denen man Alles vorbey passieren sehen kann (...)

Alles zusammen genommen, finden sich an schönen Sommertagen immer gegen 12 bis 15.000 Menschen im Prater ein.[8]

Schon kurz nach seiner Entstehung war der Prater zu einem der wichtigsten Vergnügungs- und Erholungsorte Wiens geworden, und noch heute wird auf die Frage nach den wichtigsten Bauwerken, Plätzen und Landschaften Österreichs, der Prater an 4. Stelle genannt (nach dem Stephansdom, Schloss Schönbrunn und der Ringstraße). Er zählt damit zu einem der wichtigen *lieux de mémoire* der Österreicher und vor allem der Wiener und kann als entscheidender Ort des kollektiven Gedächtnisses angesehen werden. Nach Jan Assmann prägen in erster Linie »schicksalhafte Ereignisse der Vergangenheit« das kollektive Gedächtnis, »deren Erinnerung durch kulturelle Formung (Texte, Riten, Denkmäler) und institutionalisierte Kommunikation (Rezitation, Begehung, Betrachtung) wachgehalten wird.«[9] Beim Wiener Prater finden sich jedoch kaum historische Ereignisse, die ein kollektives Gedächtnis hervorrufen könnten. Das, was den Prater zu einem wichtigen Erinnerungsort der Wiener und Österreicher machte, war nicht etwa ein politisches Ereignis, sondern die Kontinuität, die Tatsache, dass er seit über zweihundert Jahren der Wiener Bevölkerung als Erholungsraum diente. Maria Schweizer meint dazu: »Er gilt als Spiegel der ›Volksseele‹, als nicht politischer Ort, an dem man ›den Karakter unsrer Nation besser, als irgend anderswo‹[10] beobachten kann; eine Funktion, die sich wie ein roter Faden seit dem 18. Jahrhundert durch die Darstellungen des Praters zieht.«[11] Dass der Prater bald auch über die Grenzen Wiens hinaus bekannt war, zeigt der Ausruf Mephistos in Goethes *Faust*, der vom Walpurgisnachttreiben meint: »Hier ist's so lustig wie im Prater.« In ausländischen Feuilletons und Reiseberichten wurde immer wieder das Klischee vom trinklustigen und essfreudigen Wiener gezeigt, der sinnlich und unpolitisch sein Leben genießt. Es war die Politik dieser Tage gewesen, das Volk mit Belustigungen vom politischen Engagement abzulenken. Man war sich der Bedeutung von Vergnügungen und Theater zur Zerstreuung sehr bewusst gewesen, und »Brot und Spiele« sollten revolutionäres Gedankengut erst gar nicht entstehen lassen. Die Zensurbehörde kontrollierte sehr genau die veröffentlichte Literatur, und das Bild vom gemütlichen Biedermann kam ihren Interessen sehr entgegen. Aber auch wenn man bedenkt, dass die Schattenseiten dieser Epoche, das Elend und die Armut der stetig anwachsenden Arbeiterschicht, wesentlich seltener gezeigt und beschrieben wurden, so bleibt doch die Tatsache einer großen Beliebtheit des Praters. Und so scheint es, dass der Pauperismus auf der einen Seite und die große Vergnügungslust der Wiener auf der anderen, gar kein unbedingter Widerspruch ist, sondern dass vielleicht gerade finanzielle Enge und geringe Chance auf eine Besserstellung in der Zukunft die Vergnügungslust der unteren Schichten begründete: Sinnlos war es zu sparen, zu wenig war das Einkommen für Vorsorge oder Veränderung, deshalb wurde das Geld lieber für einen kurzfristigen Konsum ausgegeben. Roman Sandgruber meint dazu:

> 1. Den Arbeitern fehlte die Möglichkeit, an langfristige und dauerhafte Verbesserungen zu glauben.
>
> 2. Bestimmte Konsumgüter, vor allem bessere Wohnungen, erwiesen sich als zu teuer, sowohl in Relation zu anderen Konsumgütern, als auch in Relation zum erwarteten Einkommen.
>
> 3. Man zeigte sich zufrieden, gemessen an den Erwartungen, was vor allem für die der ländlichen Umwelt entstammenden Arbeiter galt.
>
> 4. Die Eß- und Konsumgewohnheiten waren traditionsbestimmt, und gemessen an traditionellen Standards war die Ernährungsweise prestigereicher als Sonstiges.[12]

Schon Ende des 18. Jahrhunderts schreibt Joseph Richter in seinen berühmten Eipeldauer-Briefen:

> Da hab ich so unterm Essen vis-à-vis vom Paperl dem Hutschen zug'schaut und wie die Fabriksmamsellen mit ihren Liebhabern aus den Beiseln schon um ein Uhr nach dem Essen sich von dem gemeinen Erdenleben losmachen wollen, um in einer Hutschen die Mühseligkeit der Welt zu vergessen, gegen Himmel fliegen.[13]

Das Klischee vom Wienerischen Phäaken entsteht, der sich dem Wohlleben hingibt und weder nach politischer noch gesellschaftlicher Veränderung strebt.

Den Sozialpädagogen war dieser unstete Lebensstil und die plebejische Präferenz für leichte Vergnügungen anstelle von »vernünftigen und gesitteten Lustbarkeiten« ein Dorn im Auge. Ein zeitgenössischer Vertreter dieser Volkserziehungsbewegung beklagte die Verschwendungssucht der Arbeiter: »Was er erwirbt gibt er aus; Sparsamkeit, diese schöne Tugend der Haushaltung kennt er nicht.«[14] Bedenkt man die überlangen Arbeitszeiten, die niedrigen Löhne, die beengten Wohnverhältnisse, die frühindustrielle Massenverelendung, der Anfang des 19. Jahrhunderts weder soziale Maßnahmen der Regierung noch der Widerstand einer organisierten Arbeiterbewegung Einhalt geboten, und die durch politische Krisen, Kriege sowie Ernteausfälle eingeleitete existentielle Notlage weiter Teile der Bevölkerung, so scheint das Klischee von der »Goldenen Backhendlzeit« eine Lüge.[15]

Dies ist jedoch schichtspezifisch zu differenzieren. Wolfgang Greif meint dazu:

> Das harmonisierende Klischee von der ›Wiener Backhendlzeit‹, das dem ›gemeinen Menschen‹ allgemeine Zufriedenheit ›mit dem, was er hat und bekommen kann‹ und darüber hinaus politische Apathie bescheinigt, scheint für jene Schichten im Wiener Vormärz, die weder am Luxus der oberen Gesellschaften zu partizipieren vermochten, noch auf die alltäglichen Überlebensstrategien des ›Pöbels‹ verwiesen waren, einiges an Realitätsgehalt zu besitzen.[16]

Wien war zu jener Zeit trotz des verbreiteten Pauperismus eine reiche Stadt. Als Kaiserresidenz zog sie die reiche Oberschichte an, von deren Einkommen aus Grundrenten und Handel in der Folge auch die Dienstboten und Lieferanten profitierten. Auch das wachsende Beamtentum mit seinen entsprechenden Gehältern, der bereits beachtliche Tourismus und die Ansiedlung von Gewerbebetrieben machten Wien zu einer wohlhabenden Stadt.[17] Unter diesen Voraussetzungen konnte der Prater als ein wesentlicher Erholungsort für Wiens Bevölkerung zu einem der ersten Freizeitparks Europas werden.

VOLKSGÄRTEN UND »PLEASURE GARDENS«

Neben der Umwidmung fürstlicher Gärten gab es auch immer mehr private Mäzene, Stadtverwaltungen oder politische Institutionen, die der Öffentlichkeit begrünte Freizeitareale stifteten. Noch immer war das Repräsentationsbedürfnis eine wichtige Motivation zur Errichtung von Gärten und Parks. Auch die ab der zweiten Hälfte des 19. Jahrhunderts anlässlich von Weltausstellungen und anderen großen Messen errichteten weiten Erholungsareale dienten der Selbstdarstellung der Stadt oder des Veranstalters. Zunehmend führten aber auch medizinische und sozialpädagogische Überlegungen zur Planung von öffentlichen Gärten. Erholungseinrichtungen für das Volk wurden als öffentliche Aufgabe und Verpflichtung erkannt und große Stadtgärten konzipiert, die einer möglichst großen Zahl von Besuchern einen Ausgleich zum anstrengenden Arbeitsalltag bieten sollten.[18]

Parallel zu den öffentlichen Freizeitanlagen entwickelten sich ab dem 17. Jahrhundert kommerzielle Vergnügungsbetriebe, die so genannten »pleasure gardens«, auf deren Entwicklung und Zerfall Ingram in ihrem Beitrag zur Londoner Freizeitöffentlichkeit im 19. Jahrhundert näher eingeht. Ausgehend von London entstanden sie auch in anderen englischen Städten, sehr beliebt waren sie in den Badeorten an der Küste. Als eine der ersten berühmten »pleasure gardens« können dabei die Vauxhall Gardens angesehen werden, die mit ihren fünf Hektar Fläche zu einem beliebten Treffpunkt der Londoner Gesellschaft wurden.

Eintrittsgebühren sowie Konventionen in bezug auf Kleidung und Umgangsformen führten zu einer Selektion des Publikums bei den prinzipiell für alle geöffneten Vergnügungsparks. Die Unterhaltungen reichten von Gaststätten, Tiergehegen und Wasserspielen bis zu Musik, Theater- und Tanzhallen. Mit der zweiten Hälfte des 18. Jahrhunderts entstand die Mode, die Parks mit exotischer oder romantischer Architekturstaffage auszustatten, – erste Formen des »themings« in Vergnügungsparks. Auch Feuerwerks- und Illuminations-darbietungen zogen große Scharen von Besuchern an.

Im Laufe des 19. Jahrhunderts gewannen technische Attraktionen zunehmend an Bedeutung. Ausgehend von den USA entstand eine spezialisierte Vergnügungsindustrie. Die »Tivoli-Parks,« von denen der 1843 von G. Carstensen in Kopenhagen gegründete »Kjøbenhavns Sommertivoli og Vauxhall« wohl der bedeutendste war, sowie die »pleasure parks« waren bemüht, mit immer neuen Attraktionen die Massen anzuziehen. Auch in den USA wurden während des ausgehenden 19. Jahrhunderts zahlreiche »amusement parks« eröffnet. Der Großteil der Anlagen fand sich in den Ballungsgebieten im Norden, beispielsweise Coney Island, der wohl größte und bekannteste Vergnügungspark.

Zusammenfassend kann gesagt werden, dass mit der anwachsenden städtischen Bevölkerung, der zunehmenden Bedeutung von Freizeit und dem Ausbau von Infrastruktur und Transportwesen auch die Erholungsgebiete immer wichtiger wurden. Die Ansprüche des Publikums an die Unterhaltungsindustrie stiegen, und die Unternehmer mussten stets nach neuen Reizen Ausschau halten, um ihren Freizeitpark weiterhin für die Besucher attraktiv zu gestalten. Technische Neuerungen sowie immer beeindruckendere Illusionsmaschinerien stellten die größten Publikumsmagneten dar. Von exotischer Architekturstaffage bis hin zum Eintauchen in eine andere Welt, schon früh erkannte man die Faszination, die themenbezogene Vergnügungszonen auf ihre Besucher ausüben konnten.

»THEMING«

Schon im 18. Jahrhundert fanden sich mit der aufkommenden Exotismusmode und dem verstärkten Interesse an fernen Ländern, Ansätze von »theming« in der Architektur[19] oder in der Ausstattung von Vergnügungsparks. Es handelte sich dabei aber meist nur um architektonische Zitate oder einzelne Bauwerke, jedoch nicht um ein im größeren Umfang verwirklichtes Konzept einer exotischen Phantasiewelt.

Als die ersten Themenparks können die Weltausstellungen angesehen werden. Zwar dienten sie in erster Linie der Selbstdarstellung der geladenen Länder, aber durch den Wunsch nach einer möglichst naturnahen Repräsentation wurde der Ausstellungsbesuch zum sinnlichen Erlebnis. Nicht nur Industrieprodukte und Kunstobjekte wurden gezeigt, sondern man war bemüht, einen umfassenden Eindruck von dem jeweiligen Land zu vermitteln. Dazu gehörte neben der Schau von Alltags- und Kunstgegenständen auch eine spezielle architektonische Gestaltung der Pavillons. Auch auf die kulinarischen Genüsse in einer authentisch gestalteten Umgebung legte man großen Wert.

Mitunter baute man sogar ganze Dörfer nach. Sehr beliebt waren dabei die orientalischen Viertel. Bei der Wiener Weltausstellung 1873 gab es neben einem orientalischen Viertel, mit komplett eingerichteten Gebäuden, die oft mit lebensgroßen Kostümpuppen ausgestattet waren, eine besondere ägyptische Schau. Die Gebäudegruppe umfasste ein ägyptisches bürgerliches Wohnhaus, eine Volksschule, ein Kaffeehaus, Bazare, ein arabisches Wohnhaus mit Harem, ein Herrenempfangszimmer (Mandara) Seiner Hoheit des Khediven, eine

Moscheeanlage mit Kuppel und Minarett, ein altägyptisches Felsengrab und das Bauernhaus eines Ortsvorstehers.[20] Aber nicht nur die orientalischen Länder zeigten sich in so großem Rahmen: 80 Japaner mit 6.000 Exponaten waren zur Wiener Weltausstellung angereist und errichteten auf dem Ausstellungsgelände Pavillons und Gartenanlagen mit künstlichen Wasserläufen, Brücken und Hügeln. Im Industriepalast baute man sogar eines der japanischen Nationalheiligtümer, den Tempel von Kyoto, nach.

Weltausstellungen und Vergnügungsparks sind wichtige Vorläufer der heutigen Erlebniswelten. Fasziniert von der auf der Panamerikanischen Ausstellung in Buffalo 1901 angebotenen Illusionsfahrt »A Trip to the Moon,« holte der Unternehmer Tilyou die Attraktion nach Steeplechase/ Coney Island. Als die Kreateure dieser Phantasiereise, Thompson und Dundy, im Jahr darauf mit Tilyou in Streit gerieten, beschlossen sie, ihren eigenen Park zu eröffnen und nannten ihn nach ihrem erfolgreichen Illusionstrip: Luna Park. Im Gegensatz zu anderen Vergnügungsparks, die vor allem mit mechanischen Fahrten und circusähnlichen Attraktionen die Besucher anlocken wollten, setzte man mit Luna Park auf eine Einbettung der Vergnügungen in historische, geographische oder kulturelle Themen: »Its water slide, illusion rides, Grand Promenade, Miniature Railway, wild animal show, Grand Ballroom, Electric Tower, and marching band were situated next to a German Village, Chinese Theater, Japanese Garden, Eskimo Village, Dutch Windmill, and the Canals of Venice.«[21] Als Architekturstudent und Arbeiter bei Volksfesten hatte Thompson genug Erfahrungen gesammelt, um sich der Bedeutung von Gebäudegestaltung, Illusion und Spektakel bewusst zu sein. Er erkannte, wie wichtig die Umgebung und Atmosphäre für Freiluftunterhaltungen war. Licht, Shows, Gebäude oder ganz allgemein gesprochen die richtige Szenerie, sollten die Besucher in eine andere Welt entführen, in ein Märchenland oder in eine Stadt der Träume. Um das zu erreichen, errichtete Thompson eine weite Anlage, die die verschiedensten architektonischen Stile in sich vereinigte, hielt seine Angestellten zu steter Höflichkeit an und bot den Zusehern ständig neue Spektakel.

Die Faszination, die Schrecken und Horror auf das Publikum ausübten,[22] wussten die Betreiber von Luna Park zu nutzen und boten die verschiedensten Katastrophenshows, wie den Kampf mit den Flammen beim Abbrennen eines vierstöckigen Hauses oder die Tötung eines alten Elefanten. 250.000 Glühbirnen erleuchteten Luna Park bei Nacht und gaben ihm den Beinamen »Electric City by the Sea.«

Etwa zur gleichen Zeit erbaute Gabor Steiner im Wiener Prater seine elektrische Stadt, über die das *Neue Wiener Tagblatt* kurz vor der Eröffnung schreibt:

> Gabor Steiners Sommer-Etablissement ›Venedig‹ wird am 2. Mai als elektrische wiedereröffnet. Eine helle, überaus anmutige Stadt haben die Künstler auf die Stätte des alten ›Venedig‹ hingezaubert, und Beleuchtungseffekte, wie sie noch nie und nirgends in gleich splendider Weise produziert wurden, werden diese Stadt feenhaft gestalten. Dreihundert Bogenlampen und 15.000 Glühbirnen werden nach dem elektrischen Präliminare der Saison zwei bis zweieinhalb Millionen Hektowattstunden brennen und diese leuchtenden Fronten und funkelnden Giebel werden dieser Stadt großen Reiz verleihen.[23]

Auch für die Errichtung von Dreamland auf Coney Island stand eine zuvor auf einer Weltausstellung gezeigte Attraktion Pate. Die auf der Weltausstellung in Chicago gezeigte White City inspirierte Unternehmer und führte eine Dekade später zum Aufbau von Dreamland. In reinem Weiss bemalte Säulen und Bögen und die Millionen von Glühbirnen, die das Traumland in der Nacht beleuchteten, machten die neue Attraktion weithin sichtbar und gaben ihr eine magische Ausstrahlung. Eine riesige halbnackte Staute am Eingang sollte Besucher anlocken und auf den Eingang ins Traumland aufmerksam machen. Neben den üblichen Live Shows wie ein Kampf mit dem Feuer oder der Fall Pompeiis, gab es auch ein Liliputanerdorf mit 300 Einwohnern. Außerdem bot Dreamland noch simulierte U-Boot- und Flugzeugfahrten, einen Circus, eine Show mit wilden Tieren, Wagenrennen, sowie einen Ballsaal für 25.000 Tänzer.[24]

Über die Vergnügungsparks auf Coney Island schreibt Michael Sorkin:

> Steeplechase Park, Luna Park, and Dreamland established the basic elements of this new machinery of pleasure. Their evocations of travel in time and space, liliputianization, physics-defying rides, ecstatic relationship to new technology, efficient organizing architecture of spectacle and coercion, and aspirations to urbanism – all harbinger apotheosis at Disneyland.[25]

Die Bedeutung von Coney Island für die Entwicklung von Vergnügungsparks ist unumstritten. Der Eindruck, dass diese Ausformung der Vergnügungsindustrie von Amerika ausgegangen und dann von europäischen Unternehmern übernommen worden wäre, ist jedoch falsch. Ganz im Gegenteil fanden sich in Europa Jahre vor der Gründung von Lunapark große Vergnügungsviertel. Auch die Idee einer thematisch durchgestalteten Erlebniswelt kommt nicht – wie so viele heute glauben machen wollen – aus den USA. Anhand einer Beschreibung des Aufbaus der Weltausstellungen wurde bereits die

Bedeutung einer räumlichen Inszenierung der verschiedenen Länder gezeigt. Aber auch die Vergnügungsindustrie hatte früh erkannt, welche Anziehungskraft der Nachbau exotischer Dörfer und die Kopie bekannter Sehenswürdigkeiten auf die Besucher ausübt. Auch in Wien wusste man Neugier und Schaulust zu nützen und mit immer wieder neuen Attraktionen die Bevölkerung in den Prater zu locken. Waren es nun die unter dem Deckmantel der Wissenschaft veranstalteten Völkerschauen oder Gabor Steiners »Venedig in Wien«, die Wiener strömten in den Prater, um sich diesem umfassenden sinnlichen Erlebnis hinzugeben.

ARCHITEKTUR

Die Ausstellungen des 19. Jahrhunderts stellten eine große Herausforderung für den Ingenieurbau dar. Der Bau riesiger Hallen setzte exakte Berechnungsmethoden und neue technische Konzepte voraus. Der Einsatz neuer Baustoffe wie Glas, Eisen und später der stabilere Stahl förderte durch die größere Spannweite neue Konstruktionsweisen und ermöglichte eine schnelle und kostengünstige Errichtung der Ausstellungsgebäude. Durch diese neuen Vorgaben entstanden in die Zukunft weisende Konstruktionen wie der Crystal Palace oder der Eiffelturm. Als »buildings without roots« bezeichnet Robert Brain die damals entstandene Architektur, als »orphans without progenitors in the traditional vernacular of architecture«[26] und zitiert dabei Dostojewski, der vom Crystal Palace als »epitome of soulless materialism, this apocalyptic monster of iron and glass«[27] sprach. Doch diese »celebration of decontextualisation and deracination«[28] empfanden viele Besucher als aufregend und befreiend. Heute erscheinen uns diese architektonischen Experimente eher zukunftsweisend. Die Kritik verlagert sich eher auf die vielen Gebäude, die zwar mit diesen neuen Materialien erbaut, jedoch verputzt und mit einer traditionellen, meist klassizistischen Fassade versehen wurden.[29]

Ausstellungen entwickelten sich immer mehr von Technikschauen zu Universalausstellungen. Ab der Pariser Weltausstellung 1855 wurden regelmäßig internationale Kunstschauen veranstaltet, und ab 1867 war es den Nationen möglich, sich außerhalb der Ausstellungshallen mit landestypischen Bauten darzustellen. Jedes Land sollte »ein passendes bauliches Unternehmen (errichten), welches in möglichst deutlicher und zugleich interessanter Weise die Eigenthümlichkeiten des betreffenden Volkes in bezug auf seine Sitten und Gebräuche wie auf seine ganze Lebensweise veranschaulicht.«[30] Rund um den Industriepalast entstanden so hunderte »nationale Kleinwahrzeichen«[31] wie indische Tempel, Moscheen, Pagoden, Schweizer Chalets bis zu Leuchttürmen, Bootshäusern und Musterställen. Bei der Wiener Weltausstellung 1873 gab es bereits über 170 solcher originalgetreuer Nachbauten. In vielen dieser Gebäude gab es Kaffeehäuser und Restaurants, die Erholung und Ausgleich zu dem bildungspolitischen Anspruch der Schau boten.

Mit der Pariser Weltausstellung 1878 wurde den europäischen Kolonien ebenfalls ein eigener Ausstellungsbereich zugestanden. Ganze Siedlungen und Dörfer wurden nachgebaut und mit der entsprechenden Bevölkerung belebt. Diese exotisch-ruralen Inszenierungen waren zwar nicht als offizielle Beiträge anerkannt, bildeten aber einen wesentlichen Anziehungspunkt für die schaulustigen Besucher. Für die selbe Ausstellung wurde auch die Idee entwickelt, dass Fassaden im landesüblichen Baustil die jeweiligen Abteilungen kennzeichnen sollten. So entstand die »Rue des Nations,« ein bizarres Nebeneinander von Bauernhaus-, Palast-, Bürgerhaus-, und Sakralbaufassaden,[32] eine thematische Durchmischung, wie wir sie heute in kleinerer Form öfters auch im Restaurantsektor von Einkaufszentren finden.

Auf die tragenden Stahlgerüste wurden die Gipsfassaden aufgesetzt. Das Ausstellungsgelände wurde zu einer riesigen Bühne, auf der sich die einzelnen Länder darstellten. Nicht das Streben nach Authentizität, sondern Schein und Repräsentation prägten das Bild der Schau. Der Herausgeber der Pariser Weltausstellungsberichte 1900, Georg Malkowsky, bemerkte dazu folgendes:

> (...) ›Völkerstraße‹ klingt ungemein volltönend und der Titel entspricht insofern den Thatsachen, als sich die gebildeten Nationen der Erde wirklich am Seineufer zusammengefunden haben, um dort eine Musterkarte der bei ihnen gebräuchlichen Formensprache abzugeben. Nur muß man die Sache, um sie recht beurteilen zu können, nicht allzu ernsthaft nehmen.
>
> Wer am Quai d'Orsay, wo sich in langen Reihen die Repräsentationshäuser der einzelnen Länder aufbauen, nationale Stilbildung studieren wollte, würde hier ebenso wenig zu einem nennenswerten Resultat kommen, wie der Archäologe, der in einer Maskengarderobe Material für eine Kostümkunde sammeln wollte. Mit wenigen Ausnahmen handelt es sich um eine geschickt arrangierte festliche Theaterdekoration, deren malerische Wirkung nicht zu unterschätzen ist.[33]

Man erbaute eine Scheinwelt, die sich nicht an der Wirklichkeit orientierte, sondern sich nach Belieben architektonischer Zitate bediente und somit die Verfügbarkeit sämtlicher Baukulturen demonstrierte. Nicht die Wirklichkeit, sondern das Theater schien Vorbild zu sein; gleich Bühnenkulissen reihten sich die Gebäude aneinander, mit dem einzigen und wesentlichen Unterschied, dass sie nicht bloß vom

Zuschauerraum aus gesehen, sondern durch Begehen erlebbar gemacht wurden. Weder mit dem Theater noch mit dem Panorama lassen sich diese Inszenierungen von Wirklichkeit vergleichen. Sie weisen einen neuen Weg in der Unterhaltungskultur. Über die Weltausstellungen schreibt Werner Hofmann: »Was sich als repräsentativer Querschnitt durch die Menschheit feiern lässt, ist eine Scheinwelt, die sich vom Kunstwerk die kompositorische Gebärde, von der Wirklichkeit die handgreifliche Dreidimensionalität leiht.«[34] Die Wirklichkeit wird zum Exponat präpariert, und die Idee der postmodernen Hyperrealität scheint hier ihre erste Ausformung gefunden zu haben. Gerade die Weltausstellungen, die die Geschichte und kulturelle Tradition der verschiedenen Länder aufzeigen wollten, markieren den Beginn einer Entkontextualisierung regionaler Kultursignifikanten. Trotz der Reduktion der Signifikanten kann aber nicht von einer Vereinheitlichung oder gar Auflösung nationaler Identität gesprochen werden. Ganz im Sinne Richard Wilks Bemerkungen zur Globalisierung kann auch bei den Weltausstellungen von »structures of common difference, which celebrate particular kinds of diversity while submerging, deflating or suppressing others«[35] gesprochen werden.

ERLEBNISWELTEN UND ENTERTAINMENT CENTERS

Eat-, Shop,- Info,- Edu-tainment: Die Bedeutungszunahme der Unterhaltung

Die Errichtung von Erlebnisparks ist ein weltweiter Trend. Nicht nur, dass das Disneyimperium von den USA über Paris nach Hong Kong und Tokyo den Globus mit seinen Phantasielandschaften übersät, viele, viele Unternehmer folgten und wollten teilhaben an dem großen Erfolg der inszenierten Freizeitparks. Neben den mit Comic- oder Märchenfiguren bevölkerten Parks gibt es auch zunehmend Areale, die dem Besucher unglaubliche Naturerlebnisse bieten wollen. »Just like the real thing, only better,«[36] schreibt Michael Sorkin und weist damit auf den paranormalen Charakter von Erlebniswelten hin. Ganz in diesem Sinne lesen sich die Aussagen des Austroamerikaners Ludwig Morasch, der wesentlich bei der Planung von Playcastle in Seefeld, dem Kristallpalast bei Leipzig und anderen Entertainmentcenters beteiligt war: »Ich kannte fast alle karibischen Inseln. Dann entdeckte ich bei Disney in Florida ›Taifun Lagoon‹, eine nachgebaute Karibik. Die war schöner als die Wirklichkeit. Da wusste ich: In Zukunft baue ich Traumwelten für die Konsumenten.«[37] Unabhängig von Jahreszeit und Wetter, und ohne die Gefahren, die weite Reisen mit sich bringen, kann der Besucher in sauberer, wohldosierter Form die Reize anderer Länder kennen lernen.

Die Vergnügungsindustrie boomt, und neue Wortschöpfungen wie Eat-, Shop-, Info-, oder Edu-tainment spiegeln die Ausweitung und Bedeutung von Unterhaltung. Viele Branchen entdecken die Unterhaltung als Mittel, um ihre Angebote attraktiver zu machen. Einkaufen, Essen, Hotelaufenthalte, ja selbst Bildung sollen zum Erlebnis werden. Das Konzept eines Einkaufstempels als Erlebniswelt ist ein besonders verbreitetes. Dazu muss man auch nicht über die Grenze nach Deutschland schauen, wo unter anderem in Neu-Ulm, Bremen oder Berlin Einkaufscenter mit dem Thema des mediterranen Marktplatzes, antiker Architektur oder nach dem Vorbild orientalischer Bazars gestaltet wurden.[38] Auch in Wien finden sich genügend Beispiele für eine thematische Gestaltung von Einkaufszonen in Shoppingcentern. »Entertainmentbauten sind der letzte Schrei,«[39] schreibt Paul Mayrhofer im Oktober 1999 im *Kurier*. Zunehmend setzen Investoren auf die so genannten »Unterhaltungsimmobilien«, von denen sie sich bedeutend mehr Gewinn erwarten als von der Errichtung oder Vermietung von Büro- und Wohnräumen:

> In einem Entertainmentcenter soll der Besucher (fast) alle schönen Dinge des Lebens konsumieren können: Kulinarische Köstlichkeiten aus aller Welt, Bars für jeden Geschmack, Bücher und CD-Shops, Geschäfte, die ›trendige‹ Kleidung und Schuhe anbieten, Internetcafe, High-Tech-Spielhallen und ein Virtual Reality-Center.[40]

Erst kürzlich eröffnete in Wien das Gasometer-Entertainmentcenter, eine über zwei Hektar große Einkaufs- und Unterhaltungswelt, ein weiteres Unterhaltungszentrum am Stadtrand von Wien.

Die Anlage von Themenparks

»Kein Mensch würde sich freiwillig für ein verlängertes Wochenende nach Rust/Baden im Dreiländereck Frankreich/Deutschland/Schweiz begeben. Doch auch der dort aus dem Boden gestampfte ›Europapark‹ hat sich zum Publikumsmagneten entwickelt,«[41] meint Ingrid Bahrer-Fellner und beschreibt damit ein für die meisten Freizeitparks typisches Phänomen. Fast alle der großen Vergnügungszentren werden außerhalb der urbanen und touristischen Zentren gebaut. Am einfachsten mit dem Auto gelangt man zu den neuen Zentren, urbanen Klonen, die jenseits der Realität eine neue Wirklichkeit schaffen. Das selbe Phänomen, aber aus einem ganz anderen Blickwinkel, erklärt Jon Jerde, der als der Papst der Event Cities angesehen wird. Bei seinem Vortrag in Wien anläßlich des Symposiums »Zukunft der Städte« im November 2000 sprach er von dem Wunsch der Menschen nach Zentren der Kommunikation. Nachdem die städtischen Zentren immer mehr verschwinden, sehnen sich die Bewohner nach neuen Plätzen der Zusammenkunft. Deshalb ginge es darum, eine hyper-urbane Version der ausgestorbenen Innenstädte zu schaffen.[42] Der City Walk in Los Angeles ist eines der bekanntesten Beispiele für die Erlebnisarchitektur von Jerde Partnership, die über die ganze Welt verstreut wurde und – in der Zusammenarbeit mit lokalen Architekten – die unterschiedlichsten Projekte realisiert. Nicht nur in den USA, auch in Japan, Thailand und anderen Ländern Asiens, Argentien, Israel, Polen, Deutschland, Holland, etc. entstanden neue Formen der Event Cities.

Erfahrungen der Fremde, der Geschichte

Fremde Welten – das ist seit jeher das große Thema vieler Freizeitparks. Wie bei den Weltausstellungen des 19. Jahrhunderts üben auch heute noch ferne Länder eine große Faszination aus. Sie so geschützt, ohne die Risiken und auch ohne den finanziellen Aufwand einer großen Reise, kennenzulernen, ist für viele ein Anreiz exotischer Themenparks. »Keimfreier Urlaub unterm Glassturz« – so betitelt Ingrid Greisenegger einen ihrer Artikel über Trends bei Erlebniswelten. Sie beschreibt darin die sich zunehmender Beliebtheit erfreuenden Abenteuerurlaube in der Halle. So wurde in Japan, nahe dem Meer, ein »Ocean Dome« errichtet, ein riesiges Schwimmbad unter der Kuppel für 10.000 Besucher pro Tag: »Die stärkste Wellenmaschine der Welt sorgt für meterhohe Surfwogen. Wohl dosiert ist der Wind, ohne Salzgeschmack das Meer.«[43] Die Erlebniswelten »Center Parcs« mit der Bungalowanlage »De Vossemeren« in Belgien setzen wiederum auf die Abenteuerlust von kleinen und großen Gästen. Eine Mischung aus realer Natur und künstlichen Anlagen soll die Besucher in exotische Ferne entführen. 100 Millionen Schilling haben die Betreiber in Attraktionen wie eine 20 Meter hohe Hängebrücke, Nebelschwaden produzierende Maschinen für den Tropenwald und ein Restaurant mit Piratenschiff-Kulisse investiert. Ein weiterer Publikumsmagnet ist die Aqua-Welt mit Korallenriff und Riesenaquarium, das die Taucher durch eine Glasscheibe von Haien und anderen Fischen trennt. Wie groß die Nachfrage nach diesem belgischen Tropenparadies ist, zeigen die Nächtigungszahlen: Jeder einzelne der »Center Parcs« hat so viele Übernachtigungen wie die ganze Stadt Kitzbühel.[44]

Neben Erlebniswelten, die in andere Erdteile entführen, sind aber auch die Vergangenheit und die Zukunft stets wiederkehrende Themen der Vergnügungsparks. Helga Loverseed beschreibt ein verstärktes Interesse der amerikanischen Bevölkerung für die eigene Geschichte, eine Strömung, die von Unternehmern von Themenparks sofort aufgegriffen wurde:

> The history angle is one that has not been lost on theme park operators. Along with the usual computerised rides and live entertainment, theme parks increasingly contain areas showing what life was like in the early days – pioneer villages, ›Wild West‹ store fronts, Indian encampments and the like.[45]

Auch in Europa wird die eigene Geschichte zunehmend inszeniert. Abgesehen vom traditionellen Nachspielen historischer Ereignisse an den jeweiligen Feiertagen gibt es immer mehr Ansätze, die eigene Geschichte über Erlebniswelten zu vermitteln. So gab es bei der Kärntner Landesausstellung in Friesach 2001 über das Mittelalter nicht nur eine Schau verschiedenster Exponate, sondern die ganze Stadt wurde Teil einer Inszenierung der eigenen Vergangenheit. Neben der Dekoration der Stadt und der Kostümierung von Kaufleuten und dem im Gastgewerbe tätigen Personal gab es an verschiedenen Orten in Friesach Vorführungen traditoneller Handwerkskünste. Mit dem Projekt »Leben wie im Mittelalter« war man bemüht, durch die authentische Nachinszenierung historischer Lebensformen einen neuen Zugang zur Geschichte zu gewinnen.

Zwischen Wirklichkeit und Traum befinden sich die virtuellen Welten der thematisierten Erlebnislandschaften. Im Gegensatz zur Welt des Cyberspace sind sie aber real erfahrbar. Erinnerungen, Sehnsüchte und Kindheitserinnerungen sollen geweckt werden. Die Architektur entdeckt die Welt jenseits der bürgerlichen Bildungskultur: die Welt der Kinder und des Massenvergnügens. Unternehmer von Freizeitparks argumentieren, dass die neuen Vergnügungszentren eine Art Ventilfunktion hätten, die den Menschen helfen würde, Stress, Monotonie und Vereinsamung zu entgehen. Ganz in diesem Sinn lautet auch die Firmenphilosophie von Jerde Partnership International:

> The Jerde Partnership International is attempting to answer a desperate need. Our adventure has been to reinvent the authentic urban experience. We design the appropriate vessels for a renaissance of the human communal scene – communal settings that renew a public life of richness and complexity. We create vast meeting places for a humankind that has been split apart into fractured, yet kindred souls who are beginning to participate in a global movement towards unity.[46]

Die neuen Zentren der Kommunikation wären demnach nicht die gewachsenen urbanen Kerne, sondern neu errichtete Shoppingcenter und Entertainmentcenter. Während in den meisten Städten der USA den Stadtzentren, falls überhaupt vorhanden, kaum Bedeutung zukommt, gibt es in den meisten europäischen Städten, trotz des Trends der Errichtung von Freizeitzentren an der Peripherie, noch immer zentrale Ort der Kommunikation innerhalb der Stadt. Viele Intellektuelle sehen diese Mode hingegen als Bedrohung von Individualität und Identität. Jean Baudrillard schreibt:

> We are no longer alienated and passive spectators but interactive extras (figurants interactifs); we are the meek lyophilized members of this huge ›reality show.‹ (...) Disney wins at yet another level. It is not only interested in erasing the real by turning it into a three-dimensional virtual image with no depth, but it also seeks to erase time by synchronizing all the periods, all the cultures, in a single travelling motion, by juxtaposing them in a single scenario. (...) No present, no past, no future, but an immediate synchronism of all the places and all the periods in a single atemporal virtuality.[47]

Für Michael Sorkin ist Disneyland und damit die meisten anderen Themenparks ein anti-karnevalesker Ort. Zwar gibt er vor, eine Fluchtmöglichkeit aus der bestehenden Ordnung anzubieten, und bestätigt letztlich doch nur das Existente.[48] Trotz dieser konservativen Eigenschaft von Themenparks können diese Erlebniswelten doch, wie in den folgenden zwei Fallstudien gezeigt wird, manchem Besucher einen Einblick in andere Lebensmuster bieten und damit vielleicht zu einem Testort veränderter Identität werden.

FALLSTUDIEN

THEMA 1: DER WILDE WESTEN

Die ungebrochene Faszination des Wilden Westens: Eröffnung der No Name City bei Wöllersdorf

Am 31. März 2001 wurde nach nur 11-monatiger Bauzeit Österreichs bisher größter Themenpark eröffnet: Die NO NAME CITY, eine Westernstadt bei Wöllersdorf. »Unser Konzept ist eine möglichst lebendige Westernstadt, in der die Besucher das Leben von damals nachvollziehen können und voll in die Actions eingebunden sind,«[49] erklärt Andreas Bruneder, Geschäftsführer der Errichtungs- und Betriebsgesellschaft. Auf rund 150.000 Quadratmetern Areal finden sich themenbezogene Erlebnisbereiche wie eine Westernranch, das Goldwasch-Camp (wo um 50 Schilling [3,5 Euros] jeder sein Glück versuchen kann), eine Trappersiedlung mit Übernachtungsmöglichkeit, eine Kirche (wo selbst Hochzeiten gefeiert werden können), ein Indianerlager, ein See mit Kanus, ein Streichelzoo und ein Abenteuerspielplatz. Eine Eisenbahn führt die Besucher durch den Park, auch eine Kutsche kann gemietet werden. Aus der Zeit um 1870 stammen die Vorlagen für den Saloon und die Mainstreet, die man bemüht war, originalgetreu nachzubauen. Die verschiedenen gastronomischen Einrichtungen und diversen Outfitter wie Souvenirshops stehen allerdings dem Gefühl, in den Wilden Westen versetzt zu sein, entgegen. »Alles soll möglichst authentisch sein,« wird Bruneder im *Falter* zitiert,[50] doch das richtige Wildwesterlebnis will sich nicht so recht einstellen. Und das trotz (oder wegen?) der ständigen Beschallung des Areals mit Westernsound. Vielleicht liegt es daran, dass es sich bei den meisten der Gebäude doch nur um Kulissen handelt. Abgesehen vom Büro des Sheriffs und einem Sargtischler gibt es kaum historisch inszenierte Räume, denn sowohl in die Häuser der Trappersiedlung als auch in die Indianerzelte kann man nur bei der Buchung einer Übernachtung. So gibt es in der Westernstadt zwar einiges zu sehen, aber wenig zu tun.

Stunt- und Actionshows sollen die Spannung erhöhen und das Erlebnis vom Wilden Westen intensivieren. Doch obwohl sie als täglich stattfindend angekündigt werden, findet sich unter der Woche nur ein einsamer Magier, Aladin aus dem fernen Osten (?), der am Hauptplatz seine Kunststücke zeigt. Am Abend gibt es Konzerte im Golden Nugget Saloon, und dort können dann endlich die Träume der Kindheit gelebt werden.

Die NO NAME CITY wird als wesentliches Projekt zur Förderung des Tourismus gefeiert. Den weltweiten Entwicklungen entsprechend war man bestrebt, eine neue Form der Unterhaltung auch in Österreich zu etablieren: »Internationale Trends im Freizeitverhalten zeigen, dass der Gast sich in der Freizeit bzw. im Urlaub vermehrt intensive Erlebnisse, Gegensätze zum Alltag, Genuss, Spannung aber auch den Ausflug in Fantasiewelten erwartet.«[51]

Die Welt der tapferen Cowboys, der amerikanischen Pioniere und ihre Auseinandersetzung mit den kriegerischen Indianern übt noch immer eine große Faszination aus. Die Heldengeschichten von der Eroberung des Westens werden bis heute tradiert und erfreuen sich nun schon seit fast zweihundert Jahren großer Beliebtheit.

Mitte des 19. Jahrhunderts überschwemmte eine Flut von Indianer- und Wildwestgeschichten die deutschen Verlage. Vor allem die Übersetzungen von J. F. Coopers Lederstrumpfgeschichten aus den 1820iger bis 40iger Jahren erfreuten sich größter Beliebtheit. Der wohl bekannteste Protagonist aus der Zeit der Eroberung des Westens Amerikas ist sicher William F. Cody (1846–1917), der mit seinen Shows auch den Europäern seine Abenteuer vermitteln wollte. Unter dem Namen Buffalo Bill bereisten er und seine Truppe zahlreiche Städte der Alten Welt und zeigten ein Programm, das scheinbar die historischen Begebenheiten der Besiedlung des Westens vorführte.

In Wien gastierten sie 1890 und ein weiteres Mal 1906 (in diesem Jahr auch in Graz). Dem Programmheft seiner Show wird folgende Bemerkung vorangestellt: »Diese Vorstellung hat den Zweck, den Zuschauer zu belehren, indem sie ihm lebende Bilder des einst so malerischen Steppenlebens und die berühmten Reitkünste des Westens vor Augen führt.«[52] Ganz scharf grenzen sie sich von einem reinen Unterhaltungsprogramm ab und betonen Echtheit und Authentizität des Dargebotenen:

> Oberst W. F. Cody (Buffalo Bill) und M. Nate Salsbury der bekannte amerikanische Schauspieler – Besitzer einer Ranch – haben zusammen ein grosses Unternehmen geschaffen, das zum Zwecke hat, dem Publicum ein naturgetreues Abbild von dem Leben in den Prairien zu geben. (…) Die auserlesenste Gruppe von Grenzbewohnern und Indianern – mit einer grossen Anzahl von Thieren wie man sie noch nie in Europa gesehen – wirkt in diesen Vorstellungen, die man nicht mit einer Circus – Vorstellung verwechseln darf, sondern die im Gegentheil den Reiz der Neuheit, der Ueberraschung und der Belehrung bietet.[53]

Und an anderer Stelle betont Nate Salsbury noch einmal:

> Die von Buffalo Bill's Wild West gegebenen Vorstellungen haben mit den gewöhnlichen Seiltänzer- und Kunstreiter-Aufführungen nichts gemein, deren Verdienst lediglich von einer durch Uebung erlangten Fertigkeit abhängig ist. Unser Zweck ist, das Publikum mit den Sitten und Gebräuchen und der täglichen Lebensweise der Bewohner des fernen Westens der Vereinigten Staaten, durch die Darstellung der sich dort ereignenden Scenen und wirklichen Erlebnisse bekannt zu machen (…) wir versichern Sie, dass jede Scene ein bis auf die kleinsten Einzelheiten treues Bild der Gewohnheiten der dortigen Bevölkerung bietet (…) Das ganze Material wie Pferdegeschirr usw. ist echt und schon viele Jahre in Gebrauch gewesen.[54]

Nun, die Betonung von Echtheit und Bildung ist auch in Europa nichts Neues. Denn längst waren zu Theater und Circus andere Unterhaltungsformen gekommen, die sich auf ihre wissenschaftlichen

Grundlagen beriefen. Die Popularisierung des Wissens war Mitte des 19. Jahrhunderts zu einer großen Mode geworden und Weltausstellungen wie Völkerschauen warben auf diesem Weg um die Gunst ihrer bürgerlichen Besucher.

Die Echtheit des Gezeigten war schon bei den Völkerschauen im Wiener Tiergarten viel diskutiert worden,[55] aber auch bei Buffalo Bills Wild West Show wollte man sich von der Zuverlässigkeit der gemachten Aussagen überzeugen. Die *Neue Freie Presse* berichtete am 13. Juni 1906 vom Besuch von 30 Mitgliedern der Anthropologischen Gesellschaft, die kamen »speziell um die Indianer Nordamerikas zu besichtigen und einer eingehenden Prüfung zu unterziehen.« Ganz zu ihrer Zufriedenheit, wie wir weiter lesen: »Die Mitglieder der Gesellschaft äußerten sich in anerkennender Weise sowohl über die Echtheit als auch über die prachtvollen Exemplare dieser Menschenrasse.«[56] Buffalo Bills Wild West Show war ganz darauf ausgerichtet, die Überlegenheit der weißen Rasse über die amerikanischen Ureinwohner vor Auge zu führen. Die »Indianer«[57] wurden in den Shows fast ausschließlich in der Rolle der Feinde gezeigt. Ethnologische oder anthropologische Erläuterungen fehlen. Sie sind die grausamen Gegner der weißen Siedler, die am Ende Fortschritt und Zivilisation unterliegen.

Die Kriege dienen nicht ihrer Unterwerfung oder Zivilisierung, sondern ihrer Auslöschung, sind Mittel des evolutionären Prozesses, in dem der Unterlegene »ausstirbt« und dem »Höherwertigen« Platz macht. Von der *Wiener Presse* wurde Buffalo Bills sozialdarwinistische Argumentation nicht kritisiert. Sachlich und ohne Emotion wird die Lage der indigenen Bevölkerung Nordamerikas beschrieben: »Vielleicht sieht man jetzt zum letztenmal wirkliche Rothäute aus Nordamerika in Wien; die rote Rasse ist beinahe ganz ausgestorben, und in Amerika leben höchstens 25.000 Indianer.«[58] Sensationsmeldungen ohne politischen Hintergrund geschweige denn Engagement.

Die Person Buffalo Bills

Wer war nun aber Buffalo Bill und was wurde in seinen Shows gezeigt? Martina Juen spricht davon, dass Cody unter anderem »scheinbar authentische Begebenheiten aus seinem Leben« vorführte. Mit diesem Realitätsbezug zog er das Interesse des Publikums auf sich und erspielte sich so einen nicht unbedeutenden Platz in der amerikanischen Geschichte.[59] Dabei verlief das Leben des 1846 in Iowa geborenen William Frederick Cody zunächst fernab von Stadt und Bühne. Er arbeitete als Kind als Botenjunge, später als Gastronom, Scout (Späher),

Büffeljäger, Indianerkämpfer (wie die Weißen genannt wurden, die an den kriegerischen Auseinandersetzungen um die Vereinnahmung des Landes beteiligt waren) und Soldat. Den Namen Buffalo Bill erhielt er in der Zeit, als er für die Kansas Pacific Railroad Lieferant von Büffelfleisch war, mit dem die Bautrupps der Eisenbahn versorgt wurden. Er war einer der anerkanntesten Jäger und gewann mehrere der damals sehr beliebten Wettbewerbe in Büffelschießen.[60] Seinen Spitznamen soll er allerdings aufgrund einer Episode erhalten haben, wo er zu Fuß vor einem Büffel flüchten mußte. Gut möglich, denn die Programmhefte zu seinen Shows erzählen nichts darüber.

Vom Groschenromanhelden zum Theaterstar

Zufall oder Glück führten 1869 zu der Begegnung, die Buffalo Bills weiteres Leben entscheidend prägen sollte: Ned Buntline, ein damals schon bekannter Autor, hatte einen Vertrag mit der *New York Weekly* für eine Serie von Wildwestgeschichten abgeschlossen und war auf der Suche nach einem Titelhelden. So begab sich Buntline in das umkämpfte Gebiet, um nach einer geeigneten Vorlage für seine Geschichten Ausschau zu halten – und fand Buffalo Bill. Mit einem Schlag machte die Fortsetzungsserie den damals 23jährigen Buffalo Bill berühmt. Bis 1870 lief die Serie und erschien später in Buchformat. Auch in der Alten Welt erfreuten sich Buffalo Bills Wild West Geschichten großer Beliebtheit. Insgesamt wurden 557 Dime-Novels (Groschenromane) über Buffalo Bill verfasst – und das von verschieden Autoren und in zahlreichen Sprachen.[61]

Die Tatsache, dass die literarische Figur tatsächlich existierte, zog alles Interesse auf den Helden, und Cody wurde gerne in die Salons der wohlhabenden Städter eingeladen. Buffalo Bill blieb zwar weiterhin Scout und Büffeljäger, leitete aber zunehmend hunting parties, die gerne von reichen und bekannten Gästen besucht wurden.

1872 kam das erste Buffalo Bill Stück auf die Bühne. Im Bowery Theater in New York fand die Uraufführung statt. Das Drama wurde ein großer Publikumserfolg und jahrelang gespielt. Cody spielte zu dieser Zeit noch nicht selbst, man wusste allerdings seine Anwesenheit bei den Vorstellungen werbewirksam zu inszenieren. Buntlines Idee, selbst den Part seiner Figur zu übernehmen, lehnte Cody zunächst ab. Doch noch im selben Jahr gelang es Buntline, Buffalo Bill zu überzeugen. Buntline verfasste *The Scouts of the Prairie,* und der Überlieferung nach schrieb er sich selbst eine Rolle in dem Stück, um die beiden theaterunerfahrenen Akteure Buffalo Bill und seinen Freund Texas Jack im Fall von Textschwächen unterstützen zu können. Die ursprüngliche Idee, Native Americans in den Rollen der kriegerischen Indianer zu besetzen, musste aus organisatorischen Gründen fallen gelassen werden. Geschminkte weiße Schauspieler übernahmen den Part der blutrünstigen Wilden.

Nach den Aufführungen in Nixons Amphitheater tourte die Truppe durch verschiedene amerikanische Städte. Das Interesse der Zeitungen war groß, wenn auch das Stück und Buffalo Bills schauspielerische Leistung unterschiedlich bewertet wurde. Doch das was wirklich zählte war sein reales Auftreten und seine großen Verdienste im Kampf um den Westen. Denn ungebrochen war Codys Engagement in der Armee. Sein Talent, sich und seine Taten zu verkaufen, sollte ihm in Folge noch viel Ruhm und Geld einbringen. Wesentlich für den Erfolg seiner späteren Shows war aber nicht nur seine Fähigkeit, Erlebtes unverzüglich publikumswirksam aufzubereiten, sondern auch das Zusammentreffen mit zwei Personen, die ihm bei dem Aufbau seiner Shows wesentlich unterstützten sollten: Major John M. Burke und Nate Salsbury. Burke verdankt Cody nicht nur eine konsequente Stärkung und Imageprägung der Figur Buffalo Bill, sondern auch eine sehr geschickte Pressearbeit bei allen Veranstaltungen. Salsbury war ein erfahrener Theatermann, der als Partner, Regisseur und Direktor bis zu seinem Tod zu einer der wichtigsten Stützen von Codys Unternehmen wurde.

Die erste Show fand in North Platte, Nebraska 1882 statt. Erstmals vor zahlendem Publikum wurde in Omaha 1883 gespielt. Cody machte sich die Erfahrungen, die er im Theater gemacht hatte, zunutze und wollte dennoch eine ganz andere Art von Erlebnis mit seinen Shows schaffen: »(...) the theater was too small to give any real impression of what Western life was like. Only in an arena where horses could be ridden at full gallop, where lassos could be thrown, and pistols and guns fired without frightening the audience half to death, could such a thing be attempted.«[62]

Der Aufbau der Show

Cody wollte mehr als Theater, er wollte ein gefahrloses, hautnahes Erlebnis für sein Publikum – und der Erfolg seiner Shows gab ihm Recht. Die vorgeführten Szenen waren immer ähnliche. Das *Wiener Programmheft* von 1890 gibt auf den ersten Seiten eine genaue Aufstellung der Nummern:

Einzug der Berühmtheiten und der Gruppen

Pferde-Rennen zwischen einem Cowboy, einem Mexikaner und einem Indianer, auf spanisch-mexikanischen Pferden

Fräulein Annie Oakley, berühmte Schützin, die ihre wunderbare Virtuosität im Gebrauch der Feuerwaffe zeigt

Ehemaliger Ponypost-Reiter, der zeigt wie man die Briefe und Depechen der Regierung über die großen Prairien beförderte

Überfall eines Emigrantenzuges durch die Indianer und Verteidigung desselben durch die Grenzbewohner. Nachdem der Angriff zurückgeschlagen, wird der Tanz Reel von Cowboys und Grenzbewohnerinnen zu Pferde aufgeführt

Historisches Ereignis aus dem Leben von Buffalo Bill. Der berühmte Einzelkampf mit Yellow Hand Häuptling der Sioux zu War Bonnet Creek, Dakota, und die Niederlage und Tod desselben am 17. Juli 1875 in Gegenwart der indianischen und amerikanischen Truppen

Der kleine Johann Baker. Der Cowboy-Schütze geschmückt mit den Preismedaillen der jungen Schützen der Welt

Aufheben von Gegenständen durch Cowboys vom Boden, während sie im vollen Gallop reiten, Werfen des Lassos welches die Methode zeigt, wie man das Vieh und wilde Pferde fängt, sowie Ausübung verschiedener Reiterkünste

Pistolen und Revolver-Schießen ausgeführt von Herrn C. L. Daly

Rennen zwischen amerikanischen Hinterwäldler-Damen

Angriff der Indianer auf den Deadwood-Postwagen, der von Buffalo Bill und den unter dem Befehl des Buffalo Bill stehenden Cowboys zurückgeschlagen wird

Rennen zwischen Indianer-Knaben zu Pferd ohne Sattel

Lebensgebräuche der Indianer. Indianisches Lager auf den Ebenen und Fussrennen. Verschiedene eigenartige Tänze

Col. W. F. Cody (Buffalo Bill) schiesst während des Gallop-Rittes

Büffel-Jagd. Wie es im fernen Westen Nordamerikas vor sich geht. »Buffalo Bill« und die Indianer

Angriff auf ein Grenzdorf von feindseligen Indianern. Verteidigung durch unter dem Befehl des Buffalo Bill stehenden Cowboys

Gruss am Schluss[63]

Ein Großteil der Szenen führte das besondere Geschick und die herausragenden sportlichen wie artistischen Leistungen der Truppe vor.

Auch die Westerncity in Wöllersdorf wirbt mit Westernreitvorführungen und Stuntshows. Anders als bei Buffalo Bills Show werden dort die Schauplätze gewechselt, dennoch handelt es sich hier wie damals um ein Spektakel, dem der Besucher nur als Zuschauer beiwohnen kann. Schon 1891 findet sich in einem Kinderbuch die Szene des Postkutschenüberfalls durch die Indianer, in Wöllersdorf wird auch dieses hinlänglich aus Romanen und Filmen bekannte Thema wieder zum Leben erweckt. Außerdem bietet die Westernstadt einen Banküberfall, eine Schlägerei im Saloon und den Programmpunkt »Buffalo Bill's Wild West«, der Wilde Westen aus Sicht der Legende Buffalo Bill.[64] Noch hundert Jahre nach seinem Welterfolg scheint Buffalo Bills Ruhm ungebrochen. Seine Shows waren schließlich auch sehr geschickt inszeniert, wobei die meiste Aufmerksamkeit selbstverständlich auf den Titelhelden gelenkt wurde, der durch sein Talent im Schießen und Büffeljagen einen besonderen Eindruck beim Publikum hinterlassen musste.

Einige wenige Abschnitte der Show waren der Darstellung der Native Americans gewidmet. Doch nur bei einer oberflächlichen Betrachtung kann man von einer völkerschaulichen Dimension in den Shows sprechen. Werner Schwarz schreibt dazu:

> Dem Konzept der ethnologisch-anthropologischen ›Ausstellung‹ Hagenbecks steht bei *Buffalo Bill* die dramatisierte Geschichtserzählung gegenüber, an der als Identitätsstifter die ›historischen‹ Akteure teilnehmen. Dem Statischen steht Bewegung gegenüber. Das Publikum wechselt von der aktiven in eine passive Position.[65]

Die Besucher können nicht mehr frei in dem eigens aufgebauten exotischen Dorf umhergehen, sondern müssen wie im Theater oder im Zirkus von ihren Plätzen aus dem Geschehen beiwohnen. Insofern erinnert Buffalo Bills Show viel eher an die Spektakelstücke des 19. Jahrhunderts als an die Völkerschauen Hagenbecks. Bei der Darstellung der Gebräuche und Sitten der Indianer geht es auch nicht um die Vermittlung tatsächlicher Lebensweisen, sondern um eine nochmalige Bestätigung vorhandener Klischees. Denkt man an den Misserfolg von Hagenbecks »Bella Coola« Ausstellung, die eine Vorstellung des Lebens der nordwestamerikanischen Fischer- und Jägerkulturen, jenseits der gängigen Klischees, zeigen wollte,[66] so hatte Buffalo Bill recht. In seiner Show wurden die Indianer als wilde Krieger gezeigt, die im Kampf der weißen Zivilisation unterliegen. Die europäischen Bildungs- und

Wissenschaftskonzepte spielen keine Rolle mehr: »Die ›Wilden‹ sollen nicht akkulturiert werden, sondern schlichtweg eliminiert. Sie haben im sozialdarwinistischen Sinn ihre Daseinsberechtigung verloren und der Krieg ist das Mittel der ›Selektion.‹«[67]

Das Publikum

Wie bekannt und beliebt Buffalo Bills Show war, zeigt unter anderem ein Bilderbuch zum Aufstellen für Kinder. In der Einleitung schreibt der Autor:

> Viele von Euch haben ihn wohl selbst gesehen, den mutigen Buffalo Bill, der in den letzten Jahren mit einer Schar von mehr als hundert Indianeren, amerikanischen Kuhhirten (...) und Mexikanern nach Europa herübergekommen ist und mit dieser Schaustellung, bei der es auch nicht an Büffeln, Pferden und anderen Tieren seiner Heimat fehlte, überall die größte Freude und Bewunderung erregt hat.[68]

Wieviele Kinder tatsächlich die Show sehen konnten, kann heute nicht mehr gesagt werden. Dass die Faszination über die Wildwesthelden groß war, berichtet die *AZ* am 26. Mai 1906: »(...) als aber die Wildwestreiter kamen, raste die Straßenjugend vor Entzücken. Da waren sie nun, die wirklichen, echten Indianer und Cowboys, die Beherrscher der Knabenträume.«[69] Und am darauf folgenden Tag schreibt sie:

> Es ist sicher, dass ›Wildwest‹ in den nächsten Tagen ein Wallfahrtsort für die Wiener sein wird, und es wäre nur zu wünschen, dass die Unternehmung mit Rücksicht auf die Kinder der minder bemittelten Bevölkerung, die es mit allen Fibern zu den Rothäuten zieht, auch Vorstellung zu erheblich ermäßigten Preisen veranstaltet.[70]

Sicher ist, dass sich Buffalo Bill bei den gehobenen Schichten großer Beliebtheit erfreute.[71] Vor allem bei seinem ersten Auftritt in Wien 1890 galt die Veranstaltung als gesellschaftliches Ereignis ersten Ranges. Ausführlich wurde in den verschiedenen Zeitungen über die prominenten Besucher berichtet. Am 9. Mai 1890 hatte die Truppe die wichtigsten Persönlichkeiten der Stadt zu einer Galavorführung geladen. Das *Illustrierte Wiener Extrablatt* berichtete:

> Buffalo Bill hatte das Wien der obersten Zehntausend zur Galavorstellung seines ›Wild-West‹ geladen und es waren die Meisten erschienen. Wir bemerkten, um nur einige wenige Namen zu nennen: Herzog von Nassau, Obersthofmeister Fürst Hohenlohe samt Familie, Fürst und Fürstin von Metternich, Fürstin Schwarzenberg, Gräfin Waldstein (...), Graf Herberstein, den englischen und italienischen Botschafter, den amerikanischen Gesandten, viele Generäle, Bürgermeister Dr. Prix, zahlreiche Parlaments-Mitglieder, Gemeinderäthe, Mitglieder der Wiener Theater ec ec.[72]

Die Aufteilung der Sitzplätze erinnert an die Segmentierung in den Theatern: Die Logenplätze waren dem Hofadel und dem Großbürgertum vorbehalten. Die Sitzplätze in erster Linie von einer bürgerlichen Mittelschicht belegt und die Stehplätze von einkommensschwachen Bevölkerungsgruppen besucht. Doch die wenigsten der unteren Einkommensschichten konnten sich wohl eine Eintrittskarte leisten. Bedenkt man, dass der durchschnittliche Wochenlohn eines Arbeiters um 1885 neun Gulden, einer Fabriksarbeiterin vier Gulden betrug und vergleicht man damit die billigste Eintrittskarte um 40 bis 50 Kreuzer für einen Stehplatz, so wird deutlich, dass Buffalo Bills Show kein Vergnügen für die breite Masse war. Interessant dabei ist, dass die Eintrittspreise eine Woche nach der Premiere zwar gesenkt wurden (von 2,5 auf 2 Gulden für Sitzplätze und von 50 auf 40 Kreuzer für einen Stehplatz), allerdings die Arena um 60 Logen erweitert wurde. Das kann als Hinweis für einen verstärkten Zustrom zahlungskräftiger Zuseher gewertet werden.[73]

So groß auch die Begeisterung der Arbeiterjugend für den Helden aus Wildwest war, wie viele ihn live erleben konnten, ist fraglich. Kritisch ist der Kommentar der *Arbeiterzeitung* zur heroischen Inszenierung von Buffalo Bill:

> Viel Aufmerksamkeit erregte Buffalo Bill selbst, und die Buben dachten wohl, als sie den überaus hoch gewachsenen, schönen alten Herren mit seinen wallenden weißen Locken sahen: So muss ein Held aussehen. Auch sie werden später noch rechtzeitig draufkommen, dass es noch mehr Helden gibt, die nicht hochgewachsen sind, die keine wallenden Locken haben und niemals in Gefahr waren, von Cheyenne oder den Osagen skalpirt zu werden! Dass es sogar Helden gibt im unblutigen Getriebe der Großstadt, die Schrecknisse oft größer sind als die, welche den kühnen Pionier im wildesten Western lauern.[74]

THEMA 2: VENEDIG

Und überall Venedig oder zur Rolle der Lagunenstadt in der Unterhaltungsindustrie

Von der großen Affinität der Wiener zu Venedig spricht Bartel F. Sinhuber in seinem Buch über den Prater. Nicht nur zahlreiche Operetten, Singspiele und Ballette seien ein Zeichen dafür, sondern auch Häuser wie der im venezianischen Palazzo-Stil erbaute Dogenhof auf der Praterstraße, eine Reminiszenz an das damals bereits verlorene Venetien.[75] Kein Wunder also, wenn der Unternehmer Gabor Steiner diese Vorliebe aufgriff, um eines der größten Vergnügungszentren der Jahrhundertwende zu errichten. Karl Roschitz schreibt:

> Wer in Opern und Singspielen, Operetten und Balletten, Schauspielen und Festen, aber auch im Praterbudenzauber die Wiener Träume und Sehnsüchte seit der Metternich-Ära, vor allem der Gründerzeit, Ringstraßen-und Luegerzeit, aufzuspüren versucht, stößt merkwürdigerweise immer wieder auf Venedig. (...) Etwa ein Jahrzehnt nach Makarts Tod ergibt sich das bürgerliche Wien erneut der Lagunenstadt, wenn es zu Füßen des Riesenrads sein, Venedig in Wien‹ errichtet (...)[76]

Aber nicht nur in Wien erfreute sich Venedig so großer Beliebtheit. Die Besonderheit der romantischen Lagunenstadt zog Besucher aus der ganzen Welt an, und international war auch die Bedeutung Venedigs für die beginnende Unterhaltungsindustrie. Schon 1890 hatte man in London ein kleines Venedig errichtet. Es bestand jedoch lediglich aus einer Wasserbühne und gemalten Kulissen, die berühmte Palastbauten zeigten: »Auf der Wasserstraße der Bühne kamen weltliche Prozessionen angefahren, landeten auf dem Markusplatz und entfalteten hier im Stil eines Ausstattungsstücks den Pomp der alten Kaufherren-Stadt mit dem Dogen als Mittelpunkt. Der Erfolg war grandios.»[77] Wenige Jahre später, 1894, wurde in Berlin eine Lagunenstadt nach dem Vorbild Venedigs zur Unterhaltung der Bevölkerung angelegt. Hier wurde dem Publikum schon wesentlich mehr als in London geboten. Es war nicht mehr eine Bühne, auf der sich das Geschehen abspielte, sondern der Besucher wurde selbst zum Akteur. Allerdings erinnerte wenig der Anlage an Venedig: der Eingang war als römischer Triumphbogen gestaltet, es gab ein gemaltes Colosseum und einen Concordia-Tempel, so dass die Atmosphäre eher die einer antiken Stadt war. Abgesehen von der Anlage einer Wasserstraße, auf der man mit Gondeln fahren konnte, war das Erlebnis – nicht zuletzt durch die nur mit bemalter Leinwand bespannten Bretterblenden anstelle von richtigen Gebäuden – wohl kein sehr authentisches.

Auch in Übersee, in Amerika, war der Nachbau Venedigs eine beliebte Attraktion. So bietet Luna Park auf Coney Island unter anderem auch eine Fahrt auf den Kanälen. Schöner als auf Coney Island, »as a more sophisticated version«[78] baute man 1904 in Los Angeles »little Venice in America« ursprünglich mit sieben Meilen langen Kanälen und mit Gondolen und Gondolieri, importiert aus Italien.

Dass Venedig in den USA noch immer ein beliebtes Thema der Vergnügungsindustrie ist, zeigt das erst kürzlich in Las Vegas errichtete »Venetian Resort Hotel Casino.« Mit 6000 Betten ist das 1999 eröffnete Hotel nicht nur das größte Ressort von Las Vegas, sondern der ganzen

Welt. Es enthält thematisierte Suiten, Shoppingcenters, Restaurants, ein Theater mit diversen Shows und natürlich ein Kasino. Durch den Campanile betritt der Gast das Ressort, Rolltreppen bringen ihn über Rialto- und Seufzerbrücke zum Shoppingcenter. Vor dem Hotel wurde ein Kanal angelegt, auf dem Gondeln auf und ab fahren. Das Kasino befindet sich in einem Nachbau des Dogenpalastes. Trotz der Anlage von Kanälen im Shoppingcenter und diversen Darbietungen von maskierten und kostümierten Sängern und Musikern bleibt es allerdings zweifelhaft, ob sich venezianische Atmosphäre auf diese Art inszenieren lässt. Fehlende *morbidezza* und Romantik werden durch intensives Merchandising ersetzt. Las Vegas hat damit eine weitere thematiserte Attraktion, die sich wohl durch den Aufbau, aber nicht durch die Atmosphäre von den anderen unterscheidet.

Als Gabor Steiner seine Idee zu »Venedig in Wien« entwickelte, gab es zwar so manche Vorbilder, die jedoch in ihrer Ausführung wie oben beschrieben eher bescheiden waren. Es war nun Gabor Steiners Ehrgeiz, den Wienern ein möglichst wirklichkeitsnahes Erlebnis von Venedig zu bieten und damit ein bisher nicht gekanntes Vergnügen zu schaffen.

Gabor Steiner und sein »Venedig in Wien«

Bei der »Internationalen Ausstellung für Musik und Theaterwesen,« die vom 7. Mai bis zum 9. Oktober 1892 auf dem Weltausstellungsgelände im Prater veranstaltet wurde, waren »eine Reihe ›begehbarer‹ und so direkt erlebbarer Attraktionen aufgebaut«[79] worden. Das Rotundengelände hatte man in eine französisch-italienische Gartenanlage mit blühenden Orangenbäumen verwandelt. Der auf Großausstellungen spezialisierte Architekt Oskar Marmorek hatte eine 3.500 Besucher fassende Musikhalle entworfen, der gegenüber sich ein Theater für chinesische Schattenspiele befand. Am Ende der »Haupt-Avenue« befand sich das vom renommierten Theaterarchitekten Hermann Helmer erbaute Ausstellungstheater, in dem zahlreiche Gastspiele europäischer Bühnen stattfanden.[80] Die schaulustigen Besucher zog es allerdings mehr zum Riesenpanorama, das die »Einfahrt des Dampfers ›Lübeck‹ in New York« mit einem überwältigenden Anblick der Metropole und einem Blick auf die Freiheitsstatue[81] bot, oder aber nach »Alt-Wien.« Oskar Marmorek und der k.k. Hoftheater-Maler Gilbert Lehner hatten eine originalgetreue Nachbildung des Hohen Marktes anno 1692 aufgebaut. Es gab ein reges Geschäftsleben, eine Hanswurst-Bühne, auf der mit ausgewählten Stücken die Entstehung und Entwicklung der Wiener

Posse vorgeführt wurde, und zahlreiche nachgebaute Wirtshäuser: »Die einzelnen Gaststätten waren jedoch keineswegs ›kaschiert‹, sondern echte Heurigenschenken, in denen man sich bei Volkssängern und Schrammelmusik bis in die frühen Morgenstunden trefflich unterhielt.«[82] Gabor Steiner war der Theatersekretär der Ausstellung, und der große Erfolg ließ ihn an eine Fortsetzung von dergleichen Attraktionen denken. Im *Neuen Wiener Journal* schreibt er rückblickend:

> Nach dem großen Erfolg von Alt-Wien im Jahre 1892 beschäftigte mich unaufhörlich der Gedanke, ein ähnliches Unternehmen in Wien ins Leben zu rufen. Die venezianischen Feste in der Theater- und Musikausstellung, die so großen Zuspruch fanden, ließen mich auf die Idee kommen, ein ›Venedig‹ in Wien entstehen zu lassen.[83]

Nun, es waren wohl nicht nur die venezianischen Feste der Theater- und Musikausstellung, sondern gewiss auch der Besuch des Londoner Venedig-Parks, die Steiner zu der Anlage einer Lagunenstadt in Wien inspirierten. Wenn es aber auch Vorbilder gab, die Ausführung in Wien war durch ihren gesamtinszenatorischen Charakter und die komplette Ausstattung bisher einzigartig.

Im ehemaligen Kaisergarten[84] wollte Gabor Steiner sein Venedig errichten. Das Areal war 1891 an eine englische Firma mit dem Namen »The Vienna Concessions Syndicate Limited« verkauft worden und erhielt von dieser den Namen »Englischer Garten«. Der Kaufvertrag verpflichtete die Unternehmer, die Fläche der Öffentlichkeit zur Verfügung zu stellen und einige Vergnügungsetablissements, wie zum Beispiel ein Sommertheater, zu errichten. Die dort gezeigten Attraktionen wie Schuhplattler-Gruppen, dressierte Wölfe und Seiltänzer stießen allerdings auf geringes Interesse. Die Besitzer gingen in Konkurs und mussten das Areal verkaufen. 1893 ersteigerte wiederum ein englisches Unternehmen, »the Assets Realisation Company«, das Gebiet. Gabor Steiner konnte die Besitzer für seine Pläne interessieren und den englischen Garten ab dem Februar 1895 für zehn Jahre pachten.[85]

Erst nach Interventionen konnte Gabor Steiner bei den schwerfälligen Wiener Beamten eine Baugenehmigung erwirken, und das 50.000 Quadratmeter große Areal konnte in ein kleines Venedig verwandelt werden. Wieder war es der Architekt Oskar Marmorek, der diese neuerliche Idee einer inszenierten Vergnügungslandschaft umzusetzen half. Er und sein Mitarbeiterstab kopierten eine Reihe berühmter venezianischer Bauten und Paläste. Eine topographisch genaue Wiedergabe war freilich nicht möglich, weshalb der Markusplatz als ein von den Hoftheatermalern J. Kautsky Söhne und Rottonara gemaltes Panorama gezeigt wurde. Die anderen Gebäude waren jedoch keineswegs Theaterdekoration, »sondern tatsächlich betretbare Häuser, deren Innenräume als Verkaufsläden, Kosthallen, Ausstellungsräume, Werkstätten für vornehmlich venezianische Industrien und Restaurationsbetriebe genutzt wurden.«[86] Drei inselartige Campi wurden von künstlich angelegten Wasserstraßen umgeben und durch schmale, hochgejochte Brücken verbunden. In Venedig wurden Gondeln (die für Wien allerdings etwas kürzer sein mussten) bestellt und Gondoliere, Sänger, Musiker und Aussteller angeworben. Ein authentisches Ambiente kreierte man nicht nur durch den Nachbau von Palazzi und Wohnhäusern, sondern ebenso durch die Anstellung von italienischen Künstlern und Kunsthandwerkern. Es gab Ausstellungen venezianischer Kunst, und man konnte die Produkte renommierter Firmen erwerben. Manchen Kunsthandwerkern, wie den Glasbläsern aus Murano, konnte man bei ihrer Arbeit zusehen. Außerdem gab es Verkostungen italienischen Weins und eine Reihe italienischer Restaurants. Dem Besucher wurde eine Reihe von Veranstaltungen geboten: neben italienischer Musik auch Heurigenabende, Opern- und Operettenkonzerte, Komödien, Marionettentheater und Tanzmöglichkeiten im »Römersaal.«

»Venedig in Wien« war am 22. Mai 1895 eröffnet worden und erfreute sich sofort größter Beliebtheit. Bis zu 20.000 Besucher kamen täglich, um die neue Attraktion zu sehen, und viele kamen wieder, wie uns die große Zahl von Saisonkartenbesitzern zeigt. Mit immer wechselnden Theateraufführungen und den neuesten technischen Errungenschaften der Unterhaltungsindustrie (wie dem Kinematographen oder einem Automatenbüffet) versuchte Gabor Steiner, seine Gäste anzulocken, doch nach einigen Jahren ließ der Reiz nach. 1901 wurden die venezianischen Gebäude abgetragen und auf dem selben Areal eine neue Attraktion errichtet: die »Internationale Stadt.«

ENDNOTES

1 Schinner, Barbara: Freizeitparks. Wien 1999, S. 21ff

2 Müller, Britta: Veranstaltungen Wiens im 18. und 19. Jahrhundert. Wien 1992, S. 44

3 Weschel, Leopold Matthias: Die Leopoldstadt bey Wien. Wien 1824, S. 514

4 Schrattenbach zit. nach Müller, Britta: Veranstaltungen Wiens im 18. und 19. Jahrhundert. Wien 1992, S. 45

5 Alland zit. nach Maderthaner, Wolfgang; Musner, Lutz: Die Anarchie der Vorstadt. Frankfurt/ NY 1999, S. 118

6 Maderthaner, Wolfgang; Musner, Lutz: Die Anarchie der Vorstadt. Frankfurt/ NY 1999, S. 118

7 La Speranza, Marcello: Prater-Kaleidoskop. Wien 1997, S. 15
8 Pezzl, Johann: Beschreibung der Haupt- und Residenzstadt Wien. Wien 1820, S. 236 f
9 Assmann, Jan zit. nach Schweizer, Maria: Der Wiener Prater. Funktionen und Mythen. Wien 2000, S. 8
10 Dangelmaier, M.: Der Wiener Prater. Wien 1852 zit. nach Schweizer, Maria: Der Wiener Prater. Funktionen und Mythen. Wien 2000, S. 9
11 Schweizer, Maria: Der Wiener Prater. Funktionen und Mythen. Wien 2000, S. 9
12 Sandgruber, Roman: Die Anfänge der Konsumgesellschaft. Wien 1982, S. 249
13 Richter, Joseph zit. nach Schweizer, Maria: Der Wiener Prater. Funktionen und Mythen. Wien 2000, S. 55
14 Witlacil zit. nach Greif, Wolfgang: Plebejische Kultur im Wiener Vormärz. Wien 1988, S. 131
15 Vor allem das Backhendl galt im Biedermeier als kulinarisches Wohlstandsymbol. Seine Verdrängung, im Zuge des 19. Jahrhunderts, durch die billigeren Würstel mit Kren, kann einerseits als Ausdruck vermehrten bürgerlichen Sparsinns, aber auch als Zeichen für die Verarmung der unteren Schichten gesehen werden. Vgl Sandgruber, Roman: Biedermeier-Genüsse. In: Bürgersinn und Aufbegehren. Wien 1988, S. 596
16 Greif, Wolfgang: Plebejische Kultur im Wiener Vormärz. Wien 1988, S. 48f
17 Müller, Britta: Veranstaltungen Wiens im 18. und 19. Jahrhundert. Wien 1992, S. 54
18 Schinner, Barbara: Freizeitparks. Wien 1999, S. 47f
19 vgl. Koppelkamm, Stefan: Der imaginäre Orient. Exotische Bauten des 18. und 19. Jahrhunderts in Europa. Berlin 1987.
20 Pemsel, Jutta: Die Wiener Weltausstellung von 1873, Wien1983, S. 48f
21 Weinstein, Raymond: Disneyland and Coney Island. 1992, S. 138
22 vgl. die Begeisterung für das Pariser Leichenschauhaus oder die vielen Grusel- und Wachskabinette
23 NWT, 20.4.1903, S. 7
24 Weinstein, Raymond: Disneyland and Coney Island. 1992, S. 141
25 Sorkin, Michael: Variations on a theme park. New York 1992, S. 208
26 Brain, Robert: Going to the Exhibition. Cambridge 1994, S. 119
27 Dostojewski zit. nach Brain, Robert: Going to the Exhibition. Cambridge 1994, S. 119
28 Ebd., S. 121
29 Mattie, Erik: Weltausstellungen. Stuttgart, Zürich 1998, S. 9
30 Ebeling 1867 zit. nach Rapp, Christian: Die Welt im Modell. Weltausstellungen im 19. Jahrhundert. In: Fillitz, Hermann (Hg.): Der Traum vom Glück. Die Kunst des Historismus in Europa, Wien 1996, S. 49
31 Rapp, Christian: Die Welt im Modell. Weltausstellungen im 19. Jahrhundert. In: Fillitz, Hermann (Hg.): Der Traum vom Glück. Die Kunst des Historismus in Europa, Wien 1996, S. 49
32 Ebd., S. 50
33 Malkowsky zit. nach Kuchenbuch, Thomas: Die Welt um 1900: Unterhaltungs- und Technikkultur. Stuttgart 1992, S. 181f
34 Hofmann, Werner: Das irdische Paradies. München 1974, S. 152
35 Wilk zit. nach Gay, Paul Du: Production of Culture-Culture of Production. London 1997, S. 43

36 Sorkin, Michael: Variations on a theme park. New York 1992, S. 226

37 Morasch, Ludwig zit. in: Greisenegger, Ingrid: Jedem Dorf seine Erlebniswelt. In: Kurier 1.2.2000, S. 29

38 Jöhnk, Peter: »Erlebnisräume«-Verpackung einer Illusion. In: Amusement T&M 3/97, S. 87

39 Mayrhofer, Paul: Erlebniswelten erobern Wien. In: Kurier 30.10.1999, S. 33

40 Ebd.

41 Bahrer-Fellner, Ingrid: Freizeitparks. Im Land von Show und Action. In: Freie Fahrt. Nr. 6/2001, S. 60

42 Jon Jerde bei seinem Vortrag im Rahmen des Symposiums »Die Zukunft der Städte« im Radiokulturhaus Wien, 7. und 8. November 2000

43 Greisenegger, Ingrid: Keimfreier Urlaub unterm Glassturz. In: Kurier, 3.2.2000, S. 33

44 Ebd.

45 Loverseed, Helga: Leisure Industries. Theme parks in North America. In: EIU Travel & Tourism Analyst, 4/94, S. 60

46 The Jerde Partnership International. www.jerde.com

47 Baudrillard, Jean: Disneyworld Company. In: www.ctheory.com/e32.html

48 Sorkin, Michael: Variations on a themepark. New York 1992, S. 208

49 Bruneder zit. auf der Website der No Name City, www.NoNameCity.at

50 Bruneder zit. in Falter 16/01, S. 71

51 Website der No Name City, www.NoNameCity.at

52 Buffalo Bill's »Wild West« and Congress of rough riders of the world. Offizielles Programm. O.J. Wien, S. 1

53 Buffalo Bill's Wild West. Amerikanische Spiele. Illustrierte Bilder historischer Ereignisse und Skizzen. Buffalo Bill's Wild West Company. Wien 1890, S. 2

54 Salsbury in ebd., S. 3

55 Vgl. Schwarz, Werner Michael: Aschanti-Fieber. Anthropologische Spektakel Wien 1870–1910. Diss. Wien 2000

56 Neue Freie Presse, 13. Juni 1906, S. 11

57 Die kulturelle Heterogenität der Native Americans wurde in Buffalo Bill's Shows völlig mißachtet. Die indigene Bevölkerung der USA wurde auf einen Typus reduziert: die Indianer. Seine Shows trugen damit nicht unwesentlich zu einer Stereotypisierung der Native Americans bei. Vgl. Juen, Martina: Buffalo Bills Wild West Show 1890 im Wiener Prater – ein Unterhaltungsspektakel mit ideologischer Botschaft. Dipl. Wien 1996

58 Neue Freie Presse, 31. Mai 1906, S. 12

59 Juen, Martina: Buffalo Bills Wild West Show, Wien 1996, S. 26

60 Für die Plains-Indianer hatten diese lediglich zur Unterhaltung veranstalteten Büffeljagden allerdings weitreichende Konsequenzen. Büffelfleisch zählte zu ihren Hauptnahrungsmitteln, und die stetige Reduktion des Tierbestandes bedrohte die Lebenssituation der Native Americans. Häufig anzutreffen ist daher die Ansicht, dass die bis in die achtziger Jahre des 19. Jahrhunderts andauernden und bis zu der fast völligen Ausrottung der Tiere betriebenen Büffeljagden aus politischem Kalkül organisiert wurden. Vgl. Juen, Martina: Buffalo Bills Wild West Show, Wien 1996, S. 29f

61 Juen, Martina: Buffalo Bills Wild West Show, Wien 1996, S. 31

62 Cody, Williams F.: An Autobiography of Buffalo Bill o. O. 1920, zit. nach Juen, Martina, Buffalo Bills Wild West Shows, Wien 1996, S. 40

63 Buffalo Bill's Wild West. Programmheft 1890, S. 4ff
64 Aufgrund der mangelnden Kooperationsbereitschaft des Teams der Westerncity war es leider nicht möglich, nähere Informationen über dieses Highlight des Eröffnunsprogramms am 31. März 2001 einzuholen.
65 Schwarz, Werner Michael: Aschanti-Fieber, Wien 2000, S. 156
66 Ebd., S. 154
67 Ebd., S. 156
68 Buffalo Bill's Wilder Westen. Ein Bilderbuch zum Aufstellen für Kinder. Wien 1989 (Esslingen 1891), S. 1
69 AZ, 26. Mai 1906, S. 6
70 AZ, 27. Mai 1906, S. 6
71 IWE, 27. Mai 1906,S. 5
72 IWE, 9. Mai 1890, S. 3
73 Juen, Martina: Buffalo Bill's Wild West Show, Wien 1996, S. 63f
74 AZ, 26. Mai 1906, S. 6
75 Sinhuber, Bartel F.: Zu Besuch im alten Prater. Wien 1993, S. 137f
76 Roschitz, Karl zit. nach Sinhuber, Bartel F.: Zu Besuch im alten Prater. Wien 1993, S. 138
77 Rubey, Norbert; Schoenwald, Peter: Venedig in Wien. Wien 1996, S. 41
78 Venice Canals in L.A. www. Starttribune.com/stories/425/343991
79 Horak, Roman: »Geschmackslandschaften«. Über die Formierung von Popularkultur im Wien der Moderne. In: Wiener Beiträge zur Moderne und Hypermoderne. Wien 1996, S. 334
80 Rubey, Norbert; Schoenwald, Peter: Venedig in Wien. Wien 1996, S. 39
81 Horak, Roman: »Geschmackslandschaften«. Über die Formierung von Popularkultur im Wien der Moderne. In: Wiener Beiträge zur Moderne und Hypermoderne. Wien 1996, S. 334
82 Neues Wiener Tagblatt, 8. Mai 1932, zit. nach Horak, Roman: »Geschmackslandschaften«. Über die Formierung von Popularkultur im Wien der Moderne. In: Wiener Beiträge zur Moderne und Hypermoderne. Wien 1996, S. 335
83 Steiner, Gabor in Neues Wiener Journal 1929 zit nach Schweizer, Maria: Der Wiener Prater. Wien 2000, S. 62
84 Areal zwischen Ausstellungsstraße und Hauptallee
85 Rubey, Norbert; Schoenwald, Peter: Venedig in Wien. Wien 1996, S. 42;
Schweizer, Maria: Der Wiener Prater. Wien 2000, S. 61;
Sinhuber, Bartel F.: Zu Besuch im alten Prater. Wien 1993, S. 139
86 Rubey, Norbert; Schoenwald, Peter: Venedig in Wien. Wien 1996, S. 444

Theming and the Crystal Palace: An Historical Perspective

SUSAN INGRAM

In *The Theming of America: Dreams, Visions, and Commercial Spaces*, Mark Gottdiener makes the point that while currently »themed environments derive inspiration from Hollywood, the world of high fashion, sports, and the music industry« (145), they are basically:

> a recycling of the arcade, the state fair, *the world exposition*, and the ambience of *the cosmopolitan, pedestrian city.* The themes of modernism – progress, technological wizardry, and the ›new‹ – are intertwined with themes of status, nostalgia, and fantasies derived from the most hackneyed examples of Hollywood cinema – *ancient civilizations, tropical paradise, the Wild West, ›Arabia,‹ ›Rio,‹ or ›Hawaii‹* – some fantasized geographical scene of exoticism straight out of the Saturday matinee. (151f., italics added)

In looking back not to Hollywood but rather to the 1851 Great Exhibition at the Crystal Palace in Hyde Park, this contribution tries to determine with some historical specificity how and where the practice of theming emerged at the world exhibitions. While many scholars have begun to make connections between the Disney theme parks and specific world's fairs, the 1893 Chicago Columbian in particular (see, for example, Harris, Gilbert and Wallace), my focus here is more on how the space of the world exhibitions, and of the themed exhibitionary and shopping complexes which grew out of them, was expansive enough to allow for and contain the contestatory and seemingly contradictory tendencies which might have otherwise stalled the sometimes sputtering engine of capital. As Jeffrey Auerbach has demonstrated, the Great Exhibition in 1851 »was rife with contradictions, and those who organized and participated in it were motivated both by their antipathy to industrialization — their conviction that it had ruined craftsmanship – and by their celebration of it. ... The Victorians had a love-hate relationship with technology, fetishizing it on the one hand, critical of its effects on consumer goods on the other« (172, 115), and of course they were, and are, not the only ones. It is in particular the disjuncture between »*ancient civilizations, tropical paradise, the Wild West, ›Arabia,‹ ›Rio,‹ or ›Hawaii,‹*« on the one hand, and »the works of industry,« on the other, that I will probe here in order to specify some of the cultural dynamics, functions, and fantasies that theming continues to serve.

For its organizers, the main question underlying the Great Exhibition, the first international display of the works of industry of all nations, was bound up in the name given to the organization which provided the impetus for putting things on display in Britain in the first place: the Royal Society for the Encouragement of the Arts, Manufactures and Commerce, founded in 1754 by William Shipley (Luckhurst 22). The challenge Great Exhibition organizers faced was namely: how to wed art and manufactures in such a way that the temple would not appear to be one of commerce but rather one of industry in the positive, hard-working sense of the word (cf. Auerbach 118).[1] As Auerbach details, the organizers' strategy was to disallow prices on exhibits and to place a strong emphasis on education:

> If there was one theme that united the exhibits and the organizers' objectives it was education in the broadest sense: educating producers about new materials and processes, educating consumers about new products, and educating a substantial portion of British society about the value of industry, commerce, and mechanization, and the importance of art and taste. (94)

The importance of art and taste served not only to buttress class divisions, but also as an outlet for critiquing the nature of early nineteenth-century British industrial production, which had primarily focused on quantity and utility, on making products for as many people as possible; sales were the bottom line, as British manufacturers had found that selling cheaper goods to a large portion of the population would produce higher profits than selling a few high-priced goods (114). However, those goods, produced as they were piecemeal by uneducated workers, lacked the aesthetic appeal of their continental counterparts and were roundly criticized by those »nostalgi[c] for an idealized old world of craftsmanship that had supposedly been lost (if indeed it had ever existed)« (115).

This nostalgia took on material form in the Exhibition's Medieval Court, which was located in the south-west sector vis-à-vis from the Sculpture court and incongruously between Birmingham and Canada along the main aisle (the point being that it was a prominent location quite near the central fountain). The mere presence, not to mention the popularity, of the Medieval Court at the Exhibition is worthy of comment. While its detractors derided it as »backward and outdated, antithetical to progress« and described the decorative work it featured as

»lifeless... in a more enlightened age,« it found favor with champions of a return to pre-modern methods of team-oriented craftsmanship, i.e. the William Morrises among the visitors (116-17). The Medieval Court, which also caused quite a stir by prominently displaying a cross, was designed by Augustus Welby Pugin, author of, among other things, *The True Principles of Pointed or Christian Architecture* (1841) and *Contrasts* (1836), which Auerbach describes as »a graphic satire of contemporary life and architecture, professing to demonstrate in pairs of contrasted pictures the superiority not only of Gothic architecture to modern Classic, but of medieval to modern society« (114). Pugin was one of many mid-century British design critics and reformers concerned about the deleterious effect that machine production was having on the role of artisans or craftspeople in separating design from production. And while Auerbach makes the point that this separation is inherent in the capitalist division of labor and therefore a *fait accompli* long before mechanization, it cannot be denied that industrializing production processes certainly brought this division to the fore.

That a key site of controversy at the Exhibition involved artisans and pre-modern methods of production points to what is for me one of the more striking of the Great Exhibition's seeming contradictions. While it is common knowledge that »the Industrial Revolution was a gradual process that was by no means complete by 1851,« many are not aware of the »dominance of handicrafts in the British economy until at least the late nineteenth century [which] was certainly apparent at the Great Exhibition. The very panes of glass used for the Crystal Palace, all 300,000 of them, were blown by hand, and most of the goods on display were the products not of machines, but of craftsmen« (135). While both artisans and machine-workers attended the Exhibition in great numbers, it was not the former but the latter who were the particular target of the organizers' educational hopes, just as they had been the intended beneficiaries of the government's misguided educational efforts in the first half of the century in opening mechanics' institutes and schools of design (10-12). The Exhibition, like the institutes, ended up serving what Auerbach rather inexactly describes as »the lower-middle and respectable working classes (clerks and shop assistants)« rather than the »poorer working classes« (11). It was, after all, to the clerks and shop assistants that this particular form of education (understood as incorporating knowledge and taste) was of particular importance. The basis of their distinction, it both paid and was the price of their entrance into the great exhibition that was society.

While the working-class presence at the exhibition is difficult to ascertain with any precision, it can be traced, especially through organizational efforts made on their behalf. Thomas Cook, for example, offered excursion-packages to the Exhibition:

> He and his son traveled indefatigably through the towns of Yorkshire and the Midlands, publicizing his excursions in conjunction with the Midland Railway. One of his most successful tactics was to engage bands to play outside mills and factories on Saturday nights to attract the attention of recently paid workers, to whom Cook would then sell tickets. He also arranged lodgings … [and] told his prospective excursionists that they should regard the exhibition ›not as a show or a place of amusement, but [rather as] *a great school* of science, of art, of industry, of peace and universal brotherhood.‹ (138, italics added).

In *The Yorkshire Visitors' Guide to the Great Exhibition*, published in 1851, one finds a similar admonishment: »While in London the working classes should not fritter away their time and money in seeing panoramas and shows, and paltry theatres« (136). Instead they were to congregate in the Crystal Palace and take in its instructive, sanctioned displays.

If the working classes had ignored such warnings and taken in, say, a panorama, what would they have seen that would have been such a frittering away of their time and money? Richard Altick's *The Shows of London* offers a good indication, which I would like to quote at some length for rather apparent reasons:

> Savile House had three panoramas during the season, though not at the same time. One was Charles Marshall's ›GREAT EDUCATIONAL AND PICTORIAL EXHIBITION, GEOGRAPHICAL, HISTORICAL, AND STATISTICAL, OF A GRAND TOUR THROUGH EUROPE‹ – a title that owed something, by anticipation, to the Major General in *The Pirates of Penzance*. These canvases illustrated the three routes an English tourist would most likely follow during the present year – the Thames to Constantinople by way of Berlin and Budapest, Rome to Mont Blanc, and the Rhine from Bingen to Cologne. The second Savile House ›grand moving diorama‹ was a trip up the Ganges from the point where the *Overland Route to India* at the Gallery of Illustration left off, arriving finally at the palace of Agra, ›from which is seen the splendid mausoleum, the Taj Mahal.‹ There was also a three-tableau portrayal of Paris, St. Cloud, and Versailles painted by Monsieur C. Cambon, scene painter for the Opéra and the Opéra Comique. The *coup de théâtre* here was the use of real jets of water in the scene showing the fountains of Versailles. …
>
> The Cosmorama, now renamed the Prince of Wales's Bazaar, featured an almost studied lack of novelty: its scenes included the old faithful burning of Edinburgh, St. Peter's, Mont Blanc, Versailles, and *the Grand Cairo*. … (In justice, it might be remarked that however old-hat these were to London showgoers, to visitors from the country the dew of novelty was still on them.) …

> The most popular of the panoramas as the season began, however, was the *Overland Route to India* at the Gallery of Illustration, which by the end of March had already had a total of 900 performances, before audiences totaling 200,000. (460-2, italics added)

Despite the opening claims for these panomaras to education, which resemble those made for the Crystal Palace exhibits, what one detects here, then, is the presence of what would become themed environments – the reproduction of certain exotic places which, if one thinks of the hotels in Las Vegas and the designer rooms in the Fantasyland Hotel in West Edmonton Mall, have proven remarkably and consistently popular.

These themes, however, were unwelcome as such at the Great Exhibition of 1851. Lying latent in the displays in the Crystal Palace in Hyde Park, lurking both inside and outside its gates, these themes were only allowed to come out once the Exhibition was over and due to its immense success and the Exhibition Commission's early promise to remove the building from its site at the end of the Exhibition, the original structure was dismantled, transported to the top of Sydenham Hill, on the southern outskirts of London in Kent, rebuilt, expanded, furnished as a Winter Park and Garden (Beaver 79), and reopened in June 1854. »Pugin's Mediaeval Court [was] brought to Sydenham along with the Palace and it was now joined by... Grecian, Roman, Byzantine, Romanesque, Pompeian, Chinese, Alhambra, Renaissance and Egyptian courts« (Beaver 84), the latter being particularly spectacular, »with its high pillars (in fact, half the size of the originals in Egypt), sphinxes, mummies and enormous statues« (Reeves 31-2).

> Although the building was similar, the Sydenham Crystal Palace, *a resort and theme park more than anything else*, had a very different focus to that of the Great Exhibition. Samuel Laing, MP, director of the Brighton Railway and chairman of the Crystal Palace Company, elucidated three objectives at its opening: amusement and recreation, instruction, and commercial utility. Note that only the second of these overlapped with the imperatives behind the Great Exhibition, although in the end the exhibition had indeed become a site of amusement, recreation, and commerce as well. (200, italics added)

Only instruction was encouraged at the first Great Exhibition; for commercial utility, amusement, recreation, and the re-creation or theming of environments, one had to wait for Sydenham and for future exhibitions. At the *exposition universelle* in Paris in 1855, all objects, art and otherwise, were required to have price tags (Mandell 11). By the next universal exhibition in Paris, in 1867, there were exotic restaurants with ethnic music, spicy dishes and waitresses in national costumes, and people were displayed as part of exhibits for the first time, something which would become standard and very popular practice:

> various North African exhibits were presented [in Paris] as tableaux-vivants. An Egyptian Bazaar contained crafts, people and vendors, a camel stable had real camels and Arabic attendants, an authentic Tunisian Barber Shop was open for business. Various Egyptian, Tunisian and Algerian Cafés were staffed with specially imported waiters and chefs... [and] visitors to the site were more fascinated by foreign workmen finishing off incomplete pavilions than they were by the pavilions themselves. (Greenhalgh 85)

The wider embrace of this exposition also took in gardens, an amusement park, and for the first time, sideshows of a type familiar to carnival goers. An Englishman, George Augustus Sala, attending the 1878 exposition in Paris wrote in one of his articles for the *Daily Telegraph*:

> You look in vain in these interminable corridors of shop-windows for such naive specimens of individual ingenuity and labour as were delightfully manifest in our World's Fair in Hyde Park seven-and-twenty years ago – models of Tintern Abbey or Rochester Castle in cork; Pharoah and all his Host engulfed in the Red Sea, burnt with a red-hot poker on a deal board by a clergyman in the vale of Taunton; Comical Creatures from Wurtemberg; Gulliver and the Lilliputians in wax; Susanna and the Elders in Berlin wool, by a Lady Twenty-five years Bedridden; or a Model in Ivory of the Old Temeraire, by Two Congenital Idiots. There were unpretending ›Exhibits‹ enough; but they spoke of the craft and patience of individual Man. In more recent Expositions, and notable in the gigantic Bazaar which I am at present painfully exploring, individual man, save in a very few instances, disappears, and is replaced by great Companies and great Firms solicitous of order. (cited in Allwood, 61-2)

Beginning with the 1867 Paris exposition, themed attractions appeared in the grounds outside the pavilion buildings, and with the introduction of a »midway« at the 1893 Chicago Columbian Exposition, they were given their own separate space.[2] Theming also increased as corporations, such as the American automobile manufacturers and oil companies, became more present: »In the case of American fairs, as Roland Marchand has made clear, entertainment began to surpass education as the overriding feature of pavilions organized by corporations. Indeed, technologies capable of providing entertainment – ranging from thrill rides to technologically sophisticated peep shows – became permanent fixtures of international expositions« (Ryder 2000, 137). The pavilions became increasingly themed as well. The case of the New Hampshire pavilion at the 1893 Chicago Columbian Exposition (*Ill. 1*) is particularly interesting as it was built to »by G.B. Howe ›of Boston and Omaha‹... [to] resemble a Swiss chalet because that state is ›the Switzerland of America‹« (Applebaum 86 – according to Truman, it cost $9,000 not $12,000, which was very cheap compared with the pavilions

Copyrighted by the World's Columbian Exposition.

New Hampshire Building.

(*Ill. 1* – From Truman's *History of the World's Fair*, 1893)

erected by the states of Illinois and Maine, which cost $230,000 and $20,000 respectively).

So, what are we to make of the increasingly thematic nature of exhibitions? Is what happened to the Crystal Palace in its move from Hyde Park to Sydenham similar to what happened between the London and Paris exhibitions? What happened to artisan and shop-keeper distinction and what does this have to do with cities?

An initial answer would follow Thomas Richards's convincing argument in *The Commodity Culture of Victorian England*, that the objects on display at the Great Exhibition came to life as commodities turning visitors into consumers-in-training, which effectively disrupted the smooth workings of (mostly middle-) class reproduction. Visitors, whether factory workers or shop assistants, industrialists or journalists, artisans or aristocrats, were confronted with and had to make sense of a new, dislocating reality, in which they found themselves under the roof of the same building, occupying subject positions based not on traditional social status but rather on purchasing power and disposable income. As part of this process, commodified exhibits had to appeal to the greatest number of visitors possible. The ones that succeeded were the ones with multiple significations, those which could bridge the instruction/ amusement/ commerce divides. The panorama-type displays and the exoticized cafés and restaurants were all instructional, offering forms of what would become increasingly sought after knowledge about far-away places, while at the same time amusing through difference and spectacle.

Another avenue to pursue would be to note that, for all visitors, theming enacted a kind of sublation, serving to relieve what Alexander McClung has referred to as »the tensions and anxieties of the present« (83). Scholars have tended to read the exotic elements at the world expositions in terms of their coloniality, most prominently Robert Rydell, Paul Greenhalgh and Penelope Harvey: »The world's fairs used to display the exotic alongside the technological to convince people of the necessity of *imperial* economies for the general progress of mankind« (Harvey 125-6, italics added). However, the panorama-type displays, and the exoticized cafés and restaurants, like Pugin's Medieval Court and the *»ancient civilizations, tropical paradise, the Wild West, ›Arabia,‹ ›Rio,‹ or ›Hawaii‹* mentioned at the outset of the paper, have more in common than a generic colonial exoticism: all feature specifically preindustrial settings – safe, sanitized retreats from the danger and dirt of industrial life. Commentaries on the Great Exhibition, as opposed to surveys of exposition trends, rarely fail to mention that »with a fifth of the whole British population attending without any of the rioting and disorder foreseen by the prophets of doom, [the Great Exhibition] has often been taken to demonstrate the dawning of a period of social equilibrium after the turbulent first half of the century, when British society underwent the trials of pioneering industrialisation and unprecedented urban growth« (Tyack). Modernizing urban expansion thus found in the world exhibition its first major outlet, a temporary respite from the pressures to which it gave rise, just as tourism continues to »simultaneously reaffirm... the triumph of mass consumer culture and provide... an antidote to it« (Shaffer 320); put otherwise, they can be considered a heterotopia, »a compensatory space, defined through its difference from the sites of work and of the everyday. In an interview, Foucault identified ›heterotopias‹ as: ›those singular spaces to be found in some given social spaces whose functions are different or even the opposite of others« (Philips 91).

A further avenue to explore would be to expand on the valuable work of Harris, Gilbert and Wallace in identifying key elements of exhibition-type theming by analyzing elements that the world expositions, such as the Chicago Columbian, have in common with more recent themed environments, such as the various Disney parks. A study based on Patrick Beaver's description of the Sydenham Crystal Palace in *The Crystal Palace: 1851-1936. A Portrait of Victorian Enterprise*, could, for example, productively compare it with West Edmonton Mall. Such an analysis could begin with the following points:

1. location. Beaver writes of Sydenham that: »They could contemplate the splendid rural view of Kent and Surrey, ponder on the monsters that towered amongst the trees, picnic in the woods or on the lawns – and all within a few minutes' journey from the center of the city« (99); both the Sydenham Crystal Palace and West Edmonton Mall serve as refuges from the city, at a significant yet relatively easily commutable distance from the city center, both part of the city and yet enclosed, in a recreated, non-urban setting.
2. cost. »[A] hundred years ago the Crystal Palace was unique in that it offered, for a few pence, a whole day's entertainment of a kind which hitherto had only been within reach of the well-off« (99); they both make a point of being just barely affordable for the lower middle class and in a way set a benchmark for them.

(*copyright Eberhard Reisenleitner*)

3. target audience. »For the children there was the Great Maze, the Underground Grotto, the playgrounds and the boating-lake« (99); both aim at the whole family and are careful to provide attractions for especially its younger members.
4. size. »[T]oo vast to become crowded and yet almost overflowing with a bewildering variety of things to see, all calculated to delight, instruct, astonish and amuse« (99); massive and designed to initially disorient, both overwhelm visitors, while also allowing for relatively easy mastery of their geography, especially through color-coded, frequently spaced standing maps.
5. multiple functions. »Digby Wyatt and Owen Jones were sent abroad to ransack the world's great art collections and make plaster casts of the choicest of the statuary to furnish the series of courts they had designed to demonstrate the art and architecture of all the great civilizations« (79); both aim at a kind of pseudo-sophistication in making available educational opportunities in an environment in which spectacle features prominently. Not only were water spectacles and fountains prominent features of both West Edmonton Mall and Sydenham – »Osler's Crystal Fountain was there, still in the place of honour under the now swollen central transept« (83) –, but both feature roller-coasters (the Crystal Palace's bore the name Topsy-Turvy (99)) and submarines (»Although the primary purpose of the Exhibition was to promote peace and goodwill between nations, there was a fine selection of aggressive weapons which included naval and military guns, models of warships and a submarine« (48)).

One could further note that the growth of themed exhibitionary complexes, like West Edmonton Mall, has often been as tumor-like as what Patrick Geddes termed conurbation, the »general thickening and spreading of the urban mass« (Mumford 615). Following from this observation, the expansion of the Sydenham Crystal Palace and of West Edmonton Mall, which is now up to Phase 4, could be read as a kind of *mis-en-abîme* in conjunction with its urban environs, something which holds not only for London and Edmonton, which when West Edmonton Mall was built had the largest area of a municipality in Canada, but also for Bloomington Minnesota, southern California and Florida, and even Hong Kong. However future studies proceed, they would do well to echo the cautionary pitch of Mauricio Tenorio-Trillo's study of Mexico and the world's fairs:

> for the astute observer, the short life of world's fairs was less a testimony to technological and industrial improvement than a caution about the universality and reliability of the pledges symbolized by world's fairs, a warning that all good things could not last forever. ... World's fairs are valuable for historians not to establish the falsity of modern capitalist ideologies but to situate the parameters and changing characteristics of the disparity between a presumed reality and its perception both by contemporaries and by historians. (10)

ENDNOTES

1 »At the time of the Great Exhibition, ›industry‹ had two primary meanings: sustained effort, hard work, or diligence [from the Latin *industria*, which means ›diligence‹]; and an institution or set of institutions for production or trade. The first of these two meanings predominated from the middle of the 15th century until the middle of the 19th century. In the 18th century [for example], ›house of industry‹ meant a workhouse, literally a place where people worked hard, a public institution where the indigent were fed and forced to work. It was not until the 1840s that industry as an institution began to replace industry as a human quality. Only then does industry refer to thundering machines or a largely mechanized production process, as in ›heavy industry‹« (Auerbach 95-6).

2 A list of the amusements available on the Chicago midway in 1893 begins »Algeria & Tunisia, American Indians, Bedouin encampment, Brazilian music hall...«

REFERENCES

Allwood, John. *The Great Exhibitions*. London: Studio Vista, 1977.

Altick, Richard D. *The Shows of London*. Cambridge, Mass.: Belknap Press, 1978.

Applebaum, Stanley. *The Chicago World's Fair of 1893: A Photographic Record*. Photos from the Collections of the Avery Library of Columbia University and the Chicago Historical Society. New York: Dover Publications, Inc., 1980.

Auerbach, Jeffrey A. *The Great Exhibition of 1851: A Nation on Display.* New Haven and London: Yale University Press, 1999.

Beaver, Patrick. *The Crystal Palace*. London: High Evelyn Ltd., 1970.

Fair Representations: World's Fairs and the Modern World. Ed. Robert W. Rydell and Nancy Gwinn. Amsterdem: VU University Press, 1994.

Gilbert, James. »World's Fairs as Historical Events.« *Fair Representations.* 13-27.

Gottdiener, Mark. *The Theming of America: Dreams, Visions, and Commercial Spaces.* Boulder: Westview Press, 1997.

Greenhalgh, Paul. *Ephemeral Vistas: The Expositions universelles, Great Exhibitions and World's Fairs, 1951-1939*. Manchester: Manchester University Press, 1988.

Harris, Neil. »Expository Expositions: Preparing for the Theme Parks.« *Designing Disney's Theme Parks: The Architecture of Reassurance*. Ed. Karal Ann Marling. Montréal: Centre Canadien d'Architecture and Paris, New York: Flammarion, 1997. 19-27.

Harvey, Penelope. *Hybrids of Modernity: Anthropology, the Nation State, and the Universal Exhibition*. London: Routledge, 1996.

Luckhurst, Kenneth W. *The Story of Exhibitions*. London: Studio Publications, 1951.

Mandell, Richard D. *Paris 1900: The Great World's Fair*. Toronto: University of Toronto Press, 1967.

Marchand, Roland. »Corporate Imagery and Popular Education: World's Fairs in Expositions in the United States, 1893-1940.« *Consumption and American Culture*. Eds. David E. Nye and Carl Pedersen. Amsterdam: VU University Press, 1991. 18-33.

McClung, William Alexander. *Landscapes of Desire. Anglo Mythologies of Los Angeles*. Berkeley; Los Angeles; London: University of California Press, 2000.

Mumford, Lewis. *The City in History: Its Origins, its Transformations, and its Prospects*. Harmondsworth: Penguin, 1961.

Philips, Deborah. »Narrativised Spaces: The Functions of Story in the Theme Park.« *Leisure/Tourism Geographies: Practices and Geographical Knowledge*. Ed. David Crouch. London and New York: Routledge, 1999. 91-108.

Richards, Thomas. *The Commodity Culture of Victorian England: Advertising and Spectacle, 1851-1914*. Stanford: Stanford University Press, 1991.

Rydell, Robert W. *All the World's a Fair: Visions of Empire at American International Expositions, 1876-1916*. Chicago: University of Chicago, 1984.

—, John E. Findling, and Kimberly D. Pelle. *Fair America: World's Fairs in the United States*. Washington, DC: Smithsonian Institution Press, 2000.

Shaffer, Marguerite S. *See America First: Tourism and National Identity, 1880-1940*. Washington and London: Smithsonian Institution Press, 2001.

Tenorio-Trillo, Mauricio. *Mexico at the World's Fairs: Crafting a Modern Nation*. Berkeley, Los Angeles, London: University of California Press, 1996.

Truman, Ben. *History of the World's Fair Being a Complete and Authentic Description of the Columbian Exposition from its Inception*. Philadelphia PA: Syndicate Publishing Co., 1893.

Tyack, Geoffrey. »Review of Jeffrey A. Auerbach, *The Great Exhibition of 1851: A Nation on Display*,« H-Albion, H-Net Reviews, July, 2000. URL: http://www.h-net.msu.edu/reviews/showrev.cgi?path=1580196524395 2.

Wallace, Mike. »Mickey Mouse History: Portraying the Past at Disney World.« *Mickey Mouse History and other Essays on American Memory.* Philadelphia: Temple University Press, 1996. 133-57.

The Ultra-Orthodox Pizza Joint and the Scouting Room. Enclaves in Secular and Sacred Space as Negations/Confirmations of Dominant Institutional Cultures

ANDREW COLIN GOW

Maybe Natalie Zemon Davis was right to argue, starting around 1973, that riots, carnival, Mardi Gras and inversions such as the »Fools' Mass« or charivaris were varieties of safety-valve that allowed the populace to »blow off steam,« as the industrial revolution-era metaphor puts it. By allowing only circumscribed and traditional forms of transgression, established and ostensibly tolerant authorities prevented further challenges and thus ensured that even popular disorder served a system-stabilizing function. Maybe Mikhail Bakhtin was wrong to argue, even longer ago, that such festivities expressed a deep folk culture that was everywhere in retreat by the sixteenth century, and that such events were always deeply troubling to the earnest moralists of monastic, aristocratic, patrician or administrative elites. But the deep-seated functionalism of both approaches presents problems for understanding how resistance and (re)integration work in real-life situations. Both approaches assume tension, but in a specific direction, with calculable vectors: away from disorder, towards »modern« forms of social control; and the Middle Ages and early modern period appear on these stages as ramshackle but promising forecourts to the rationally planned palaces of absolutism. As a historian of culture, I am forced to deal with the approaches of Davis and Bakhtin as canonical authors, yet I am so unsure of how to engage their inherent whiggism without simply dismissing them that the opportunity to examine a couple of contemporary enclaves of resistance simply seemed too good to pass up. By enclaves I mean not merely things surrounded by something else but also have in mind the multiple surrounding frames and contexts in which institutions, persons or objects relate to each other, often in contexts of resistance. I shall not rehearse here the theoretical literature on sacred space, partly because I am not trying to engage it in a systematic (or any other) fashion.

LIFE IS A CARNIVAL AT WEM?*

The West Edmonton Mall is a gigantic shopping theme-park-cum-swimming pool complex in the west end of the city of Edmonton (pop. 960,000), capital of the province of Alberta. The first phase of the WEM opened in 1981 during Edmonton's second oil boom and has posed a serious problem for the old business core of the city ever since. When a reporter for the *Daily Telegraph*, Robert Philip, wrote during the 2002 World Athletics Championship that Edmonton's charms were »less than obvious« and described it as a »visually unappealing corner of Canada« (i.e. boring; he seems to have seen little more than the rather depressed core and the Mall), there was predictable outrage from boosters. The discussion of Philip's comments on the BBC website tells a great deal about the place of the Mall in outside views of the city: »I am forced by nature to agree with Robert Philip. Ever since the ice hockey player Wayne Gretzky left for L.A., Edmonton has truly been a one-show town – the West Edmonton Mall! Admittedly, it's some mall, but I think that says it all right there, doesn't it?« (Nicolas Zekulin, United Kingdom).

Ills. 1-3

Ill. 4a-c

The Mall is an early example of its genre, a massive congeries that is meant to be one: Christopher Columbus (*Ill. 1*), Palm Beach (*Ill. 2*), New Orleans's Bourbon Street and »Olde Europe« (*Ill. 3*) compete for theme-space and head-space in this enormous snow-shelter. A rather aged amusement park (*Ill. 4a-c*) and a gigantic indoor swimming-pool-beach-water-slide (*Ill. 5a&b*) constitute the main »family« entertainments, along with a host of smaller venues, ranging from cinemas through rides in small submarines on rails (*Ill. 6*), a dolphin show, a skating arena and indoor golf to quaint little remote-control boats and coin-operated plastic kiddy horses. The many dozens of fast-food outlets cater to the carbohydrate cravings of Canadians suffering from cabin fever, offering the usual big-city commercial multi-ethnic choices toned down for suburban palates. This is a consistent explicit and implicit theme of the Mall, in fact: safety, predictability, standardization, the taming down and digestion of raw realities. As the mall's builder said of his creation, seeing »Olde Europe« would suffice to keep Mum and Dad at home. One wonders just what other motives might have been in play in this semi-elitist, semi-populist criticism of bourgeois »grand tour« activities, e.g. trotting off to admire the restored facades and bildungsbürgerlich self-importance of Deutschnyland. The themed environment »Olde Europe,« in any case, is even more of a rhetorical gesture than any of the other heavily themed spaces: it consists merely of three rather unconvincing facades of which there certainly were no originals: simulacra in Baudrillard's sense.

Unusual in this by-now predictable range of aesthetic, climactic, ideological and cultural inducements to spend, to enjoy, and to enjoy spending, was a single restaurant: the ultra-orthodox pizza joint, King David, a little deli with only dairy and parve items. There was no proper seating area, just formica tables in »public space.« Alone among the Mall's hundreds and hundreds of shops, amusements and food sales points, King David followed a very different rhythm from that prescribed by the Mall's owners, Triple 5 Corporation. One informant, a student who had worked long shifts in a toy shop directly across from King David, told me how amazed he was that the owners were allowed to close on Friday night and Saturday, the two biggest sales periods of the week, when every other shop was required to be open; he was also surprised and pleased that it was clearly a family-run, »mom-and-pop« business, unlike the Hard Rock Cafe, GAP stores (two), and Hooters franchises that dominate the retail boulevards. The owners were in their sixties and would not have looked out of place in a kosher deli on St. Urbain Blvd. or in Brooklyn in 1973, and the shabby homeliness of

Ill. 5a-b, 6

their establishment would have fit in too. The food was also very fresh and very good, typical for the genre but certainly not for the Mall. On Sundays and weekday afternoons, boys in peyyot and girls in long blue denim dresses came with their mothers to eat falafel or Israeli salads or a pastry at the only establishment in all of Edmonton to serve warm kosher food. Maybe I am painting a Noam Rockwellski portrait – and yet it felt as though a piece of my Jewish Montreal, with buildings and people dating from somewhere between 1930 and 1980, had been transplanted as a special »themed environment,« perhaps even unintentionally. The Mall was built and partly financed by a family of ultra-orthodox Jews originally from Iran, the Ghermazians, and although they permitted/encouraged the King David to follow the rules that require a strictly kosher establishment to close over shabbat and the religious holidays, and even though King David is said by community leaders whom I interviewed to have paid a reduced rent (Triple 5 management did not answer my calls), it has now closed, which is why I have no photos to offer, merely a nostalgic portrait of moments by the WEM skating rink, with peyyot: a tiny Crown Heights in the »one great big Idaho« that is Canada, according to the daughter of a former American ambassador to Ottawa.

That the King David attracted people who otherwise would not have spent two minutes in the WEM – crowded as it is, especially in winter, with highly secular teenagers displaying their bodies in ways ultra-orthodox Jews find offensive – already made it a very odd space. There are so few Jews, especially visible ones, in Edmonton, that one or two haredim attract stares and sometimes odd comments; even wearing a kippa makes a person exotic. The King David resisted the cultural pressures of its environment for various reasons, including preferential treatment from management. I think it is reasonable to suggest that it simultaneously affirmed the culture and religion of the Mall's builder/owners and resisted the hegemony of commercial ideologies grouped around the well-known complementary pair »shopping – entertainment«. Perhaps the ultra-orthodox (haredi) customers constituted a themed entertainment, an exoticum... or a safety-valve to relieve the intolerable pressure created by so much concentrated white-bread suburbia. It did for me, anyway.

Edmonton, the winter city par excellence, has many quasi-public indoor spaces. In a city where it is usually very unpleasant to shop, eat or relax outdoors at least seven months of the year, it makes sense, from a retail perspective, to build, maintain, light and heat large buildings. However, not only commercial malls in Edmonton, but also public establishments such as libraries, schools, city hall, the main federal government office building, and even the morgue, offer large, sun-lit atria with a combination of seats, fountains, service establishments, and the like. The WEM is merely the largest and most consistently themed of all these spaces, with the one little exception just discussed.

While one group might well own a building, it might not set all the rules. While malls are arguably the most important socio-architectural idiom of 20th-, and now 21st-century western society, churches had that distinction (or shared it with city halls) until comparatively recently. Edmonton's Holy Trinity Anglican Church (*Ill. 7*), a clinker-brick hulk begun in 1911 and finished in 1913 (*Ill. 8*), represents the cultural pretensions and social ambitions of the pre-WWI Anglo-Canadian bourgeoisie: it is massive – when it was built, it was one of the largest buildings between Winnipeg and Vancouver – and the use of brick, extremely uncommon and expensive in the Canadian west before the 1950s and even relatively rare right to the present, signaled the community's wealth and its ties with its two »mother countries«, Ontario and England. Holy Trinity was also a community establishment, a meeting place for all sorts of groups, some of which still use it. In fact, the church is stuck with a contractual, deeded obligation to provide for one of those groups that restricts and shapes the church's ability to use some of its most-used areas, the basement with its classrooms and social hall. When the church was being built, it was in the midst of a newly developed residential area 20 minutes' walk from the university, a middle-class area characterized by the Anglo-Canadian identity that would remain dominant everywhere in Canada (with the debatable exception of Québec) until the end of the Second World War. The Boys' Brigade of the Anglican Church and Baden-Powell's Scouting movement were in their enthusiastic, militant and militaristic infancy, and most of their members were imperialist Anglo-Canadians – and, given the name of the church, Anglo-Catholics as well. What more natural alliance, then, than between the Anglican Church and what became the First Strathcona Scout Troop (*Ill. 9 a&b*), after the Boys Brigade was folded into the Scouts by Archbishop Alan George, a friend of Baden-Powell? During the early 1920s, the Scouts and Guides had raised money to equip a new Scouting room, but there was no building on the south side of what was by then the booming city of Edmonton large enough to house it. Holy Trinity Church was to receive the money that had been raised to fund an addition in which the Scouting room would be located. The Depression and war delayed building, but when ground was broken in 1949, the Scouts and Guides received a written guaran-

Ill. 7

tee that they would at all times have access to a room (*Ill. 10a&b*) 24 by 12 feet, with wood-clad walls, a blackboard and a cupboard. One or more of the Scouts, Guides, Venturers, Rangers, Pathfinders, Brownies, Sparks, Cubs and Beavers, some of which are mixed and some female-only, meet on every weekday evening and require both the Scouting room and one or two of the large function rooms. They pay no rent, as the agreement stipulated, and their membership has not had even a sizable minority of Anglicans for a long time. Every ten years or so, ac-

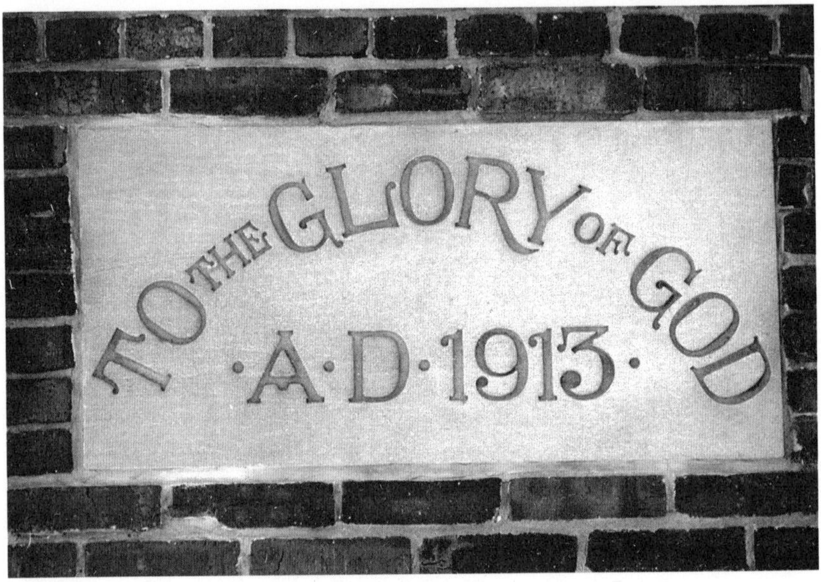

Ill. 8

rangement and attempts to reclaim »its« space, and the scouting group produces the document that ratifies its privileges, rather as cloisters or cities did in the face of rapacious bishops or territorial lords in medieval and early modern Europe. The scouting groups, relatively diverse organizations with 21st-century political, gender and cultural agendas, actively resist the repeated attempts of what once was »the Scouts at prayer« to dislodge them. The Anglican Church as a whole and this parish in particular constitute an especially white, middle and upper-middle-class enclave in a multi-ethnic, multi-cultural city shaped by waves of French, Anglo-Canadian, Ukrainian, German, Vietnamese, South Asian, Vietnamese, Fijian and eastern Canadian immigration. The Anglican Church in Canada is not merely in demographic decline; it is in serious danger of bankruptcy over legal cases involving sexual abuse and the theft of culture in so-called residential schools for First Nations children between the 1890s and 1950s; by comparison, the Scouting movement not only looks healthy but, shorn of its ugly imperialism and nativism, represents an effective agency for the inculcation in school-aged children of tolerant pluralism and the civic values of a self-avowedly multi-cultural society. I shall not pause here to elaborate upon the mechanisms of social control and the control over identity formation wielded by the multi-culturocracy.

What do these two very disparate examples of resistant spaces, enclaves and relationships have in common? How can we read them as

6TH EDMONTON PACK
DO YOUR BEST
WOLF CUBS
1ST STRATHCONA
EST 1910
6TH EDMONTON
OLDEST CONTINUING
SCOUT GROUP IN CANADA
AT HOLY TRINITY ANGLICAN CHUR

Ill. 9a&b

Ill. 10a&b

anything other than randomly chosen examples of anomalous relations of power/possession? In each case, resistance is complicated by commercial, cultural or confessional conformity to certain aspects of the dominant/surrounding culture. In each case, resistant use defines spaces over against the hegemonic practices that frame them and make them possible. In each case, tension that does not necessarily imply or spring from either directions or vectors holds the opposing pair together and at the same time apart: ultra-orthodox/unworldly versus ultra-commercial/secular and artisanal/family-run versus industrial/franchised; mono-ethnic/upper middle-class versus multicultural/socially mixed. Far from merely providing safety valves for a (putative) populace to »let off steam« and thus postpone or cancel out serious opposition, in each of our cases we see some measure of serious opposition to the hegemonic cultural, ideological or religious surroundings and practices, opposition that is *sui generis* and designed to anchor and safeguard very different interests and agendas from the framing ones. Are these oppositions more stable than dynamic/vectored? I have suggested that they are without arguing the point. I do not know. Does medium or long-term stability rule out sudden change or collapse? Probably not, as the case of the King David suggests. The complex nature of resistance is illustrated all the more powerfully when groups share some essential goals but not necessarily all, or not in the same measure: the Ghermazians did not force the King David out of business, but they have not replaced it either.

And then there are the opposing possibilities: are the Anglicans of Holy Trinity in fact resisting the dominant culture of urban Canada, represented by the scouting troop? And perhaps the King David was fulfilling a hidden agenda of resistance on the part of the Ghermazians to their own vision of a commercially and culturally »complete,« regulated, standardized, profit-maximizing and predictably conformist indoor world.

ENDNOTES

* All photographs were taken by the author.

1 Natalie Zemon Davis, in the famous collection of her early articles: *Society and Culture in Early Modern France: Eight Essays* (Stanford: Stanford University Press, 1975).

2 Mikhail Bakhtin, *Rabelais and his World*. Trans. Helene Iswolsky (Cambridge, MA: M.I.T. Press, 1968).

3 See Norbert Elias, *The Civilizing Process*. Trans. Edmund Jephcott with some notes and revisions by the author (Oxford: B. Blackwell, 1982).

4 »West Edmonton Mall is situated at the junction of 87th Avenue and 170th Street

in Edmonton, Alberta, Canada. The complex was built in four phases opening in 1981, 1983, 1985, 1998. The Fantasyland Hotel opened in 1986. Total cost to build West Edmonton Mall was $1.2 billion Cdn. West Edmonton Mall is listed in the Guinness Book of World Records for the ›largest shopping centre in the world‹ and ›world's largest parking lot.‹ Open 365 days per year. WEM TRIVIA: seven major attractions; two theme streets; over 800 stores and services including six major department stores; 26 movie theaters; 110 eating establishments; bingo hall; world class casino; aquariums; chapel; works-of-art; bungy jumping; Jubilations Dinner Theatre; Playdium; IMAX 3-D Theatre; 100,000 square foot family rec room features 10 pin bowling, dining and dancing in Red's Rec Room; [...] 58 entrances; 325,000 light fixtures; over 23,500 employment opportunities; parking for over 20,000 vehicles; RV and trailer parking available while shopping; total cost $1.2 billion Cdn; 493,000 sq. meters (5.3 million sq. feet).« Other details include »four real submarines, self powered and propelled, capable of reaching a depth of 46m (151 ft)«; »the coral is real, some being over 2000 years old«; the »SANTA MARIA SHIP IS AN EXACT REPLICA OF COLUMBUS' SHIP built at False Creek, in Vancouver, British Columbia, Canada; hand carved and painted; transported in flat-bed trucks across the Rocky Mountains to Edmonton; available for receptions and special functions, ie. weddings, etc.« All this, and, of course, much, much more, can be found on the mall's website at http:// www.westedmall.com/info/fastfacts.html.

5 http://news.bbc.co.uk/1/hi/talking_point/1482034.stm

6 Another comment deserves to be reproduced: »There are many boring places on earth (most of them English speaking). Here are some warning signs. Claims at ›world's biggest,‹ ›world's longest,‹ ›world's tallest‹ (ask yourself why are they trying so hard). Boasts of a vibrant multicultural atmosphere (outside of Reykjavik, what city isn't multicultural now). Any place with a monorail or a revolving restaurant. Any mention of equally second rate ›sister cities‹ (clearly they're desperate). Can you think of anyone truly interesting from that city (and do they still live there)? The one city that wins (or loses) in all of these categories is Toronto (any city that has a shoe museum as its second biggest attraction should really be avoided).« Blair, Sydney Australia. While Edmonton has no monorail, it does have a revolving restaurant.

7 As theming (of malls and other attractions) has been dealt with extensively both in the scholarly literature and in other articles this volume (see in particular Hilje van der Horst's »Multicultural Theming: Pacifying, Essentializing and Revanchist Effects«), I have resisted the temptation to clutter the footnotes with duplicate bibliography.

8 With perhaps 5,000 Jews out of a total of almost one million inhabitants, Edmonton has an atypically low proportion of Jews and Jewish infrastructure for North American cities – probably the lowest of any major city on the continent.

9 The oldest continuously functioning Scouting troop in Canada: see photographs of the Scout room.

10 Robert E. Milks, *75 Years of Scouting in Canada* (Ottawa: Scouts Canada, 1982).

11 The Scouts Canada website (www.scouts.ca) lists under the principles of Scouting: »Duty to Others: Defined as, Loyalty to one's country in harmony with the promotion of local, national and international peace, understanding and cooperation, and Participation in the development of society, with recognition and

respect for the dignity of one's fellow-being and for the integrity of the natural world.« (http://www.scouts.ca/inside.asp?cmPageID=80).

12 William H. Katerberg, *Modernity and the Dilemma of North American Anglican Identities, 1880-1950* (Montreal: McGill-Queen«s University Press, 2001).

13 David Napier, *Sins of the Fathers* (Toronto: Anglican Church of Canada, 2000).

14 See, for example, Leo Driedger, *Multi-Ethnic Canada: Identities and Inequalities* (Oxford and Toronto: Oxford University Press, 1996).

»Des Pudels goldener Kern«: Legitimate Theater and Notions of European Culture in Dawson City, Yukon*

MARKUS REISENLEITNER

When tourists use the short summer months to travel way up north to Alaska and the Yukon, the restored historical buildings of Dawson City are a required stop. »You'll Need A Week To See It All« promises the official tourist brochure, which also features a dance-hall girl kicking up her heels in an iconographic representation of bawdy good times (*Ill. 1*). *Man spricht deutsch* in Huskyland (*Ill. 2*), and in the restored Palace Grand Theater, visitors are treated to daily performances of the »Gaslight Follies« from May to August. The official brochures lure visitors with the picture of a mining camp that we have come to expect from the Northern frontier: a rough-and-tumble, lawless society of greedy miners and loose women where entertainment is music-hall style and scarcely-clad dance-hall girls double as prostitutes for a rough, mostly drunk and ill-behaved male audience.

Dawson City owed its very existence to the discovery of gold in the Yukon in 1897, which triggered the most frenzied gold rush in North American history. In the course of three years, a mining camp and tent city became the largest city north of San Francisco and west of Winnipeg, with an estimated population of 30,000 (surpassing places like Victoria, BC and Seattle, WA). The lure of gold brought people to a place difficult to reach and isolated from the rest of the world from September to May; the route by boat went from Seattle or San Francisco to Skagway, Alaska, then over the infamous Chilkoot pass, where Canadian border police checked provisions – you had to bring enough for at least a year, which meant that people who could not afford native carriers had to make the steep ascent up to 100 times –, and finally down the Klondike, which only became navigable in mid-May, by boat to Dawson (Guest). The alternative land route via Edmonton was 2600 km and took some people three years (Romig). Remote definitely qualifies as a description of Dawson City around 1900.

The fortune hunters came mostly from the larger cities of the American West to Canada's North and were apparently not only looking for gold, either by mining or by selling overpriced goods to the miners (Graham and Bowles), but also for entertainment. The Palace Grand Theater was not the first theater to open in Dawson, but it was definitely the most ambitious. When its opening was announced in the local paper on June 28, 1899, its official name was the »Grand Opera« (Yukon Archives: Victoria Faulkner Collection. MSS 135 f. 3 83/50). While at this point there already existed a few theater/saloon establishments in Dawson, seating around 100-200 people and combining vaudeville with dances and gambling, the Palace Grand had more ambitious cultural aims from the very beginning. The presence of many men (and women) who had been in San Francisco, Seattle or Chicago only a few months before would seem to have created the need for a lavish playhouse, large enough to stage major productions and to seat 600 to 700 people.

At first sight, and according to the – few – existing historical descriptions, Dawson's Palace Grand Theater seems little more than a bigger version of the saloon/playhouse type of establishment characteristic of the frontier theater of the American West, with a saloon as an integral part.[1] During its first seasons, it was owned and managed by »Arizona« Charlie Meadows, a self-proclaimed former Indian fighter with a larger-than-life reputation who had toured Europe and Asia with a wild west show which he claimed »outbuffaloed« Bill Cody's and who also claimed experiences of hand-to-hand combat with Geronimo. When his theater opened on July 18, 1899, the Klondike Nugget announced that »at last Dawson is to have a theater« (Coutts 16). Yet it was, perhaps unsurprisingly, a vaudeville show that first lured an audience to the Palace Grand, consisting of a melodrama, a chorus line, a juggling act and a rendition of popular songs (Coutts 21-2).

As much as this program seems to conform to our image of a frontier society, the Palace Grand's repertoire was by no means restricted to »popular« entertainment, and this is true for most periods of its existence. From the beginning, it was Arizona Charlie's aim to bring professional troupes to Dawson, as well as to provide a place for benefits, socials, balls, concerts and sporting exhibitions. Even the style of the building seemed to reflect this double claim to high culture and popular entertainment by combining »European« elegance in the building's decorative fittings with a rougher style in the lumber walls and balco-

Includes Carmacks, Dempster, Faro & N. Klondike Hwy Info
FREE
DAWSON CITY
HEART OF THE GOLD RUSH CENTENNIALS • 2000
www.dawsoncityinfo.com
11th year
You'll Need A Week To See It All!
www.DawsonCity.com

Yukon
Huskyland
Eines der letzten Abenteuer ...
... unserer Zeit
...Lieber Asche als Staub. Es ist besser, dass meine Flamme erlischt in einem letzten brillanten Schein, als dass sie ausgeht in einem müden Flimmern. Ich wäre lieber ein Meteor mit einem prächtigen Glühen als ein schlafender Planet. Die Funktion eines Mannes ist zu leben, und nicht zu existieren. Ich werde meine Tage nicht verschwenden, sie zu verlängern. Ich werde sie nützen.
Jack London
BLUE KENNELS

nies of traditional boomtown architecture. This is even more visible in the more ambitious productions of European plays that have hardly been mentioned in research (or only as experiments and curiosities, aberrant preludes to the dance, and mostly doomed to failure in a »frontier« society).

When the Palace Grand Theater in Dawson City was renovated in October 1899 by its second manager, George Hillyer, its opening production was Goethe's *Faust*, which was hailed by Dawson's newspapers as a »meritorious production« (Coutts 33). It »won the admiration and applause of all the audience,« and »it is rarely ever in the Yukon or elsewhere, that the public is given so much in return for its money« (ibid.).

Faust among the lawless miners does not seem appropriate, and yet it was not the only occurrence of what I call, for lack of a better word, »high« culture in a city that had only existed for three years by 1900. Pictures show well-dressed couples at social events and balls; lavish productions of legitimate theater, even if not dominating the playlists, at least received public attention; and concerts of classical music became a regular feature of Sundays in the Yukon. These attempts at bringing high culture to Dawson City were fairly successful and, perhaps more importantly, were consistently appreciated by the newspapers. Dawson was included in the circuit of many companies who traveled up and down the west coast, and even Viennese culture reached Dawson as early as 1899:

> The people of Dawson are to be extended a rare treat on next Thursday evening at the Grand Opera House when Mme. C. Bluett [sic], the Prima Donna soprano of the Imperial Grand Opera House in Vienna, will appear in a repertoire of concert song. ... It is a safe prediction that this cosy and handsome house will be well filled on this occasion. (*The Sunday Gleaner* July 30, 1899. Yukon Archives: Victoria Faulkner Collection. MSS 135 f. 3 83/50.)

Examples like the one quoted can be found in great numbers in the Yukon Archives in Whitehorse. At the end of 1899, a St. Andrew's Day Ball was held, which again saw well-dressed couples in white ties and ball dresses dancing under chandeliers that would do London ballrooms proud and, as a *Klondike Nugget* journalist wrote, »positively precluded this scribe from overpainting and teaches him the paucity of his vocabulary« (Coutts 34). This is by no means an exception: the New Year's Event of 1900 was similarly splendid, and in the same vein, on January 10, 1900, a concert of classical music was held:

> The excellent concert given at the Palace Grand last Sunday evening and the large audience in attendance that crowded every available seat in the theater,

> prove two things conclusively, namely first, that a concert can be given suitable to a Sunday evening performance, void of coon and other shady songs and made up of classical and high-class modern music; and, second, that Dawson contains a population today sufficiently large, intelligent and educated, to fully appreciate it and who will be ready to encourage a continuance of the same by their presence. The success of the prison scene from *Il Trovatore* is a cue to its managers. (*Dawson Daily News* January 9, 1900. Yukon Archives: Victoria Faulkner Collection. MSS 135 f. 3 83/50.)

The following seasons saw productions of *La Bohème* as well as of the play on which it was based, Dumas's *Camille*. This play could still be seen in Dawson in 1903, when the *Dawson Daily News* reported enthusiastically:

> *Camille*, the famous play by Alexander Dumas, Jr.... was one of the successes of the evening. Mrs. Hall [the female lead] surprised the most critical. She carried the difficult part with confidence and displayed unquestioned talent. In the last act she was so realistic in the impersonation of a dying woman that scarcely a dry eye remained in the audience. Hardy miners and other strong men in all parts of the house wept. For the first time in years their eyes were dimmed. (*Dawson Daily News* July 7, 1903)

Even if this might be interpreted as a particular form of cultural boosterism by self-appointed guardians of high culture, this passage, as well as the repertory to which it refers, bears witness to an obvious esteem and appreciation of culture imported from Europe, which seems grossly inadequate for the location and history of a place that seemed to constitute a last »frontier experience« around 1900.

The disconcerting presence of Beethoven, Verdi, Goethe and Dumas has been explained by a »stabilization« of society after the first years of the gold rush, with a few respectable women and more sophisticated, middle-class men setting the tone while the rougher elements left for more promising mining in Nome, Alaska (Guest). A closer look at the archive material, the many existing diaries, travel reports and photographs begs the question as to when the »wild« days of Dawson, the uninhibited frontier, actually were – when the reporters got there in 1899, they could already attend opera performances.

There are no reliable sociological data on the population of Dawson City around 1900, but it does not seem very probable that this was at any point after 1897 a lawless frontier society. Most descriptions stress the law-abiding nature and good behavior of its inhabitants and attribute it to a large extent to the presence of the formidable North West Mounted Police. Yet it seems unlikely that twelve »Mounties« were solely responsible for keeping the peace in Dawson. Others have put forward the theory that »the severity of life in the Yukon had kept out many desperate characters, and the people who had come in were honest citizens accustomed to regulations« (Guest 38).

This seems to be closer to the truth. The people who could actually afford to take a ship from San Francisco or pay for an overland trip and the necessary provisions were rarely dirt-poor adventurers (or professional miners) but rather middle-class people from fairly big, mostly American cities, caught in the frenzied acceleration of a greedy capitalist system. Their cultural background around 1900 was already constituted by a firm division between popular entertainment and »highbrow culture,« which by then meant: European. A comparison to other mining communities, especially California's 49ers, is of limited value as distances, the speed and social basis of the Gold Rush, as well as the cultural backgrounds of the people involved were completely different. »The theater in the first half of the nineteenth century played the role that movies played in the first half of the twentieth: it was a kaleidoscopic, democratic institution presenting a widely varying bill of fare to all classes and socioeconomic groups« (Levine 21). Tempting as this might seem as an interpretation of the Palace Grand, the situation there was completely different. Due to its claims to a shared cultural tradition and process of institutionalization that contributed to the formation of taste, theater in Dawson confirmed the already existing hierarchy of cultural values and distinctions that was characteristic for its predominantly middle-class society.

Let us return to the Palace Grand: What we can indeed observe – from the very start of the theater – is an oscillation between popular and highbrow forms of entertainment, where legitimate theater, particularly theater of European origin, art music and opera represent highbrow. Despite the fact that both highbrow and popular entertainment generally enjoyed the popularity of a wide audience, there is never any doubt as to the cultural value of the program, and the cultural mediators (critics, reporters, newspapers) rely on a firmly established system of cultural criticism and value. Where 49ers in California cheered at Shakespeare in the same way they supported their favorite in a boxing match, the Dawson audience knew the difference. During theater performances, men in the audience were asked to remove their hats and refrain from smoking, a request that, according to witnesses, was almost eagerly complied with (Coutts 48) – a clear sign that the general success of high culture in disciplining and training audiences had not bypassed the Far North.

In Dawson City, the cultural transfer from Europe actually served – very much like in the rest of the continent – to set up, and confirm, a

(Ill. 3 & 4 – The reconstructed Palace Grand in April 2000, copyright Susan Ingram)

middle class legitimized by its cultural taste. This form of distinction, however, constantly has to compete with cultural crossover in regard to space, a situation not unfamiliar to the theater historian. The position of competing cultural spheres in the Palace Grand as an institution consistently oscillated between separating those spheres within the building (setting up a distinct boundary between the saloon-bar and the theater hall) and alternating the program from sacred concerts on Sundays to prize fights during the week or even at periods trying to relegate the less prestigious performances to other theaters (Coutts 43). What we see is the attempt of the – and I would claim not emerging but from the beginning clearly visible – middle class to express their cultural preferences within as well as apart from »popular« entertainment, and their hierarchy of values was firmly established by the time the Palace Grand opened, with European culture meaning high culture. The Palace Grand may thus be regarded as a contested space between hierarchies of taste that remain firmly tied to processes of middle-class identity formation. From the fact that the theater also served as a movie house after the First World War, it could be surmised that movies fulfill the same function of providing a shared public culture stratified through hierarchies of taste, rather than through different genres or places.

The frontier myth has thus to be read against the apparent history of »high« culture and a civilized and settled form of behavior that dictates the standards of taste, and to a certain degree also the repertoire, of the Palace Grand. Why has this tradition of high culture disappeared from the histories of the Palace Grand? One reason is definitely the attempt to see it as an example of a tradition of frontier theater in a mining situation and to apply and generalize – misleadingly, as I think I have shown – a pattern of mining theaters to the situation in the Yukon.[2] But I think the situation is at the same time more complex and yet simpler.

What seems to manifest itself in the current presentation of the history of Dawson City – a history that was uncovered by the Department of Northern Affairs and National Resources in the early 1960s when the foundation of the Park was laid – is a pattern of identity consumption manifest in an area that streamlines history – in other words, a theme that works very much like nationalism for imagining communities: highbrow, European-style theater is not very suitable for marketing the »wild frozen north,« created on the basis of a democratic myth of the frontier and presented as an environment themed accordingly. In the case of Dawson, this image is a deliberate recreation, which shows clearly in the decisions as to which buildings to restore/rebuild in order to best exploit the tourism potential and market what by the end of the 1950s had nearly become a ghost town.[3]

The Gold Rush had indeed been a very short-lived affair, and after 1900 the population of Dawson had seen a steady decline; the great majority of its population moved on to Nome, Alaska. When Dawson was revived as a frontier theme park in the early 1960s, it was precisely the frontier myth – a myth popularized by Hollywood Westerns – that provided a convenient narrative for the revival. That is why today tacky vaudeville performances are performed in Dawson during the summer months and not *La Bohème*, and why it pleases the masses of German tourists frequenting the place in search of the authentic frontier, *urgemütlich* and *romantisch*, as a tourist brochure in German states. But it is also a myth that has its roots in popular entertainment, as well as in the events of the past themselves: as well as bringing opera and legitimate theater to Dawson, Arizona Charlie helped to perpetuate this myth as a form of popular entertainment (notwithstanding the fact that he probably did fight Indians) by staging and dramatizing it.

What is elided today by foregrounding just one of the cultural discourses of the few years around 1900 is the complexity of the cultural contest that took place between clearly differentiated, and firmly established, hierarchies of taste, in which European culture had a special place. In Dawson, the cultural hegemony of European culture around 1900 has been replaced by the hegemony of the frontier myth. As this paper has tried to demonstrate, the theater in Dawson institutionalized hierarchies of taste in which »European« drama, alongside other forms of »legitimate« theater and high culture, formed the basis of the social identity of a respectable society.

ENDNOTES

* The author gratefully acknowledges the generous help of Shannon Olson from the Yukon Archives, and of Susan Ingram, who faithfully chronicled our trip way up north and provided invaluable insights. This article first appeared in *Kultur – Identität – Raum: Kulturelle Praktiken und die Ausbildung von Imagined Communities in Nordamerika und Zentraleuropa*, eds. Susan Ingram, Markus Reisenleitner and Cornelia Szabó-Knotik (Vienna: Turia+Kant, 2001): 257–67.

1 »The historian David Lavender describes this saloon-theater combination as stemming from a phenomena he calls ›urban schizophrenia‹ which he saw developing in the American west during the 1880s. The social composition of western communities, he maintained, could be reduced to two component parts: one group clearly emulating the staid urban life of the metropolitan east,

the other wanting to hang onto the frontier legacy of the mining towns« (Coutts 13).

2 For a good overview of the topic, see Evans. For a romanticized notion of »the miners« and their theater, see Booth.

3 A good example of this painstaking and well-intentioned, but deliberate selection is the »list of recommended sites and areas of historic interest in the Dawson area,« which starts with the administration building where »the walls must resound with the voices of our [!] Pioneers.« Most listed items specify the value of a building as a tourist attraction. The list concludes with a »Suggested Tourist Attraction,« an exhibition of mining equipment. Despite the obvious attempt at being neutral, there is a very noticeable interest to present the town in the light of a primitive mining society (Yukon Archives: Victoria Faulkner Writings. MSS 136 f. 15. 83/50).

REFERENCES

Booth, Michael R. »Gold Rush Theatres of the North.« *The Beaver* (Spring 1962).

Coutts, Robert, and Parks Canada. *The Palace Grand Theatre, Dawson City, Y.T. : An Interpretive History.* Manuscript Report; No. 428. Ottawa: Parks Canada, 1981.

Evans, Chad. *Frontier Theatre: A History of Nineteenth-Century Theatrical Entertainment in the Canadian Far West and Alaska*. Victoria, B.C.: Sono Nis Press, 1983.

Graham, Harry, and Frances Bowles. *Across Canada to the Klondyke: Being the Journal of a Ten Thousand Mile Tour through the ›Great North West‹ (July 19th to October 13th) 1900*. Toronto: Methuen, 1984.

Guest, Hal, and Parks Canada. *Dawson City, San Francisco of the North, or Boomtown in a Bog: A Literature Review*. Manuscript Report; No. 241. Ottawa: Parks Canada, 1978.

Levine, Lawrence W. *Highbrow/Lowbrow: The Emergence of Cultural Hierarchy in America*. Cambridge, MA; London, England: Harvard University Press, 1988.

Romig, Emily Craig. *A Pioneer Woman in Alaska*. Caldwell, Idaho: [s.n.], 1948.

Multicultural Theming in the Netherlands: Pacifying, Essentializing and Revanchist Effects

HILJE VAN DER HORST

INTRODUCTION

There is an ever-growing amount of academic research on the deliberate construction of images of place. Two strands can be distinguished in this research (see also Hannigan, 1998). The first takes a positive view of place promotion. It sees image building, city branding, and urban tourism as tools in urban regeneration and other positive developments (see, for example, Gold and Ward, 1994; Paddison, 1993; Caffyn and Lutz, 1998). These new images are seen as necessary to overcome negative images of urban areas that are generally associated with urban decay and bankrupt industries (Young and Lever, 1997). This line of research is predominantly concerned with the link between images of the city and commercial interests and usually focuses on ›fun‹ industries.

The second strand is much more cynical and stresses the ›fake‹ construction of identity. Cities like Los Angeles, Miami and Las Vegas are called cities of ›façade.‹ Social control, power and capitalism are alleged to be hidden in an architecture that suggests fun, entertainment and fantasy (Zukin, 1991). Goldberger (1996) focuses on the ›unreal‹ representations of the city to be found in diverse ›urbanoid environments,‹ such as shopping malls and theme parks. Writers with this perspective often have a negative perception of initiatives for urban image building, finding that they obscure the realities of capitalism and city life. The ›real‹ in this strand seems to have a certain inner value that should not be concealed.

In this paper I do not wish to make distinctions between the real and the unreal and their respective merits. This would easily end up in discussions on what is more real, the original or the copy, the model or the simulacrum; it is a discussion that Baudrillard and Deleuze have actively engaged in, and one I would prefer to leave to them. More interesting is the question of what the effects of the unreal representations are. What happens when spaces are shaped after unreal images or are remodeled to represent new versions of themselves?

The aim of this paper is to look at the effects of one specific type of urban image construction that has received far less attention than the ›screaming‹ architecture and imagery of Walt Disney and other fun industries: the construction of a multicultural identity in neighborhoods. Diverse urban neighborhoods are multiculturally themed through festivals, marketing campaigns and artifacts in the built environment. The expected benefits of this particular multicultural landscape construction are both economic and social in nature.

Landscapes are both a tool and an outcome of power relations. Landscapes are shaped by those with power to construct landscapes and fill them with meaning. In turn the constructed landscape exerts power by naturalizing and reifying social realities (Duncan and Duncan, 1988). It is hard to imagine landscapes in other ways because of their material visibility and normality. Landscapes give rise to ideas that ›it could not have been otherwise‹ and ›everything and everyone is in its rightful place‹ (see also Harvey, 1989). Landscapes are not immobile backgrounds to human interaction, but the result of power relations.

Kong and Law (2002) argue that cultural geography and especially the study of landscapes should therefore be concerned with issues of power and oppression. Multicultural theming is rarely associated with the exercise of power in public discourse, but rather with emancipating ethnic minorities. However, there are certain concerns arising out of the effects of multicultural theming and questions of power and oppression. It is those concerns that I will look at in this paper.

I have grouped these issues of power under three general headings: multicultural theming as a pacifying project, as an essentializing project and as a revanchist project. The first heading refers to the depoliticizing effect of multicultural theming (see also Jacobs, 1998). The people who construct the multicultural landscape aim to portray a certain kind of multicultural society that is positive, exotic, tolerant, harmonious, and often has an emphasis on consumption. This kind of multicultural society can be seen as designed to prevent ethnic resistance and foster consumption. The issue underlying the second heading is that multicultural projects may exclusively attribute certain archaic and essentialized identities to ethnic groups. This concern is linked to the wider critique of multiculturalism. The third heading refers to Smith's book on the revanchist city (1996). The revanchist theme is concerned with the struggles of the white middle class to retake the city from ethnic minorities and the poor. Multicultural theming, though it should not be seen to be as polemical as the revanchism described by Smith, has certain revanchist characteristics.

This paper will discuss the above topics in the light of different examples of multicultural theming. The paper starts with a review of the literature on the strategic and non-strategic construction of place identity. This theoretical background will be narrowed down in the second section on the construction of ethnic identity in place. Subsequently I will look at the three ›concerns‹ of multicultural theming: multicultural theming as a pacifying project, as an essentializing project, and as a revanchist project. With the theoretical background thus established, I will turn to four case studies and look at the role of the three identified ›projects‹ in them. My analysis will pick out recurrent themes in the four case studies. The conclusion will discuss in how far multicultural theming in the three case studies can be seen as pacifying, essentializing and/or revanchist projects.

CONSTRUCTING PLACE IDENTITY: A REVIEW OF THE LITERATURE

The idea that built environments are filled with features that convey symbolic meaning for their inhabitants is not new and has been taken up by, for example, environmental psychologists and cultural geographers. The latter have, notably in the last two decades, given more thought to the ways in which power is intertwined with identities, meanings, and representations of place. Cosgrove & Jackson (1987) have argued for the importance of considering how power relations structure the construction of landscapes. They see important benefits to be gained from the combination of cultural geography with contemporary cultural studies because of the latter's emphasis on »the various strategies of *resistance* that subordinate groups employ to contest the hegemony of those in power« (98). Identities of place are contested. Places are part of discourses that assign meanings and identities to them. The explicit interest in ›landscapes of power,‹ the title of Zukin's often quoted book (1991), is of relatively recent origin but has grown steadily.

The features of place that convey meaning are diverse. This is exemplified by Hull et al. (1994), who have researched the sorts of icons that had memories and meanings attached to them. Their data were collected from residents of Charleston, South Carolina, after Hurricane

Hugo caused considerable damage there in 1989. In order of importance, the features mentioned were urban forest, churches, homes, public buildings, places associated with historic events, and retail structures. These icons, according to Hull et al., may be used as orientation points; they may trigger certain memories or may be seen as representing an aspect of the area's identity.

Because their focus is on the individual experience of meaning, Hull et al. (1994) and other environmental psychologists fail to address the social context in which the construction of meaning takes place. Even though residents and passers-by are free in their thoughts and associations, they are not independent. They are influenced to a large extent by the construction of meaning by others and by dominant discourses on the ›correct‹ meanings. For example, the media are very influential in constructing an image and directing attention to certain icons or characteristics and leaving others under- or unrepresented (see also Martin, 2000).

Identity construction takes place continually and unintentionally. Identity production can, however, also be part of strategic plans. Because place is socially constructed, people in positions of power can try to impose certain meanings on the built environment. They can do this by changing the built environment to comply with their proposed image; they can design advertising campaigns to focus attention on certain aspects of an area and use festivities as a means of promoting a favored image. For example, planners, architects, and other designers of urban space to a large degree create the material reality and can try to manipulate meanings of place.

This kind of place promotion is often characterized by simplicity. There is an underlying assumption that the target public will uncritically take in what is being said. It seems to rely on the assumption that by saying that a city is as the campaign says it is, the city will become this representation. Young and Lever (1997), however, have shown that the public has a mind of its own. Their research demonstrates that office managers display considerable diversity in their responses to place promotion. The same hypothesis can be formulated for those encountering multiculturally themed places.

Pine and Gilmore (1996) convincingly show that place identity plays a large role in the experience economy. Place is an important tool in the shaping of experience. Identities of place can provide a large surplus value. This is illustrated by the almost classic example of the price people are willing to pay for a cup of coffee on San Marco Square in Venice. The coffee is identical to that served three streets away, where the price is a fraction of that in the cafés on the square. People are not only buying coffee, however; they are buying the identity of the place. Place is commodified and consumed and, in turn, is used to express a certain identity or lifestyle.

It is not difficult to see the potential economic gains of making a San Marco square, or in other words a place that is saturated with identity in such a way that people are willing to consume this place. The most extreme examples are theme parks and shopping malls. Place identity is manipulated to encourage consumption.

The manipulation of place identity is not solely a tool for urban regeneration and economic allure but takes other forms as well. It may, for example, be used to represent a certain vision of society. There have been numerous accounts of the nationalist inscription of meaning in place (see for example Vale, 1992). Another favorite site for image creation is the neighborhood. The neighborhood is modeled on an ideal image of what a neighborhood should be like. In this ideal the neighborhood is a community, a socially integrated area. The idealized neighborhood stands as the opposite of the supposed downfall of community in the typical suburb or problem-ridden inner city areas and is intended to look nice and friendly. The »new urbanism« movement, most influential in the U.S., represents the ideal image of a neighborhood in architecture and neighborhood planning (Huxtable, 1997). A frequently quoted example is the Walt Disney-owned neighborhood of Celebration, some twenty kilometers south of Orlando, Florida. This neighborhood is designed on an ideal image of neighborhood life: safe, friendly, socially integrated, and pretty.

REPRESENTING ETHNIC IDENTITY IN SPACE

Images of place are not separate from people and their identities. People consume places to shape their own identities, but places are also imaginatively linked to groups of people. The dominance of men in the public sphere of the streets and the morally charged placement of women in the private sphere of the home and its immediate vicinity have been described by several (feminist) writers (see, for example, Wilson, 1991). This has not only affected representations of men and women, but also of place. The public sphere became a masculine sphere and the private sphere feminine. Places in similar fashion become racialized and ›ethnicized,‹ i.e. imaginatively linked to ethnic and racial groups. This racialization of space is caught in binary oppositions:

black versus white, strange versus familiar, safe versus unsafe, suburb versus inner city (Sibley, 2001).

It is, however, not only a question of representation. Men and women, the young and the elderly, people with different ethnic backgrounds, all have different geographies, which are heavily influenced by processes of exclusion (Sibley, 1995). Women let their use of space be influenced by fear of attack and of being morally contaminated. They are excluded and exclude themselves from certain areas at certain times. Ethnicity also immensely affects individual geographies. Ethnic minorities in Western Europe and the U.S. are utterly urban and occupy certain spaces in the city. Kobayashi and Peake's (2000) claim that the spatial expression of American life is racialized can also be made for diverse European societies. There are distinct concentrations of ethnic groups in certain areas or neighborhoods. And ethnicity plays a large role in imaginative urban geographies.

There is a long tradition of measuring the degree of separateness/intermingling and expressing the result in segregation indices (see, for example, Bolt, Hooimeijer and van Kempen, 2002). This highly quantitative work tends to overlook the social construction of ›white‹ and ›ethnic‹ spaces. This work may actually add to the geographic imagination of ethnicity because of its frequent use of maps. The city is visually represented in white, black and different shades of gray. Different spaces of blackness and whiteness are often represented as distinct, recognizable areas (see also Zukin, 1998). The suburbs are associated with white inhabitants, whereas deprived urban areas are frequently equated with blackness. The term ›black neighborhood‹ can be frequently heard in public discourse.

The percentage of ethnic minority inhabitants is often implicitly used as a measure of urban problems, and the ethnic minority population is often portrayed as one of the *causes* of the problems in the neighborhoods. Crime, juvenile delinquency, litter and poorly performing schools are implicitly and explicitly connected to the high proportions of ethnic minorities in the neighborhood. »The other is treated as the scapegoat for all sorts of urban problems,« as Baeten (58) puts it. White inhabitants resist segregation because they do not feel like living in a ›black‹ space. They claim that the ›burden‹ should be equally shared. This claim is represented in the policy debate on ›social balance‹ in neighborhoods (see, for example, Goodchild and Cole, 2001).

Regarding ethnic identity, we see a similar combination of a non-strategic construction of place identity with more strategic approaches. Ethnic diversity is used as a positively charged signifier in attempts at multicultural theming in order to achieve certain economic and social goals. In the food courts of American malls, and elsewhere, there is usually an array of foods linked to different ethnic identities. Because of its duplication in malls throughout the U.S. this creates a uniform diversity. Many cities host multicultural festivals, and often these are not limited to one, such as in the two largest cities in the Netherlands, Amsterdam and Rotterdam, where you can find multicultural festivities almost weekly during the summer months. In the following sections we will look at the issues of power and subordination that are raised by multicultural theming.

THE PACIFYING PROJECT

Inequality and exclusion are intertwined with space, and space also works as a medium to produce inequality and exclusion. Some places are more desirable than others, and those with less power often inhabit and occupy the less desirable places. The urban landscape shows, for example, the relegation of weaker groups to less desirable areas. People considered deviant are actively barred from certain places, for example, homeless from the tourist areas and non-consumers from the shopping malls.

Space can, however, also be used as a means of resistance, for example by occupying certain places (Beazley, 2002). Neighborhoods with concentrations of ethnic minorities can be seen as both the result of exclusion and as resistance. The concentration is often the result of lack of access to other neighborhoods, but the concentration can also be used to empower the ethnic minority members and may be the result of positive choices.

Multicultural theming is situated in these landscapes of power and necessarily plays a role in it. According to Harvey (1989), catering to multicultural eclecticism in urban areas obscures the real geographies of ethnicity.

> The geography of differentiated tastes and cultures is turned into a pot-pourri of internationalism that is in many respects more startling, perhaps because more jumbled, than high internationalism ever was. When accompanied by strong migration streams (not only of labor but also of capital) this produces a plethora of »Little» Italies, Havanas, Tokyos, Koreas, Kingstons, and Karachis as well as Chinatowns, Latino barrios, Arab quarters, Turkish zones, and the like. Yet the effect... is to draw a veil over the real geography. (87)

Multicultural theming distracts from the issues of power, exclusion and resistance that may be seen as the most important forces in the creation of city landscapes. The ›veil‹ that is made of multicultural consumerism defines the separation of ethnic minority groups in Chinatowns and Little Istanbuls solely in terms of heightened choice for the eclectic, cosmopolitan consumer. It suppresses the question of whether locating themselves in Chinatown is a positive choice of Chinese immigrants, or is induced by lack of good alternatives.

Multicultural theming, in line with Harvey's thinking, can be seen as a strategy to depoliticize race relations. The festivals, multicultural building projects, and promotion campaigns all promote a harmonious image of relations between ethnic groups. They suppress very relevant information about resistance and the disadvantaged position of many ethnic groups. Jacobs (1998) underlines this view of the depoliticizing nature of many multicultural projects. She describes a project in Australia on the aboriginal heritage. This project represented only the uncontroversial aspects of ethnic diversity. »These works conformed precisely to the way in which non-aboriginal Australians prefer to encounter their indigenous cohabitants – linked to a primitivized past which is viewed as more spiritual than political« (272-3). The multicultural ideal is shaped according to the terms of the dominant group, in this case white Australians, which does nothing to emancipate aborigines, but actually underlines their distinctness. This distinctness is, however, devoid of all political content.

THE ESSENTIALIZING PROJECT

The Netherlands has received substantial numbers of immigrants throughout its history. In a rather fanciful recollection of history, the current era is often seen in rather exceptional, sometimes apocalyptic terms with regard to the numbers involved. The large cities are, so much is true, steadily moving towards a majority of ethnically non-Dutch inhabitants in the years to come (Veenman, 2002). The Netherlands is also growing increasingly ethnically diverse as the number of countries from which immigrants move to the Netherlands increases because of the influx of asylum seekers, who come from a much wider range of countries than the former *gastarbeiter*. Just like other European countries, the Netherlands is struggling with a new multicultural identity. Multiculturalism, which is seen here as an ideological standpoint, is one of the reactions towards this ethnic diversity.

Young (1999) sees multiculturalism as a moral doctrine. This doctrine describes the social world as consisting of a plurality of cultures, not limited to ethnicity or, for example, sexuality and subcultures. This inherent cultural diversity is celebrated, nurtured and elaborated by diverse institutions, such as education, politics, and the mass media. Moreover, all cultures are deemed equal. No culture can claim priority over other cultures. Related to this is a reluctance to morally evaluate other cultures. Certain aspects of cultures that are not easily accepted, such as clitoridectomy, are seen as excesses and are separated from the culture as a whole. In the multiculturalist doctrine all cultures are seen as having essential natures formed through long historical processes. The emphasis is on historical, and not on future, change. All cultures that are there now should be carefully ›preserved.‹ Belonging to a certain culture starts with birth. Individuals may drift away but can always come back to ›recover‹ their roots. Contact between cultures is characterized by distance. Deep personal contact takes place between members of the same culture. Contact between cultures is characterized by gazing at, and consuming, each other's differences, for example by visiting Chinatowns and Little Istanbuls, and by eating in ›ethnic restaurants‹ (Young, 1999).

The multiculturalist position is very different from the classic model of integration, which also had strong moral connotations. In this view, immigrant groups would increasingly conform to the dominant culture. Ultimately it would no longer be possible to differentiate the immigrant groups from the rest of the society. This perspective can be traced back to the Chicago School in the early twentieth century. For many people this expected process of assimilation is a desirable one. They assume that the beliefs of the recipient community are the norm to which immigrant groups must adapt. In this view, ethnic diversity represents a threat to the unity of a country.

Multicultural theming of place, on the other hand, is part of the multiculturalist agenda. The focus of multicultural theming is on ›cultural folklore‹; on the things tourists are looking for when going abroad. As Jencks (1991) says, we all carry with us a *musée imaginaire* drawn from experience of other places through tourism and television images. Multicultural theming materializes these *musées imaginaires* in place. The projects make sure that visitors will encounter what they expect, by staying fairly close to the familiar and to expected difference. The deprived neighborhood is remodeled as an exotic environment where one goes on safari (Hajer and Reijndorp, 2001). With multicultural theming the ›exotic‹ is brought to the doorstep. This ›exotic‹ portrayal of the ethnic ›other‹ bears many parallels with the orientalism described so eloquently by Said (1978).

What is essentialized by multicultural theming is not only ethnicity, however, but identity of place as well. Identity of place is always contested and subject to diversity. The marketing of place can be seen as an effort to claim the true meaning of place. However, neighborhood struggles to resist ›yuppification‹ and preserve the ›true nature‹ of the neighborhood make a similar claim: »All of these have been attempts to fix the meaning of places, to enclose and defend them: they construct singular, fixed and static identities for places, and they interpret places as bounded enclosed spaces defined through counterposition against the Other who is outside« (Massey, 168). Even though in multicultural theming the emphasis is on a plurality of ethnic identities, it promotes a singular identity of place, namely that of a tolerant multicultural community. This stands in opposition to those who, for example, would like to define the place of the neighborhood as a ›Dutch working class neighborhood,‹ in which ethnic minorities are seen as out of place.

THE REVANCHIST PROJECT

The revanchist theme goes back to nineteenth-century French history and encompasses a revengeful re-taking of the city by the middle classes, who feel that their city has been stolen from them by the poor. Smith describes the gentrifying process as a revanchist class struggle (1996). The application of revanchism as an urban movement is, however, much wider.

> Revenge against minorities, the working class, women, environmental legislation, gays and lesbians, immigrants became the increasingly common denominator of public discourse. Attacks on affirmative action and immigration policy, street violence against gays and homeless people, feminist bashing and public campaigns against political correctness and multiculturalism were the most visible vehicles of this reaction. In short, the 1990s have witnessed the emergence of what we can think of as the *revanchist city*. (45, italics in original)

The ways in which this revenge is carried out are diverse; however, they all aim at making the city environment more hospitable to middle-class whites, often by removing what they consider offensive. The homeless, prostitutes and drug addicts are displaced so that those who are better off can feel more at ease. Smith links this revengeful course of action to the issue of gentrification. The processes of cleaning up space are both accompanied by and reinforced by gentrification processes. The cleaning up makes sure that gentrification can take place, while gentrification in itself is part of and intensifies the processes of displacement.

City theming is linked to the revanchist project. The theming of cities is select in terms of who it is intended to appeal to, namely middle-class tourists and business people. Therefore representations and images are chosen that are appealing to those groups. In these representations things not corresponding to their romanticized visions of the city are simply left out. In the case of multicultural theming, certain ›dark sides‹ of cultural diversity are underrepresented as well. For example, Islamic fundamentalism or Islam in general is hardly ever represented because of its unpopular connotations for the white middle class. Multicultural theming must be seen as benefiting the middle classes.

A themed image can become mistaken for reality. By theming the city as a friendly, unproblematic place, this becomes a vision of reality. Instead of seeing that the theme is flawed and overly positive, the dark sides or the personages representing these dark sides are seen as unfitting. By providing a certain, partial vision of reality, theming may have the effect of writing people out of the script, instead of adjusting the script to the realities encountered. Islam itself may be seen as an ›unnatural‹ element of the multi-ethnic community. As only those images that underscore the communal multiculturalist vision are accepted, a religion that is considered to be a dividing force comes to be considered alien to the neighborhood.

Multiculturalism is, above all, a middle-class lifestyle. It is the middle class, especially those with higher education and a left-wing political orientation, who are drawn to the multicultural ideal and who go to ethnic restaurants, visit the multicultural festivals and celebrate cultural tolerance (see also Ward, 2000). Multicultural theming caters especially to this group. Gentrification in Smith's revanchist city is described as class struggle, but it is also very much a cultural or lifestyle phenomenon, a form of distinction. Gentrification can to a large extent be explained by the appeal of romanticized working-class or ethnically mixed neighborhoods. Difference becomes fetishism.

Smith sees revanchism in opposition to multiculturalism and political correctness, both being very much related. Revanchism would therefore be opposed to multicultural theming. This seems to be a partial truth. Multicultural theming incorporates the multicultural theme and redefines it in a new and inoffensive way. Ethnic diversity is not fought but colonized and reused and becomes a part of revanchism. Multicultural theming can also be considered revanchist because it may have gentrifying effects. The neighborhood is designed to appeal to the middle classes and may actually make it a more popular place to live.

And using the multicultural theme to attract customers may drive up rents if those customers actually come.

CASE STUDIES

The following part of this paper deals with four case studies of projects of multicultural theming. Two projects are aimed at neighborhood regeneration. Two others consist of the construction of dwellings. Project organizers and initiators were interviewed, and written material was studied. For each case study I give a short description of the project and assess how multicultural theming works in terms of essentializing, pacifying and/or revanchist projects.

Rotterdam: Social and Economic Regeneration in ›Schatten van Noord‹

As part of the ›strategic neighborhood approach‹ in the *Oude Noorden* neighborhood in Rotterdam attempts are being made to reformulate the ethnically mixed population as one of the assets of the neighborhood instead of its problems. In 1998 the district council launched a program under the title *Schatten van Noord* (*Treasures of Noord*) in which art and culture have been promoted to generate a positive image of the neighborhood. This is an attempt to break down the stigma of a ›problem neighborhood‹ and to make the neighborhood attractive and unique for residents, visitors, and other users. The approach consists of video events, theater productions, music performances, cultural courses in primary schools, architectural exhibitions, and initiatives related to public space. It also employs the concept of waterfront development, this time with a multicultural tint. The thrust of the approach is to stress the ethnic diversity of the population of the neighborhood. The foundation *Stichting Culturele Wereldwijk Noord* is responsible for the program, while *Bureau Medelanders* is responsible for the execution of the different subprojects.

The goal of the multicultural theming in this program is bipartite: first, the promotion of a multicultural society with high social cohesion based on respect for each other's differences; second, economic regeneration through multicultural theming. This dual goal is clearly revealed in a description of the approach by Wigmans (2000). He believes that the arts and culture projects in the *Oude Noorden* neighborhood help to bring people together, encourage debate and confrontation and stimulate the strength of different cultures. In addition, investments in the image of the neighborhood should attract cultural entrepreneurs, something which, according to Wigmans, can have spin-off effects for shops, businesses and employment.

The first objective of the initiative is to shape art and cultural activities in such a way that they reinforce multicultural society. The *Treasures of Noord* are in fact the residents, claims the project leader in an interview. He believes that the projects promote integration because they reflect reality: the multicultural nature of society. The initiative clearly fits with the multiculturalist doctrine that sees ethnic diversity as something positive to be emphasized and integration as taking place through understanding each other's differences.

According to the project leader, the initiative is based on the cooperation of residents and on their cultures. He believes that culture is the instrument through which people can be reached. »It is something they are proud of and which they are happy to share with others.« The project approaches residents in terms of their ethnic identities and differences between those identities. This leaves little space for those who do not wish to present themselves ethnically, which is an effect of essentializing ethnic identity.

The social aim of the approach is most clearly revealed in a subproject, which was realized on a demolition site where the land was to remain empty for some years. At first the gap between the remaining houses (some 36 meters long) was closed off with a wooden partition. After a short time, residents began to complain about the view and how they felt unhappy and unsafe. The *Stichting Culturele Wereldwijk Noord* developed a conceptual framework for the space, which would fill it in a way related to the different cultures in the neighborhood. The concept was symbolically called »*De Afbraak van de Muur,*« which means »breaking down the wall.« The ideological idea was to help reduce unfamiliarity and misunderstandings between cultures or, in other words, to break down barriers between cultures. The first plan for a work of art took this ideal literally. The different components would show symbolically a wall between cultures being pulled down.

On the basis of this conceptual framework, attempts were made to find local artists who could express the concept in their designs. However, it proved difficult to find artists in the neighborhood. The ethnic minority artists felt uneasy about the project because they had been asked to contribute because of their ethnicity rather than their talent. The artists resisted attempts to limit them to their ethnic identity. When it became clear that it would be impossible to find neighborhood artists, the project looked further afield to the rest of the city. In the end, two of the five artists did come from *Oude Noorden*, and only one was of ethnic minority origin. The artists that participated resisted the highly ideological symbolism of the project. They felt that the concept of breaking down a wall was too highly charged. In the end, each artist painted a tableau, which was then hung on a specially designed construction. The tableaux do have ethnic themes and are therefore still considered to fall within the *Treasures of Noord* approach.

Another subproject is the ›makeover‹ of a shopping street in the neighborhood. This project supports the second goal of the approach: economic regeneration of the neighborhood. The majority of shopkeepers and businesses in the street are of ethnic minority origin. The native Dutch population perceives the street mainly as rundown and unsafe. However, the ethnic minority entrepreneurs often see the street as a step on the road to a brighter future.

In order to raise the street into the multicultural sphere, an art festival was held in the street and the surrounding area during three weekends in 2001. The aim of the festival organizers was to provide a platform for intercultural communication, corresponding to the first goal of the approach. But another clear objective was to attract tourists and purchasing power to the neighborhood. In addition to the festival, the multicultural theme was also communicated through the built environment, for example by redecorating shop fronts. »This is all about correct and attractive deployment of high artistic quality with a multicultural flavor« (*Bureau Medelanders* 23, my translation). The buildings in the area are used as a platform to represent the desired multicultural society.

Following the festival, the *Bureau Medelanders* formulated the following vision for the Zwaanshals:

> A tourist guide to Rotterdam could contain the following recommendation: In the old town of Rotterdam North, there is an area where artists have decorated a complete street (Zwaanshals). It is like an open air museum, where you can enjoy art and at the same time shop in the many multicultural shops or eat in small exotic restaurants. It is next to the river Rotte, which gave Rotterdam its name... (ibid., 23)

This fits in the revanchist aim to make the neighborhood more attractive for the middle class. The other revanchist process described by Smith (1996), gentrification, is not very likely to take place on a large scale, however. Rotterdam has very little ›gentrification potential‹ (see for example Burgers and Van der Land, 1997). It would take much more than this approach to catalyze gentrification to the extent that displacement of poorer residents would take place.

The representation of multiculturalism in the built environment, as promoted in the approach, is not universally accepted. A Moroccan fountain built in the neighborhood is a case in point. In 1999 the Moroccan community in the *Oude Noorden* neighborhood in Rotterdam took the initiative to build a Moroccan fountain on the central square in the area known as the *Noordplein*. The local council embraced the idea as it would underline the multicultural character of the neighborhood and therefore fit into the strategic neighborhood approach. The fountain represents a non-political, non-religious vision of Moroccan identity. In addition, the mosaic is both a traditional element of Moroccan culture and is also recognized by non-Moroccans as distinctly Arabic. It almost perfectly fits the image of ethnic diversity favored by the proponents of the strategic approach. However, there is one important difference: the fact that the fountain is mono-cultural, whereas the approach is *multi*cultural.

This mono-cultural quality seems to foster resistance in the Dutch population of the neighborhood. One of the initiators and supervisors of the project talked about resistance encountered during the planning process, from the native Dutch population, who viewed the fountain as a provocative assault on their trusty square. Their resistance was based on the fear that the *Noordplein* would now be annexed by Moroccans, who would hang out around the fountain, or use it for cultural and religious purposes.

The resistance to the Moroccan fountain is exemplary of the Dutch population's general resistance, both in this neighborhood and in other deprived, ethnically mixed neighborhoods, to growing ethnic minority populations and the effect this has on neighborhood character. Recent municipal and national elections demonstrate the strong electoral appeal of anti-immigrant policies. The *Treasures of Noord*, with the exception of the fountain, which was added later, can in some ways be seen as pacifying by focusing on *multi*culture. This multicultural approach is more acceptable to the Dutch population than *one* ethnic group claiming space for expression. It recasts ethnic diversity in an unthreatening fashion for the Dutch population.

The Hague: Consuming Multiculturalism in the ›City Mondial‹

The theming of environments is often perceived as a catalyst for consumption. In neighborhoods with an ethnically mixed population it does not take much imagination to take the multicultural identity as a guiding theme for attracting consumers. The marketing of Chinatowns and Little Istanbuls fits this approach. The same approach has been applied in The Hague in a number of projects with the overarching name *City Mondial*. It is the aim of these projects to market existing ethnic minority business initiatives under a new name in order to attract new clients and tourists to the area. *City Mondial* targets the middle-class multicultural consumer in a fundamental way, which is, as pointed out above, an important element of revanchism.

The multicultural theme is used as a tool for attracting the public. The neighborhood is reshaped as a theme park with different attractions such as guided walks, the ›working-class neighborhood museum,‹ a Chinatown and an area featuring a concentration of multicultural restaurants called *avenue culinaire*. What distinguishes this neighborhood from other leisure activities in the city is the overarching theme of multiculturalism. An advantage is sought by marketing existing shops and businesses in a new way: i.e. theming. Spatial design also plays a role in the project. Given that *City Mondial* does not have one specific location but rather multiple locations throughout the area, the project has to use various public spaces to communicate the project's objectives. In the street called Paul Krugerlaan, for example, shop fronts are being renewed and used to communicate cohesiveness in the area.

The aim of the project is an essentialized ethnicity that can be consumed visually. ›Colorful‹ inhabitants and shops form a decor in which visitors can enjoy Turkish pastry and buy a sari or other ethnic tokens. Differences rather than similarities between people form the attraction and are stressed.

One of the key objectives of the project is to recast the identity of the area, transforming it from a neighborhood with a reputation for problems and a lack of safety to a bustling multicultural ›fun neighborhood,‹ which Harvey described as pacification. The neighborhood is made more welcoming to tourists; however, the real problems of the inhabitants are not dealt with. Not all residents own shops or restaurants and can benefit from the new clientele. Unemployment rates still remain high. Redefining a poor neighborhood into an exotic neighborhood directs attention away from the mechanisms behind segregation and leaves this issue unaddressed. Segregation may be partly caused by choice, but is also attributable to a lack of choice.

What is the attraction of multiculturally themed shopping areas? We are all too familiar with the standard high streets and malls full of the same kind of chain stores. A multicultural shopping area offering exotic products, people, décor, and possibly even a hint of danger may be a response to the need for new experience. Shoppers become tourists; in the words of Bauman, »... in the tourist's world the strange is tame, domesticated and no longer frightens; shocks come in a package deal with safety« (29).

Another explanation may be found in Ritzer's widely read book on the MacDonaldization of society. Ritzer states that the strategies of fast-food restaurants are quickly invading the rest of society (1996). This means that people expect the same kind of efficiency, calculability, predictability, and control in different kinds of places. In multi-ethnic shopping areas there seems to be a reverse appeal: an inefficient, unpredictable, and less controlled environment. The multicultural shopping area is dominated by small shops, which are neither franchises nor chains. Some would say they are less efficient as they do not operate according to industrially standardized training and operating manuals. They are unpredictable because you never know what's for sale, which cultural customs you should abide by and which language is spoken. In addition the environment often qualifies as relatively uncontrolled. Multicultural theming transforms these areas and creates a predictable unpredictability, a more efficient inefficiency, a controlled uncontrollability and a domesticated diversity by adapting it to the white middle-class consumer.

Amsterdam: Multicultural Neighborhood Community in ›Mi Akoma di Color‹

As emphasized before, theming is not only used to attract customers but can also be used to theme residential neighborhoods. The same applies to multicultural theming. One characteristic of deprived neighborhoods in the Netherlands that receives frequent mention and is generally considered a problem is the large number of different cultures living together. Segregation in the Dutch context is typically multi-ethnic in contrast to the American context, where segregation is often more mono-ethnic. In the Netherlands there is always mixing, and it is often assumed that this cacophony of difference must cause aggravation. The multiculturalist position on ethnically diverse neighborhoods, however, sees diversity as something binding in itself. This is the starting point for a new housing development project containing 20 rental dwellings and 20 privately owned dwellings called *Mi Akoma di Color* (*My heart of color*), which is going to be built in one of the most infamous neighborhoods of the Netherlands: the *Bijlmermeer*.

The future residents are to be the current residents of the neighborhood. They come from a range of ethnic backgrounds. Project organizers have attempted to put together a mixed group with a balanced ethnic distribution. »*Mi Akoma di Color* brings together all cultures. It is truly multicultural,« says someone from the organizing team. This does not correspond with Dutch society as a whole or the reality of the *Bijlmermeer* neighborhood. In Dutch society, Dutch culture dominates, whereas in the *Bijlmer* certain ethnic groups, in particular from the former Dutch colony of Surinam, are numerically predominant. This emphasis on balance pacifies relations between ethnic groups as it obscures the imbalances in power.

As the project is aimed at the current residents of the neighborhood, it can hardly be called revanchist, in Smith's sense of a *re*taking of the city. However, seen in the wider context of the neighborhood, it may add to a revanchist trend. Many of the original high-rise buildings in the *Bijlmermeer* are being demolished. Single-family dwellings often replace them. The *Bijlmermeer* has long been considered a no-go area by the white middle class. The current massive restructuring and the positive emphasis on a multicultural identity can be considered a way of opening up the neighborhood to the middle class.

Like the other case studies under discussion here, this project also emphasizes people's cultural differences. »We stimulate people to come forward with their own culture,« says a woman responsible for assisting residents during the process. If people have certain culturally determined wishes regarding their homes, the building design team attempts to satisfy them. Cultural differences are the project's *raison d'être* and are therefore stressed. The text on the website is a good example of the essentializing tendency of the project:

> *Mi Akoma di Color* means my colored heart. It is a name in five languages: Ghanese, Papiaments, Surinam, Antillian and Spanish. The name refers to the colored heart of the Bijlmer, which will be expressed in a special way in the new neighborhood. In *Mi Akoma di Color* different cultural values regarding housing and building are given a voice. Together they add color to the neighborhood and are a positive stimulus for people to live in the Bijlmer. (www.patrimonium.nl, my translation)

The name symbolizes unity amidst difference. Differences between ethnic groups are still there, but taken together, all the differences form a unity. The name points to the way ethnic identity is considered an essential characteristic of the residents and the neighborhood: not superficial but enshrined in the heart. This symbolic naming corresponds to other Dutch projects, such as an initiative in the city of Den Bosch called *Wijk van Werelden* (*Worlds in One Neighborhood*) and the terms *Plein der continenten* (*Square of the Different Continents*) and *Straat van duizend culturen* (*Street of a Thousand Cultures*) from the urban renewal plans for the *Bijlmer* submitted by the architects Kuiper Compagnons. All these names are intended to symbolize a tolerant ›salad-bowl-society.‹

The logo that the project uses is a case in point as well. It is a picture of a heart with the name of the project in the middle. It is very colorful, representing the different ethnicities that are part of the project, but also the differences between the different ethnic groups. The heart symbolizes the harmony among the different participants and among the different ethnic groups. The heart also seems to hold together the different words, thereby symbolizing unity. Also, the use of different languages to form one sentence can be seen as the creation of unity through difference.

Rotterdam: Exclusion and Inclusion in ›Le Medi‹

In Rotterdam, a plan for a multicultural housing development project, called *Le Medi*, is being developed, which is in many respects very different from *Mi Akoma di Color*. It is the aim of this initiative to create a neighborhood with a Mediterranean flavor. One of its initiators explains part of the motivation behind the project: »The houses in which we live are... very monotonous, whereas Dutch people like to go abroad on vacation and enjoy other architectural styles. So, what keeps us from doing that here as well?« (Idrissi, my translation). The project explicitly tries to appeal to the ›tourist experience‹ and aims to provide a decorative ethnic identity.

A working group comprised of people from a range of ethnic backgrounds has started reflecting on this concept. The objective is to build some 500 dwellings, including some 100 to 200 dwellings for private ownership. This number is deemed the minimum necessary to ensure a multicultural imprint on the environment. The proposed location is the Delfshaven neighborhood, which is undergoing major restructuring and has a large ethnic minority population.

The city of Rotterdam is struggling to maintain its middle-class population. Rotterdam has little attraction as a place to live for the middle class. The reasons for this are not completely clear. The paucity of attractive houses and neighborhoods is one explanation. Another, probably more important factor is the lack, compared to other Dutch cities, of a historic center due to the bombing during WWII. The municipal government is very eager to win the affection of the middle class because this middle class is considered essential for a healthy city, both economically and socially. The main target groups of *Le Medi* are both ethnic minority and Dutch middle-class groups. This initiative therefore fits the municipal policy aims and helps to open up the neighborhood to the middle class, which fits the revanchist theme, especially since it is located in a disadvantaged neighborhood.

The working group seems to be struggling with issues of inclusion and exclusion. This is most apparent from the debate about the cultural direction of the initiative. At first the project intended to use Moroccan architecture. However, this was considered by some to be too exclusionary, and the scope was broadened by using the term ›Mediterranean.‹ However, uncritically incorporating Mediterranean architecture was also considered undesirable, especially since it was unclear what the common denominator of the very diverse architectural styles found around the Mediterranean would be. Some of the people involved in the project are therefore aiming at ›something new‹ with a Mediterranean flavor. One of the architects involved believes that the scope of the project is broader than one single country. It seeks forms in which everyone can feel at home, irrespective of their background. The project is searching for a new style of architecture, inspired by Moroccan architecture without simply copying it. By creating ›something new,‹ the project initiators also hope to overcome resistance to a Moroccan or Mediterranean neighborhood. One of the project's ambitious aims is to rise above exclusionary ethnic identities. The aim to create ›something new‹ can be seen as an attempt to overcome the essentialization of ethnic difference. The project does not wish to build copies of Moroccan houses, but rather aims to take elements of Moroccan houses and mix them with other styles. This gives rise to the question of which elements of different cultures will be combined to create this ›new architecture.‹ Idrissi (2001) mentions pillars, mosaics, fountains, gardens, and the use of specific material. These are rather uncontroversial elements, and the emphasis placed on those elements can be described in terms of pacification.

Nonetheless, the project is encountering some resistance. One of the initiators relates that »certain organizations are worried about whether there is in fact a market for something like this. What is it you actually want, they asked us. Surely not a ghetto? Some people were also afraid that the application of Islamic building styles would strengthen Islam in the Netherlands« (Idrissi, 2001, my translation).

ANALYSIS

Certain themes recur in these four diverse case studies. I will summarize them in this section before drawing conclusions. The first common theme is the emphasis on the positive aspects of multicultural society. Multicultural society is represented as full of flavor, fun and excitement. Diversity is considered an integral part of modern life, and that diversity is considered an asset. Other realities of the multicultural world, such as the economically depressed situation of many immigrants, and the deep gaps between the different cultural groups and lack of interaction in the local context, are deliberately omitted. Multicultural society is represented in a positive fashion as something to be desired. This is in sharp contrast with another discourse, which focuses on the problems associated with multicultural society.

Secondly, the case studies are similar in focusing on certain aspects of ethnic diversity. The four projects focus on rather stereotypical aspects of cultural diversity, such as architectural designs, crafts, and food, thereby running the risk of oversimplifying ethnic diversity. For example, second generation immigrants differ from the Dutch of their own age group in many aspects, such as clothing, consumption, and body language, but they also differ from their parents. These forms of difference are not usually represented. The focus is often on rather archaic aspects of identity. The image portrayed is characterized by ›shallowness.‹ The projects claim a fixed vision of ethnic identity. They bring the ›vacation experience‹ close to home, explicitly in the case of *Le Medi*. The fact that ethnic identities are multiple, variable and contingent and that being away from the country of origin has profound effects on ethnic identity is scarcely addressed. Symbolic representation can hardly ever do justice to diversity. Indeed, the case studies demonstrate that the projects do not manage to reach much complexity.

The projects are also similar in what they do not address, such as Islam. Islam has a very controversial position in Dutch society. This did not start with the bombing of the Twin Towers on September 11th, 2001. This event did, however, make openly expressing suspicion of Islam more acceptable in public discourse. The portrayal of ethnic identity in the case studies here is very apolitical and non-religious. Controversial elements are left out of the representation.

The fourth shared theme is an emphasis on balance. The stress is on multi-culture rather than mono-culture. In real life multicultural society is very seldom balanced. Some groups have a numerical majority; often the same groups also have financial and political power. There is usually a hierarchy of ethnic groups ranging from the most disadvantaged to the most powerful. In neighborhoods there is very seldom an even mix of people from different ethnic origins. In the projects no one ethnicity is allowed to claim a central position; rather, all the different ethnicities blend into something new. This also seems to be a strategy to smother resistance. Everybody is treated in the same way; therefore nobody has cause for complaint. In two of the projects, apparently mono-cultural elements attracted resistance.

CONCLUSION

Can the case studies be interpreted as pacifying, essentializing and/or revanchist projects? The answer is at least partly affirmative. In all four case studies, pacifying, essentializing and revanchist processes take place, which I will discuss in this concluding section.

The depoliticizing or pacifying effect takes place in various modes in the cases. Multicultural theming projects are usually assumed to be good for people in ethnically mixed neighborhoods. They redefine the mixed neighborhoods as nice areas. But is it really fun to *live* in these neighborhoods? And are people really benefiting from the images produced? Research in the Netherlands suggests that non-Dutch inhabitants of mixed neighborhoods are, generally speaking, quite dissatisfied with the neighborhoods in which they live (Bolt, 2001). Multicultural theming, namely in the *City Mondial* and *Treasures of Noord* projects, creates a nice decor for the visitor and the tourist but does not really change the reality of those living in these areas. Badly performing schools and low employment rates, for example, are not improved.

Pacification is also furthered by the fact that the projects tend to obscure who really benefits from them. The multiculturalist ideal is essentially middle class. In all four projects members of ethnic minorities participate, but they are the educated professional elite. The aim of the projects is to make the environment more in line with multiculturalist ideals and more inviting to consumers, tourists, and middle-class inhabitants. The projects all present themselves as favoring the lower-class inhabitants of the neighborhoods, but in reality they promote a predominantly middle-class and consumerist ideal. This is not to say, however, that the lower income minority groups do not benefit from the projects. It is not unlikely that some local shopkeepers do benefit from middle-class consumers and that some members of ethnic minorities do like to live in a neighborhood with a positive multicultural image.

Another depoliticizing effect is the unproblematic representation of ethnic diversity. The emphasis on visual culture in the projects, such as architectural styles and crafts, is much less controversial than religion and political ideas. In all four cases the focus is on the superficial, the *musée imaginaire*. Ethnic diversity is portrayed in an unthreatening fashion and as a tourist experience. Notably *Mi Akoma di Color* and *Treasures of Noord* also promote a socially cohesive kind of multicultural society in which people respect each other's differences. Difference in this vision does not lead to conflict but to mutual understanding.

As well as a pacifying project, multicultural theming can also be seen as an essentializing project. It imposes an identity on people that may very well be different from the way people perceive themselves. As Harrison claims, it may only reflect »part of their own understanding of their social, cultural or economic locations« (797). The multicultural projects often represent the dominant cultural group's vision of ethnic diversity. In the four cases a quite shallow and uniform image of ethnicities emerges, with little emphasis on other sources of difference than ethnicity. The dividing lines among people which are stressed in the projects are based on ethnic differences, and not for example class or youth culture. This emphasis essentializes ethnicity.

Another essentializing effect of multicultural theming is that it may fix cultural boundaries (see also Bowes et al., 2000). It overlooks the fact that identity is never a fixed category and is constantly reconstructed. In addition, the people who are included in the same social identity may differ greatly from each other. First-generation elderly immigrants often differ enormously from their descendants, who are second- or third-generation immigrants. In the case studies there was an emphasis on ›traditional‹ visual cultures of the countries of origin. The fact that changes take place within cultures, and that many people continually cross cultural boundaries, is conveniently overlooked.

Multicultural theming can also be seen as a way of essentializing the identity of place. Notably *Treasures of Noord* and *City Mondial* can be interpreted in this manner. Both projects aimed to redefine the neighborhood in a positive manner. They promoted the neighborhood as multicultural, ›unique‹ and rich in experience. The same can also be said of *Le Medi*. Its organizing group is aiming for a certain scale that would allow for it to become a distinctive place with a ready-made identity.

Lastly multicultural theming was considered in this paper as a revanchist project, or a retaking of the city by the middle class from the weaker groups. The emphasis on a middle-class version of ethnic diversity in the four cases can be considered revanchist, as well as the fact that all four projects aim to attract people with higher incomes. The four projects are all located in deprived neighborhoods with high percentages of ethnic minority households. Multicultural theming may make them more attractive or open them up for the middle class. The two housing development projects had substantial percentages of privately owned dwellings. The two regeneration projects aimed to attract tourists and customers. The impact of the projects must not be overrated, however. It is questionable whether they alone can truly lead to anything that may justify the term ›retaking‹ or gentrification. They are part, however, of a wider effort to draw higher incomes, customers as well as inhabitants, to deprived neighborhoods.

This ›revanchism‹ must not be seen in terms of complete opposition between classes and ethnic groups. The revanchist theme supposes an intentional class struggle. This is certainly too far-fetched. The projects are not solely in opposition to the interests and ideas of all the inhabitants of the concerned neighborhoods, and the initiators are acting in what they sincerely believe to be the best interests of the neighborhoods and their residents.

In sum, multicultural theming, of which I have looked at some examples in this paper, can to some extent be described as part of pacifying, essentializing and revanchist projects. It should, however, be noted that the degree to which this applies varies from project to project. Also, multicultural theming should not be seen as a deliberate attempt at pacification, essentialization and revanchism or as complete opposition between classes or ethnic groups.

REFERENCES

Baeten, G. »Clichés of Urban Doom: The Dystopian Politics of Metaphors for the Unequal City.« *International Journal of Urban and Regional Research* 25.1 (2001): 55-69.

Bauman, Zygmunt. »From pilgrim to tourist – or a short history of identity.« *Questions of Cultural Identity.* Eds. Stuart Hall and Paul du Gay. London: Sage, 1996. 18-35.

Beazley, Harriot. »Vagrants wearing make-up: negotiating spaces on the streets of Yogyakarta, Indonesia.« *Urban Studies*, 39.9 (2002): 1665-1683.

Bolt, Gideon. *Wooncarrières van Turken en Marokkanen in ruimtelijk perspectief.* Utrecht: Faculteit Ruimtelijke Wetenschappen Universiteit Utrecht, 2001.

—, P. Hooijmeijer and R. van Kempen. »Window on the Netherlands, Ethnic Segregation in the Netherlands: New Patterns, New Policies.« *Tijdschrift voor Economische en Sociale Geografie* 93.2 (2002): 214-20.

Bowes, A., N. Dar, and D. Sim. »Citizenship, Housing and Minority Ethnic Groups: An Approach to Multiculturalism.« *Housing, Theory and Society* 17 (2000): 83-95.

Bureau Medelanders. *De weekenden van Noord. Zwaanshals Rotterdam. Een intercultureel beeldend kunstproject van De Schatten Van Noord. 27 april tot en met 13 mei 2001 te Rotterdam*. Rotterdam: Bureau Medelanders, 2001.

Burgers, Jack and Marco van der Land. »Thuis in de uitstad.« *Leefstijlen, wonen in de 21e eeuw.* Eds. A. Reijndorp, V. Kompier and L. de Haas. Rotterdam: NAi, 1997. 123-9.

Caffyn, A. and J. Lutz. »Developing the heritage tourism product in multi-ethnic cities.« *Tourism Management* 20.2 (1999): 213-21.

Cosgrove, Denis and Peter Jackson. »New directions in cultural geography.« *Area* 19.2 (1987): 95-101.

Duncan, J. and N. Duncan. »(Re)reading the landscape.« *Environment and Planning D: Society and Space* 6.2 (1988): 117-26.

Gold, J.R. and S.V. Ward. *Place promotion, the use of publicity and marketing to sell towns and regions.* Chichester: John Wiley and Sons, 1994.

Goldberger, P. »The rise of the private city.« *Breaking away: the future of cities.* Ed. J. Vittulo Martin. New York: The Twentieth Century Fund, 1996.

Goodchild, Barry and Ian Cole. »Social balance and mixed neighborhoods in Britain since 1979: a review of discourse and practice in social housing.« *Environment and Planning D: Society and Space* 19.1 (2001): 103-21.

Hajer, Maarten and Arnold Reijndorp. *Op zoek naar nieuw publiek domein, analyse en strategie*. Rotterdam: NAI uitgevers, 2001.

Hannigan, J. *Fantasy City: Pleasure and profit in the postmodern metropolis.* London and New York, 1998.

Harrison, M. »Theorising Exclusion and Difference: Specificity, Structure and Minority Ethnic Housing Issues.« *Housing Studies* 13.6 (1998): 793-806.

Harvey, D. *The condition of postmodernity: an enquiry into the origins of cultural change*. Oxford: Blackwell, 1989.

Horst, H.M. van der, A. Haars and A.L. Ouwehand. »Multicultureel bouwen, de weerslag van culturele diersiteit op de gebouwde omgeving.« *Smaken verschillen: multicultureel bouwen en wonen, advies 032.* Vrom-raad. Den Haag: VROM-raad, 2002. 51-187.

Hull, R.B., M. Lam and G. Vigo. »Place identity: Symbols of self in the urban fabric.« *Landscape and Urban Planning* 28.2-3 (1994): 109-20.

Huxtable, A. L. *The unreal America, architecture and illusion.* New York: The New Press, 1997.

Idrissi, A. Hassani. »Mediterraan wonen aan de Maas.« *Migranten Informatief* oktober, 2001.

Jacobs, Jane M. »Staging difference, aesteticization and the politics of difference in contemporary cities.« *Cities of difference.* Eds. R. Fincher and J.M. Jacobs. New York, London: The Guilford Press, 1998. 252-78.

Jencks, C. *The language of post-modern architecture*. London: Academy Editions, 1991.

Kobayashi, A. and L. Peake. »Racism out of Place: Thoughts on Whiteness and an Antiracist Geography in the New Millennium.« *Annals of the Association of American Geographers*, 90.2 (2000): 392-403.

Kong, Lily and Lisa Law. »Introduction: contested landscapes, Asian cities.« *Urban Studies* 39.9 (2002): 1503-12.

Martin, D.G. »Constructing place: Cultural Hegemonies and Media Images of an Inner-City Neighborhood.« *Urban Geography* 21.5 (2000): 380-405.

Massey, Doreen. *Space, place and gender*. Cambridge: Polity Press, 1994.

Ministerie van VROM. *Innovatie Programma Stedelijke Vernieuwing. 476 keer innovatieve ideeën plannen en projecten. IPSV Inzendingen 2001*. Den Haag: Ministerie van VROM, 2001.

Paddison, R. »City Marketing, Image Reconstruction and Urban Regeneration.« *Urban Studies* 30.2 (1993): 339-50.

Pine B. Joseph and James H. Gilmore. *The experience economy: work is theatre & every business a stage*. Boston MA: Harvard Business School Press, 1999.

Ritzer, George. *The McDonaldization of society: an investigation into the changing character of contemporary social life*. Thousand Oaks: Pine Forge Press, 1996.

Said, Edward W. *Orientalism*. London: Routledge & Kegan Paul, 1978.

Sibley, David. *Geographies of exclusion, society and difference in the West*. London: Routledge, 1995.

—. »The Binary City.« *Urban Studies*. 38.2 (2001): 239-50.

Smith, N. *The new urban frontier: gentrification and the revanchist city*. London/ New York: Routledge, 1996.

Stichting City Mondial. *Jaarverslag 2000 Stichting City Mondial*. Den Haag: Stichting City Mondial, 2000.

Stichting Culturele Wereldwijk Noord. *Rotterdam Waterkant. Van een droom naar werkelijkheid?* Rotterdam: De Schatten van Noord, 2001.

Vale, Lawrence J. *Architecture, power and national identity*. New Haven: Yale University Press, 1992.

Veenman, J. ed. *De toekomst in meervoud, perspectief op multicultureel Nederland*. Rotterdam: ISEO, 2002.

Ward, Alan. »Eating globally, cultural flows and the spread of ethnic restaurants.« *The ends of globalization, bringing society back in*. Eds. Don Kalb, Marco van der Land, Richard Staring, Bart van Steenbergen, and Nico Wilterdink. Lanham: Rowman & Littlefield Publishers Inc., 2000. 299-316.

Wigmans, G. *Strategische wijkaanpak Rotterdam*. Delft: Publikatiebureau Bouwkunde, 2001.

Wilson, Elizabeth. *The Sphinx in the city, urban life, the control of disorder, and women*. Berkeley: University of California Press, 1991.

Young, C. and J. Lever. »Place promotion, economic location and the consumption of city image.« *Tijdschrift voor Economische en Sociale Geografie* 88.4 (1997): 332-41.

Young, Jock. *The exclusive society, social exclusion, crime and difference in late modernity*. London: Sage, 1999.

Zukin, Sharon. *Landscapes of power, from Detroit to Disney World*. Berkeley: University of California Press, 1991.

—. »How bad is it?: Institutions and intentions in the study of the American ghetto.« *International Journal of Urban and Regional Research* 22.3 (1998): 511-20.

Music City Unlimited?
A Case Study of Contemporary Vienna

CORNELIA SZABÓ-KNOTIK

INTRODUCTION

Theming has become an important part of contemporary urban *mis-en-scène*. In Vienna it has helped give shape to the most prominent element of the city's clichéd identity: that of »Capital of Music.« Through many activities (both permanent and temporary), the cityscape has recently been staked out with symbols of that image, both real (buildings) and virtual (screens and loudspeakers), transforming the whole city into a kind of a theme park of (classical) music.

My paper analyzes these recent developments, contextualizing them on the basis of the Central European history of urbanization and of music life. The three objects of this case study are the *Haus der Musik*, the *Music Mile Vienna* (a »Classical Walk of Fame«) and the *SoundEllipse ID* (a »sound artwork«).[1]

MARKING PUBLIC SPACE – TOPOGRAPHY AND ITS MEANING

The *Haus der Musik* has a sophisticated architecture that is not apparent from the street. It first impresses itself on the visitor in the courtyard and is only obvious in the interior. Its symbolic importance for the cityscape is enhanced by the fact that it is a »Haus,« i.e. a solid building, which is a characteristic element of the general function of the architecture of public spaces and signifies »urban quality,« establishing the cultural memory of a community and creating identity. Since the early days of the nineteenth century, having an entire building dedicated to one's agenda has been the most superior form of official recognition, often either linking political issues to, or expressing them through, cultural practices.

In the case of the *Haus der Musik*, it was in the late 1990s that a successful entrepreneur, Stefan Seigner, convinced both the electronics megacorporation *Siemens* and a large insurance company to take the building over and sponsor a center for a special experience in the so-called Capital of Music: »Conceived as a hub for all musical venues in Vienna, the HOUSE OF MUSIC VIENNA provides room and space for aesthetic, scientific, popular and artistic encounters with music.«[2]

The building, situated prominently in the heart of the city, had been transformed into a Baroque palace by its pawnshop owners before being redesigned for its next owner, Archduke Charles. It also has a special connection to music history: for some years the composer (of the well-known opera *Die lustigen Weiber von Windsor*) Otto Nicolai, the musical director of the *Hofoper* and one of the founders of the Vienna Philharmonic, lived there.

»Fully renovated, air-conditioned and up to date with the latest scientific research,«[3] the *Haus* features a remarkable mix of attractions (that will be discussed in more detail in the second part of this paper), a stylish ambience for relaxing and shopping, a computerized adventureland devoted to the worlds of acoustics (*Sonosphere*) and of »hyperinstruments« (Todd Machover's *Brain Opera*), and a museum devoted to some of the great masters of (classical, romantic, and not too modern) music.

Taking advantage of the possibilities of electronic media, the *Haus* also reaches out into its surroundings, establishing a, so to speak, virtual presence. There is an underground arcade allowing pedestrians to cross from the *Ringstraße* and the *Opera House* – the southern perimeter of Vienna's downtown inner city area – to the *Karlsplatz*, the *Musikverein* and the *Secession*. At the arcade's (invitingly) broadening exit to the *Karlsplatz* it widens to a square, which is used as a shelter from bad weather and as a meeting-point by the marginalized of consumerism, the homeless and the drug-addicted. And it is in this liminal zone of urban society that the *Haus der Musik* is present too, if in a different way; and significantly this second presence does not leave any traces in its web-presentation.

This underground staging is due to a co-operation with *Vienna Public Transport* dating back to the *Haus*'s opening in 2000, when several underground stations were »filled with sound,« and for two weeks a so-called *virtual singing teacher* was installed in the station located right beneath *St. Stephen's Cathedral*. Now *Vienna Public Transport* again seems to have asked for a music presentation, this time in the *Karlsplatz-Passage* (as this arcade is called), and to have provided »space and logistics« for that purpose: three niches in the wall, formerly used as information desks, not only display conventional advertisements for the *Haus der Musik* (the logo and images from the web-presentation, arranged as a kind of mobile suspended from the ceiling) and a presentation on video screen, but familiar pieces of classical music are also piped in from the ceiling. PR- and Event Manager Katharina Springer refuses to consider this setting a virtual branch of the *Haus* and explains that it merely serves as »an advertisement.« But at the same time she stresses the fact that the music broadcasts do not just provide background music but are of special importance, first because it is part of the *Haus*'s philosophy to »change space through sound,« and second because all the examples chosen (a selection for which no explanation is given) represent composers to whom, »amongst others, Vienna owes its reputation as a ›capital of music‹ and who are each presented in the *Haus der Musik* in a separate room.«[4]

Remarkably this place's (recently acquired) symbolic quality as a musical museum is enhanced by something not in the *Haus*'s advertisements: stars set into the floor engraved with composers' names, images and personal data. These stars belong to another recently installed feature of the musical museum, the *Music Mile Vienna.* There is no information to be obtained on how the placement of the stars was designed (the selection of names is ascribed to a cross-section of prominent members of all aspects of music life,[5] and will apparently also be the subject of web-polls in the future), but examples like the star for Wolfgang Amadeus Mozart in front of *St. Stephen's* or the one for Herbert von Karajan on the *Kärntner Ring* in front of a center devoted to his work indicate a governing principle of relating names and places. It is therefore at least interesting to draw attention to the fact that in the case of the *Karlsplatz-Passage* the placement of the stars seems to correspond to fundamentally traditional prejudices – the stars frequently covered by litter and the sleazy traces typical of such spaces bear the names of Béla Bartók, Bed ich Smetana, Alfred Schnittke, Hugo Wolf and Leoš Janá ek, that is, of composers born in Hungary, Moravia, the Czech Republic, Russia and Slovenia, regions that stood for the closest and oldest Viennese experience of an ethnic and social *other*. Currently the *Music Mile Vienna* presents us with 73 stars named after composers, musicians and conductors, and is supposed to be extended annually. In regard to how media are used, it is rather conventional. It is a »strip,« just like the famous model in Hollywood, a notion perhaps even to be related to »paths to heaven« like *St. Jacob's ladder* or, to offer a somewhat less ancient example, Dorothy's brick-walk in Viktor Fleming's famous 1939 *The Wizard of Oz*.[6]

The whole design of the *Music Mile* reveals a highly meaningful demarcation of space. The stars form a path, leading from *St. Stephen's* to the *Theater an der Wien*, i.e. from the very heart of the city (the 1st, so-called »inner« district, inside the *Ringstraße*) to a place still within the limits of a pronounced urbanity (that is, districts numbered 3 to 9 inside the *Gürtel*, the outer ring road). *St. Stephen's* is said to be »the city's beating heart« (Marboe 361), a place laden with symbolic relevance for Vienna's cultural memory, a monument to Habsburg Catholicism as well as to the development of the Second Republic (Breuss et al. 253f.),[7] and as such of mythical importance in the construction of an Austrian identity after World War II. The *Theater an der Wien* also plays a role in this construction because it was where opera performances took place most frequently when, between 1945-1955, the *Opera House* on the *Ringstraße*, after having been considerably damaged by bombing, could not be used – a traumatic experience for locals. Performances started immediately after the collapse of the Third Reich and were promoted as signs of the resurrection of an Austrian cultural identity. They proved to be of strategic importance in cultivating the country's image abroad, and this period – of the so-called *Mozart-Ensemble* – has become a particularly beloved legend in the narrative of Austria's music life.

At each end and in the middle (in front of the *Opera House*), the *Music Mile* is marked by Info-Points providing additional material: a small catalogue containing biographical notes and images of the composers and musicians in question, together with a list of commemorative places (sites, memorials and plaques) and musical institutions near the path, some of which are described in detail. Audio guides offer the same information in a somewhat expanded form, plus a soundtrack of sound effects and excerpts of prominent works. A CD-edition by *Deutsche Grammophon* – not yet available, but advertised – is also part of the package and will contain the audio guides' music examples in full length. Thus the *Music Mile* represents one of those tours of the »city walk« genre that are regular parts of guide books and travelogues, but with additions (mostly due to electronic recording) from the realm of museums and exhibits (the catalogue, the audio guide) and with CDs as a possible souvenir or gift.

Both the *Haus der Musik* and the *Music Mile* are new attractions in the musical museum that are (more or less) permanently attached to the city's topography and target, in the first instance, tourists, yet do not exclude locals. The *Haus* has become a popular spot for field trips, with music teachers regularly bringing pupils of all ages; and it hosts a wide variety of both cultural and technological events. The *Music Mile* also passes on the message about Vienna's important position in music life to Viennese passers-by, whose awareness of the stars may be occasionally furthered upon encountering groups of tourists led by a licensed guide or tourists walking into them absentmindedly, distracted by their audio guides.

In this context it is worth noting that the marketing of a city's image is no longer exclusively aimed at investors and tourists. Since the mid-1980s it has also been a matter of domestic policy, aiming to swell inhabitants with motivating pride and to provide a substantive, potentially strong identity, just as it did during the process of nineteenth-century urbanization, when not only technical but also cultural infrastructure was a matter of image in the sense of providing a modern, desirable place to live (Schiffer et al). In today's Vienna this type of marketing is not centralized but, as is evident from the numerous logos and slogans that exist, there are many different groups acting independently and with different strategies (Freund), not only communicating the city's urban qualities but also creating them (such as the open-air screenings of music films at the *Rathausplatz* during the summer season, while in winter the *Christkindl-Markt* and an open-air ice rink provide major attractions for locals and tourists alike). For the sake of ongoing urbanization the cityscape must constantly be renewed, so-called »*Stadterneuerung*« (often with funding from the EU) possibly aiming to inspire new life and activity in all the dead corners that result from the adverse effects of migration or from public transport measures and policies.

These measures mainly affect the remoter parts of the city, districts outside the *Gürtel* or north of the Danube. One of these projects, a rather expensive and spectacular one, has a pronounced musical aspect. The *SoundEllipse ID* is a sound installation created by the same artists (Sha and GTT) that rose to fame by creating the *Haus der Musik*'s soundsphere. This time their work was commissioned and funded publicly, by the City Council of Vienna and the EU. It is located on the *Dornerplatz*, a central square in Vienna's seventeenth district, which is nowadays largely inhabited by what are known as »residents of foreign descent.« Its atmosphere is therefore especially multicultural and seems to call for measures enhancing tolerance while also providing a common urban identity. The *SoundEllipse's* architecture (by space artist Burkhardt) is spectacular – 14 large metal plates forming an elliptical space that, depending on the angle of vision, provides two different views: either framing an invitingly opening space or seeming to be a group of needle-like metallic columns. From the point of view of its use of electronic media, this is a rather ambitious and quite avant-garde project. The plates are monitors, collecting radio and TV signals from satellites and interacting with the movements of every single visitor, who can hear the original signals when standing still in front of a single monolith but is treated to their digital abstractions – produced by the sound-artists – when moving around. Oscillating through the installation, visitors thus »compose« their own personal musical aggregate states; the results of this live processing of sounds are fed back into the public media space, to which you can tune in from all over the world.

As a feature of the cityscape, the way the *SoundEllipse* occupies space resembles a monument. The carefully chosen design seems to evoke self-reliant aesthetic principles of art; its cool quality is fashionable, and the task of »embellishing a dead corner« is a rather prosaic measure of urban politics. From the outside this is the most »contemporary« site of all the displays discussed here, with the most ambitious use of electronic media, and perhaps the site targeting tourists the least. But one important question remains: the meanings produced by these sights. In all three cases technology signifies up-to-date-ness for topographically more or less conventional phenomena. In the next section I want to consider how the contents of each site relate to their fashionable packaging.

CONTENT: MEDIATED IMAGES OF MUSIC HISTORY

Bypassing the *Haus der Musik*'s first-floor exhibit on the *Vienna Philharmonic*, which is traditionally designed and only accessible for an extra entrance fee, one enters the *Sonosphere*, a sound installation devised by a partnership of Austrian composers (Sha + GTT). The *Sonosphere* is a counterpoise to the traditional: it defines the internal architecture of the whole floor (reversing the usual principle of the design process) and does not aim to be awe-inspiring in the sense of romantic art, but rather to create something which is educational while featuring a major »fun-factor.« Visitors enter to sounds like those a fetus hears in the womb; next they see a series of six touch screens devoted to explaining basic physical aspects of music, such as pitch, virtual tones or the Shepard scale. The evolution of hearing is demonstrated in an aquarium with seahorses and by larger-than-life instruments that clunk and wheeze in computer-generated rhythmic patterns. Further screens provide experiences of the advanced possibilities of sound design, and in the so-called *Sea of Voices* three interactive columns provide material for complicated singing in response to visitors' touching them. In the last section, the *Polyphonium*, all kinds of sounds – »from the micro- and the macro-sphere, environment and the human body,« as the catalogue booklet states – are collected, condensed and spread throughout the room at different speeds up to the limits of perception, while screens on the ceiling show »corresponding images« and a *Sound Gallery* in the next room exhibits these sounds in their singular forms. In a next step these materials are also the basis for visitors' own experiments in sound design, which they are encouraged to burn onto a CD and take home as a special souvenir.

Similar activities are encouraged on the fourth floor, where Todd Machover's *Brain Opera* is installed, a collection of »hyper-instruments« developed at the Massachusetts Institute of Technology Media Lab. Complexity and sophistication – such as the question of the degree to which the sounds heard are pre-composed or in fact manipulated by the player, or the options and influences of hyperspace on the contemporary understanding of composing – are disguised or remain in the background; on the surface everything is presented as pure fun, a kind of colorful version of »kitchen concerts« (such as beating pans with a spoon or clinking glasses).

Between these attractions – on the building's third floor – you can find a so-called *history zone*, where it is striking to realize that in spite of new media / multi-media possibilities and gimmicks, the musical tradition can still be presented and exhibited in a manner which is completely oblivious of current discussions on questions of the canon or aspects of music history other than the »life and work of great masters« approach. In fact this approach exclusively provides the background for the combination of sound, software and objects for this museum, basically recycling altogether romantic ideas that date back to the nineteenth century.

The great composers' sequence inevitably starts with Haydn, Mozart, Beethoven and Schubert, interestingly followed by Johann Strauß and Mahler (note: no Brahms, no Bruckner). Up to this chronological point in music history, each master has a room of his own, crowded with exhibits (manuscripts, pictures, articles of everyday use), property (such as the puppet shaped like a parrot in Haydn's room), info screens, video walls, games (one »var[ies] the instrumentation of *A Little Night Music*«) and gimmicks (the feng shui of Beethoven's apartment, a hologram of Mozart's and Constanze's faces). The settings are completed by music exactly limited to the room in question, changing without the slightest leakage or any visible barrier – the way this is done is kept as a technological secret by the management – with the commentary on an optional audio guide also changing according to the visitor's movement between displays.

Most remarkable is the fact that the »older« the composer, the more »directly« he seems to be presented. While in the three so-called »classical« rooms one finds many tidbits of information and items related to their personalities and everyday lives (some of doubtful value, such as the notion that Haydn had a life-long problem with orthography), symbols start to prevail once we reach Schubert (the friends), Strauß (marketing) and Mahler (nature) – in the latter case artificial trees with autumn leaves on the floor, perhaps to evoke the cliché of fin-de-siècle melancholy. The impression of losing track gets stronger with every step in this zone, as history approaches the present. After Mahler, only one room is devoted to the so-called Viennese School of Schönberg, Berg and Webern, and this is also the first room without background music – visiting tourists don't want to be irritated too much by this kind of music, one is led to assume.

After that, it is just names. At first, in the *Exodus room* dedicated to exiled musicians and to those murdered by the Nazis, they are written on the wall in golden letters, then on the staircase to the fourth floor in light-blue writing, naming some contemporary Austrian composers, chosen according to a principle that isn't obvious. No information is given about what they did, nor are there any music examples or objects. This creates a strange impression – as though the presence of all the new media and new technology in other parts of the building is far from enough to prevent the same old prejudices from being repeated, reviving a golden age of music that creates an everlasting treasure out of tradition, after the end of which (somewhere around 1900) music as art and music history (the history of material progress) apparently came to an end. And although the catalogue, as well as the website, promises that the exposition in the *history zone* will be regularly extended, as the exhibits from different collections and museums are always loaned for limited periods only, there is no indication that its approach to or the understanding of music history can or will be changed in principle.

At first glimpse the *Music Mile* seems to offer a different image, as the names on the stars stretch (by their sheer number) the traditional canon of Viennese composers (from Gluck and Haydn to Brahms, Mahler and Schönberg, Berg and Webern), including performing artists and thus representing a good deal of twentieth-century music history

(*Table I*). The choice of composers reflects the music life of the twentieth century rather than its musical repertory and is in general, for obvious reasons – with some astonishing exceptions such as Gounod, Tchaikovsky and Weill – strictly local: if not of Viennese origin, then having made frequent visits to the city and/or having a special attachment to its institutions seem to have been the criteria for selection (*Table II*).

The information given in the catalogue and on the audio guide is the usual assemblage of biographical data and artistic facts that also characterizes the seemingly comprehensive and logically chosen information in traditional tourist guides. And, as in the case of the *Haus's history zone*, this material is illustrated with the anecdotal elements typical of the culturally interested *Bildungsbürger's* approach to history, providing a safe feeling of immediate access to, and immediate comprehension of, genius and high art, necessary to support the illusion of safely possessing cultural value. As for the *Music Mile's* function in the context of presenting the *City of Music* as a notion that for more than a century has been mainly defined in terms of museum-like qualities, such an understanding of history is as little surprising as the image of musical tradition related to it. Again the more interesting message can be found in the details of this image of music history, revealed by a closer reading of the path's lay-out (*Table III*), which marks the important spots such as *St. Stephen's*, the *Opera House* or the *Secession* with names that belong to the center of the music culture in question. Some names are not clear at first glance, but generous explanations are provided, which show how the connections are intended.

Take, for instance *St. Stephen's* square, the sacred »heart« of this path. Haydn and Mozart are clearly important as the ancestors of the *Viennese Classic*, and there is Strauß Father, representing local color in music instead of his Son, probably because Johann Jr. has to mark the walk's other end at *Theater an der Wien*. Then there is an apparently less prominent figure, Gaetano Donizetti, who also stands for an important element of the tradition: the relation of court (Emperor) and opera. During his stay in Vienna from 1842 to1844, Donizetti wrote two operas for the Emperor (*Linda di Chamonix* and *Maria di Rohan*) and served as courtly music director, chamber music director and court composer.

Or take the *Annagasse*, where Otto Nicolai is commemorated because the prominent founder of the *Vienna Philharmonic* lived in what is today the *Haus der Musik*. Next to his name, Fritz Kreisler and Arturo Toscanini are mentioned, two important figures in Viennese music life: Kreisler, the violinist, representing yet another kind of light music in local color (perhaps as an allusion to the Ronacher, an establishment close by), and Toscanini standing for the *Vienna Philharmonic's* prominent conductors, together with Kreisler (without this being mentioned in the catalogue) forming the part of the music culture that was banned by the Nazis.

The names between these special locations partly reveal what these walks are meant to connect. On the *Wienzeile* the names closer to the city center refer to concert life (Klemperer, Korngold, Krenek), while those farther away relate to the *Theater an der Wien* (Lortzing, Bernstein). In the *Kärtnerstraße* the last names before the walk reaches the *Opera House* are Puccini, Abbado, Wagner and Vivaldi – the latter, as the catalogue suggests, for his role in the genre of Violin concerto, which reflects the importance of strings to the *Vienna Philharmonic's* sound, an integral part of the orchestra's celebrated identity.

Another way of explaining this design is that it partly refers to the notion of music culture's center (situated in the German-speaking realm) and its periphery (what has once been called the nineteenth-century *National Schools*). This is clearly the case in the *Karlsplatz-Passage* with its series of (South)-Eastern European composers (Bartók etc.), and in the adjacent subway to the *Naschmarkt* – a rather seedy underground walkway –, in which mainly French and Scandinavian romantic composers (Sibelius, Debussy, Saint-Saens) are featured, while Rossini and Weill are perhaps meant to prefigure the *Theater an der Wien*'s entertainment qualities. (This theater has, during the past several years, mostly been dedicated to the performance of musicals).

The opening phrase of the then head of Vienna's Association of Theaters in the introduction to the catalogue is programmatic: »Unlike practically any other city, Vienna is connected to classical music. Almost every outstanding composer, conductor, musician and singer has made a stop-over in Vienna during the course of his or her career, has lived and worked here and left artistic traces.« This quote is a clear reference to the topic of a *City of Music* (cf. Szabó-Knotik), similar references to which can be found in both popular and scholarly Austrian publications throughout history, as for instance in the following statement:

> There was some sort of enchantment in the musical ground where Vienna stood. Great musicians trod this ground and were held fast by it. ... There were but a few musicians in recent times who either could not find a footing in Vienna or were pushed aside by it. ... But such phenomena and manifestation were exceptions. In general, through the centuries, Vienna showed an astounding force in attracting and holding musicians fast. Their various nation-

> alities and races joined to create the great tradition which made Vienna's music rich and colorful. (Graf 57; 58f.)

In contrast to these two examples, *SoundEllipse ID* must be considered different, as it is not first and foremost a historical site and does not relate to a particular tradition of representing »cultural memory.« Rather, it seems to be telling people something new, even disregarding its moral message, which is also strikingly contemporary. It represents new media not only in its design and technology but also in its playful approach to a highly educational, one could even say moral, task. The entire installation has, according to the slogans in both its press material and web-presentation, ambitious aims, such as »art as a means to integrate urban problem areas« and »a symbol of tolerance amongst world cultures«; it is advertised as »a digital Stonehenge,« »a sacred space for the urban dweller of the twenty-first century.«

These phrases draw attention to the fact that this avant-garde artwork is not completely de-linked from cultural history, from ideas about the inherent value of art music in the sense of a so-called classical, i.e. Western tradition. Since the late 1780s, when music was increasingly esteemed as an art form, possibly even as the highest of the arts, a sacred dimension has been conferred to the product itself, but also to its context, its creators (the composers) and interpreters (the performers). The notion spread that the purpose of music was not only to create a link to the celestial spheres (which, in the case of *SoundEllipse ID*, would be true in the very technical sense of the plates' relation to the satellites), but also to connect people through its »humanizing« ability – an ability to which, for instance, the famous quote attributed to Joseph Haydn pays homage: upon being asked how he would be able to live in England without sufficient knowledge of the language, the 60-year-old composer is reputed to have answered: »My language is understood by the whole world.« It is precisely this traditional notion of the value of music lying in its making our world a better and a more peaceful place that is quoted as the basic idea of this installation. And this same notion, which is frequently mobilized as an argument for maintaining classical and romantic music as values of the Western tradition, also formed the basis of the original optimistic belief in the world wide web's democratic structure, which was, of course, just as illusory.

Apart from the question of the possible (cultural, moral etc.) values this site stands for or may transport, it remains doubtful how many local passers-by, the »users« of this space, are (made) aware of its ideals. An occasional visit to the *Dornerplatz* seems to demonstrate that even those who actively enjoy the place in a pleasant and playful way do not read the plates that explain the *SoundEllipse*'s purpose. Thus the question may be raised whether the overall concept could possibly still work, perhaps even more powerfully, on an unconscious level? Details of the *SoundEllipse*'s setting (the surrounding stone benches) even seem to prevent people from walking through, rather making them pass by the installation on its outside, which means that they cannot interact with the installation in the suggested way. The wheezes of the plates are clearly heard and lend the whole space a particular atmosphere, even if on workdays the *Dornerplatz* can be quite a lonely spot. Is this, in terms of the so-called interactive technique, another, more »contemporary« form of »*Kunst am Bau,*« similar in its educational and its decorative aspects to the statues and reliefs that traditionally belong to the setting of »Red Vienna's« publicly funded apartment blocks? And on a more general level: it may also be worth reflecting on how much such an »unconscious« educational effect could be at work in these cases, which means also in terms of the entertainment quality that all these sites share.

CONCLUSION: ANOTHER CULTURAL BATTLE?

There is yet another aspect to this process of turning the entire city of Vienna into a kind of artificial paradise of classical music: the history of nineteenth-century urbanization in Central Europe shows that the demarcation of public space is not exclusively tied to contemporary cultural practices (in which space has become, on top of everything else, a category of increased importance on account of the internet, raising the awareness of spatial processes reflected by current developments in the humanities, in geography and cultural studies). Rather, space was already an important category in the context of more traditional cultural practices during the nineteenth century, when monuments, halls and private buildings represented the importance of a specific (musical) culture. This development was concomitant with an increasing professionalization of music life and made the topography of Central European cities a battlefield for struggles over the definition of culture in the course of developing national identities.

Considering public space a field of struggles generally points to an ongoing conflict between a dominant and a marginalized form of culture. And this may well be true for the current theme-park trend in Vienna, as this trend developed parallel to an increasing worldwide awareness that Western musical »elite culture« is perhaps about to be, or is in the process of being, marginalized. Fundamental changes are taking place on many levels in bourgeois music life, affecting the identity of composer, performer and audience, the aesthetics of music and its forms of distribution and reception (Scheib), while at the same time the relationship between high art and popular culture is undergoing a profound transformation. The popularization of elite tastes for mass audiences can be described as a characteristic development in contemporary culture. In the course of this development, classical music's business has (successfully) adopted strategies of promotion and distribution from popular culture, while popular culture has increasingly made refinement and the acquisition of taste its business.

> The reconciliation of the ease of access and rarity of expression serves as the foundation of the popular connoisseurship which comes after the Pop art moment; it insists on *apartness* of genuine aesthetic expression, but at the same time promises to deliver that experience to a mass audience, an evaluative maneuver made possible by redefining the delivery system *vis-à-vis* content. Where the standard form of the ideology of mass culture made mass distribution an evil unto itself, the mode of transmission precluding the possibility of genuine art as the content of that widely disseminated message, the taste ideology that authorizes the pleasures of high-pop distinguishes between the two, uncoupling the Modernist pairing of rarefied content and exclusivist delivery system, by insisting that knowledge, rather than money, is the only thing required in order to appreciate the *apartness* of the object, even as it becomes ever more widely available. (Collins 24)

It is in the case of the *Haus der Musik* that this relation can be observed most clearly. When in the late eighteenth century the idea of music as an art in the emphatic sense became popular, it resulted in a cult of the genius as creator that was also applied to its interpreters; the performers were venerated literally as the high priests of this new religion. In other words, it was the composer and the musician – mostly the virtuoso and the conductor – who gained new status. And it is exactly those two personifications of Western music's aesthetic values that are – or better: seem to be – central to the visitors' »experiences« in the *Haus*. »Be your own composer« is a slogan that guides you through the *Sonosphere* right to its last attraction, the *Sound Gallery*, where one can »burn the personal, unique and unrepeatable composition on a CD and take it home as a special souvenir.« This is part of the fun provided by the possibility to change *A Little Night Music*'s instrumentation in Mozart's room, and this is the guiding principle in the *Brain Opera* section, where the *Mind Forest*'s hyper-instruments supposedly let the audience »create music,« in itself an illusion as much as the notion that the experience of a creative composer could really be made available to everyone. And then, of course, there is the *Haus*'s most popular, most spectacular attraction: the *virtual conductor*. Situated at the end of the *history zone*, a large screen shows none less than the Vienna Philharmonic, waiting to provide the »conduct the Vienna Philharmonic« experience. One selects a title from the list of classical hits provided (mainly Johann Strauß), picks up the baton, and *presto* – the musicians follow every movement, playing softly or loudly, quickly or slowly. If the »conductor« does well, they offer standing ovations at the end, and one can fetch, or rather buy, a certificate in the museum shop; but if there are too many mistakes in rhythm or speed, then the orchestra breaks into sharp protest and refuses to continue playing.

The *SoundEllipse* also makes use of technology to give its »audience« (the passers-by) the impression of creating sound; but these sounds are clearly based on pre-fabricated material (broadcasts) and – though relating to enlightened ideas of education and humanization through music – lack the emphasis of a musical artwork: if there is any notion of »being a composer,« the concept itself has changed its meaning.

The fundamental question, the answer to which is by no means straightforward, remains: is the theming of the Music City the sign of a battle for the maintenance of the values attributed to or embodied by Western music in times of a cultural shift which marginalizes the culture of those to whom those values were important? Or should this form of theming rather be interpreted as a form of restoring traditional cultural values intended to make the musical museum more consumable? Both options would seem to be intertwined. The classical music theme park features a whole range of attractions, ranging from the mere disguise of the traditional museum in a fashionable wrap to a meaningful contemporary adaptation.

Therefore the only conclusion this paper can reach might be that if it is all too true that cultural studies has to deal with culture in an emphatic sense (Collins 13-16), critical analysis is needed to properly describe the detailed meaning of these complex adaptations of elite tastes, as traditional prejudices and pretensions come with it and may still have kept their potential for political/social effects. The question of what »cultural values« represent is in this context not to be overlooked and not to be answered simply.

TABLE I

Music Mile Vienna: A Chronology of Stars

17th-18th century: 7 names	*19th century:* 29 names	*20th century:* 33 names
Bach, Johann Sebastian	Beethoven, Ludwig van	Abbado, Claudio
Gluck, Christoph W.	Berlioz, Hector	Bartók, Béla
Haydn, Joseph	Brahms, Johannes	Berg, Alban
Monteverdi, Claudio	Bruckner, Anton	Bernstein, Leonard
Mozart, Wolfgang A	Chopin, Frédéric	Böhm, Karl
Schikaneder, Emanuel	Czerny, Karl	Boulez, Pierre
Vivaldi, Antonio	Donizetti, Gaetano	Debussy, Claude
	Dvo ak, Antonin	Furtwängler, Wilhelm
	Gounod, Charles	Hindemith, Paul
	Lanner, Joseph	Janá ek, Leoš
	Liszt, Franz	Karajan, Herbert v.
	Lortzing, Gustav A	Kleiber, Erich
	Mendelssohn-Bartholdy, Felix	Klemperer, Otto
	Nicolai, Otto	Knappertsbusch, Hans
	Offenbach, Jacques	Korngold, Erich W.
	Paganini, Nicolai	Krauss, Clemens
	Rossini, Gioacchino	Kreisler, Fritz
	Saint-Saens, Camille	Krenek, Ernst
	Schubert, Franz	Lehár, Franz
	Schumann, Clara	Mahler, Gustav
	Schumann, Robert	Menuhin, Yehudi
	Smetana, Bed ich	Messiaen, Olivier
	Strauß, Johann Vater	Puccini, Giacomo
	Strauß, Johann Sohn	Ravel, Maurice
	Tschaikowsky, Pjotr I.	Rubinstein, Arthur
	Verdi, Giuseppe	Rysanek, Leonie
	Wagner, Richard	Schnittke, Alfred
	Weber, Carl M. v.	Schönberg, Arnold
	Wolf, Hugo	Sibelius, Jean
		Strauss, Richard
		Strawinsky, Igor
		Toscanini, Arturo
		Walter, Bruno

TABLE II

Music Mile Vienna: Relationship of Persons to Vienna

Born &/or lived in Vienna	Years in Vienna	Often in Vienna	Visited Vienna	Weak or no links
Beethoven, Ludwig van	Abbado, Claudio	Bernstein, Leonard	Bartók, Béla	Bach, J. S.
Berg, Alban	Donizetti, Gaetano	Furtwängler, Wilhelm	Berlioz, Hector	Boulez, Pierre
Böhm, Karl	Dvo ak, Antonin	Kleiber, Erich	Chopin, Frédéric	Gounod, Charles
Brahms, Johannes	Janá ek, Leoš	Klemperer, Otto	Debussy, Claude	Hindemith, Paul
Bruckner, Anton	Karajan, Herbert v.	Knappertsbusch, Hans	Offenbach, Jacques	Mendelssohn-Bartholdy, Felix
Czerny, Karl	Lortzing, Gustav A.	Krauss, Clemens	Paganini, Nicolai	Messiaen, Olivier
Gluck, Christoph W.	Sibelius, Jean	Menuhin, Yehudi	Ravel, Maurice	Monteverdi, Claudio
Haydn, Joseph	Vivaldi, Antonio		Rossini, Gioacchino	Puccini, Giacomo
Korngold, Erich W	Wagner, Richard		Rubinstein, Arthur	Schumann, Robert
Kreisler, Fritz	Walter, Bruno		Saint-Saens, Camille	Smetana, Bed ich
Krenek, Ernst	Weber, Carl M. v.		Schnittke, Alfred	Strawinsky, Igor
Lanner, Joseph			Schumann, Clara	Tschaikowsky, Pjotr I.
Lehár, Franz			Toscanini, Arturo	Weill, Kurt
Liszt, Franz			Verdi, Giuseppe	
Mahler, Gustav				
Mozart, Wolfgang A				
Nicolai, Otto				
Rysanek, Leonie				
Schikaneder, Emanuel				
Schönberg, Arnold				
Schubert, Franz				
Strauß, Johann Vater				
Strauß, Johann Sohn				
Strauss, Richard				
Wolf, Hugo				
Zemlinsky, Alexander				
Vienna Philharmonic				

TABLE III

The *Music Mile Vienna*'s Layout

- *Stephansplatz*: Haydn, Mozart, J. Strauß Father, Donizetti

- *Kärntnerstraße* (heading to the *Opera House*): Kleiber, Strawinsky, Rubinstein, Chopin, C. Schumann, R. Schumann, Liszt, Czerny, Gounod, Mendelssohn, Weber, Paganini, Berlioz, Gluck, Walter, Menuhin, Tschaikowsky, Puccini, Abbado, Wagner, Vivaldi

- *Annagasse*: Nicolai, Kreisler, Toscanini

- Special Sites:
  1. *Opera House*: Knappertsbusch, Rysanek, Verdi, Böhm, Strauss, Mahler, Berg
  2. *Kärntner Ring*: Karajan
  3. *Musikverein*: Hindemith, Furtwängler, Zemlinsky, Brahms, Bruckner, Schubert

- *Karlsplatz-Passage*: Bartók, Smetana, Schnittke, Wolf, Janá ek; Saint-Saens, Debussy, Weill, Sibelius, Ravel, Messiaen

- Special Site:
  Secession: Schönberg, Webern

- *Wienzeile*: Klemperer, Korngold, Krenek, Monteverdi, Offenbach, Dvo ak, Lanner, Lortzing, Bernstein

- Special Site:
  Theater an der Wien: Lehár, Schikaneder, Strauß Son, Beethoven

ENDNOTES

1 cf. the presentation of these sites on: www.haus-der-musik-wien.at; www.musikmeile.at; www.project-id.at/concept_e.pdf; all July 2002
2 Press Information, May 31, 2000.
3 Catalogue of the Music Mile Vienna, 79.
4 E-mail communication to the author. This paper lacks illustrations of the *Haus* because, tellingly, she made a point of only being willing to provide them after having personally approved the content of this article.
5 The election committee for the *Music Mile* as listed in the catalogue (8) consists not only of all the officials of Austrian music institutions, including the International Mozart Foundation and the Bregenz Festival, but also of leading figures from international orchestras and institutions such as the Royal Opera Stockholm, the Lincoln Center Festival New York and the Opera Australia.
6 The reconstruction of this brickwalk was advertised at the time as a desirable item for the design of trendy children's rooms' interiors.
7 On the south end of St. Stephen's roof there is a crest of the Habsburg eagle dated 1831, and on the north end the Austrian and the Viennese coat of arms dated 1950.

REFERENCES

Breuss Susanne, Liebhart Karin, Pribersky Andreas, eds. *Inszenierungen*. Wien: Sonderzahl, 1995.

Collins, Jim, ed. *High-Pop. Making Culture into Popular Entertainment.* Malden – Oxford: Blackwell, 2002.

Freund, Michael. »Wien ist Parallelaktion.« *Der Standard (*1 June 2002*)*. Album: 4.

Graf, Max. *Legend of a Musical City*. New York: Philosophical Library, 1945.

Marboe, Ernst. *Das Österreich-Buch.* Wien: Österreichische Staatsdruckerei, 1948.

Scheib, Christian. »Nur keine Angst vor der Unübersichtlichkeit.« *Österreichische Musikzeitschrift* 7 (2000): 18-27.

Schiffer Josef, Antje Senarclens de Grancy, Monika Stromberger, Heidemarie Uhl, and Peter Wilding. »Urbanität und Moderne. Kultur, Wissenschaft, Architektur und Technik als Symbole städtischer Identität um die Jahrhundertwende.» *Zeitgeschichte* 23 (1996): 213-42.

Szabó-Knotik, Cornelia. »Musikalische Elite in Wien um 1900: Praktiken, Prägungen und Repräsentationen.« *Identität. Kultur. Raum.* Eds. Susan Ingram, Markus Reisenleitner and Cornelia Szabó-Knotik. Wien: Turia+Kant, 2001. 41-58.

Illustrations

1. Béla Bartók's star in the *Karlsplatz-Passage*

2. The *Haus der Musik's* advertisement in the *Karlsplatz-Passage*

3. The Transition from *Karlsplatz* to *Naschmarkt* with more «national composers«

4. The SoundEllipse from the «needles« perspective

5. The *SoundEllipse* from the »space« perspective

6. The setting of the *SoundEllipse* in the city-scape

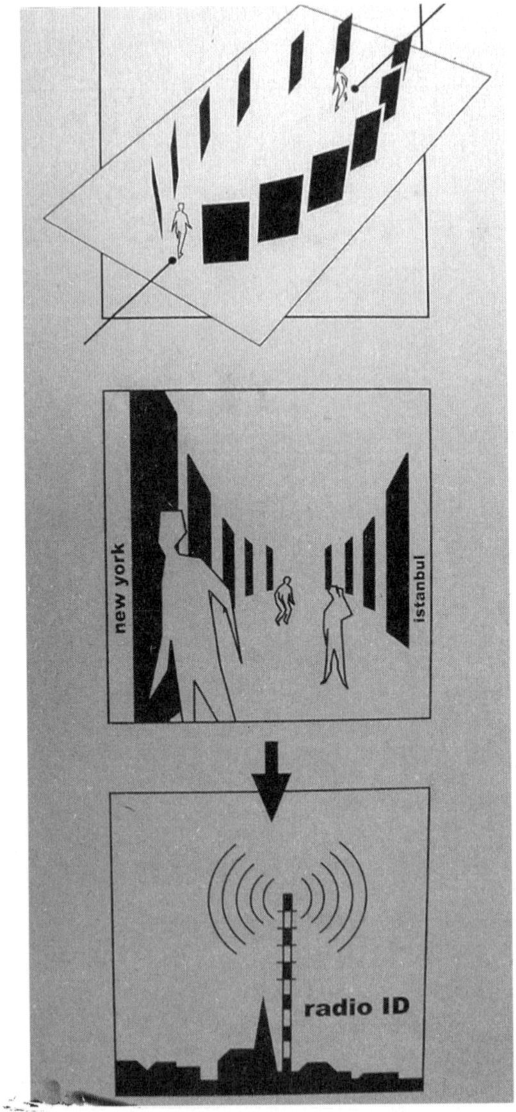

7. The explanations of technology (excerpt)

Imaginationen von Los Angeles zwischen Ramonaland und noir-Apokalyptik

MARKUS REISENLEITNER

Im Juni 2001 fanden in Los Angeles Bürgermeisterwahlen statt, und erstmals seit über hundert Jahren bestand eine reale Chance für einen Latino, in die Eliten der Macht einzusteigen. Dazu kam es nicht. Aber nicht nur seit den letzten Bürgermeisterwahlen ist die starke Präsenz von Latinos in Los Angeles ein viel diskutiertes Thema, bei dem es um Fragen der Zukunft globaler Städte (und der mangelnden Zukunft vieler ihrer Bewohner) geht. Am Beginn des 21. Jahrhunderts ist Los Angeles die erste kontinentalamerikanische Stadt der Vereinigten Staaten (nicht Kanadas), in der Weiße (wieder) keine Mehrheit mehr bilden. Das Latino-Element hat auch in der Vorstellungswelt, in den Bildern und Mythen, die das Bild von Los Angeles als Stadt seit dem Ende des letzten Jahrhunderts bestimmt hat, eine wesentliche Rolle gespielt. Es bildet einen Strang einer dominanten Mythologie von Los Angeles, die ich im ersten Teil dieses Beitrags nachzuzeichnen versuche. Im zweiten Teil werde ich dann auf einen dominanten Gegenmythos eingehen, den ich lose als noir bezeichne und zu dem ich nicht nur die literarischen Werke wie Paul M. Cains *The Postman Always Rings Twice* zählen möchte, sondern auch deren filmische Umsetzungen so wie das bedeutende Sub-Genre der »hard-boiled detective« Romane Raymond Chandlers und Ross McDonalds.

DAS RAMONA-THEMA

Als Kalifornien 1848 als Bundesstaat an die Vereinigten Staaten von Amerika fiel, war die Ausgangsposition von Los Angeles, sich als urbanes Zentrum zu etablieren, denkbar ungünstig. Im Zensus von 1880 Census rangierte die Stadt an 187. Stelle (Davis 25). Nur durch eine clevere Kombination von Grundstücksspekulation, einem durch die Eisenbahnen forcierten *land rush*, und frühen Formen der Konsumorientierung – charakteristisch auch eine ausgeprägten Gewerkschaftsfeindlichkeit (im deutlicher Abgrenzung zum »roten« San Francisco) – konnte jene wirtschaftliche Ausgangsposition geschaffen werden, die den rasanten Wachstum der Stadt seit den 80er Jahren des 19. Jahrhunderts erlaubte.

Als urbanes Zentrum ohne wesentliche industrielle Produktionsbasis wurde Los Angeles als »erste postmoderne Metropole« (Soja, Davis) bezeichnet. Erforderlich dafür war die Erschaffung von Mythen, die Süd-Kalifornien im allgemeinen und Los Angeles im besonderen als utopisches Arkadien darstellten und andererseits die Wachstumschancen und Möglichkeiten des Raums promoteten. Diese Werbe-Kampagnen wurden bereits sehr früh von den wesentlichen Machtzentren in Los Angeles (der Chamber of Commerce unter dem Einfluss von Eisenbahnmagnaten und Grundstücksspekulanten und der Los Angeles Times unter General Harrison Gray Otis (gest. 1917), und seinem Schwiegersohn Harry Chandler, beide selbst in hohem Maße an den Landverkäufen beteiligt) in sehr zielgerichteter Weise durchgeführt. Es ging einerseits darum, Touristen und Siedler anzulocken, um den Grundstücksboom in Schwung zu halten, andererseits aber auch der Stadt selbst im Sinne der durchaus bereits existierenden Städtekonkurrenz eine Form von wieder erkennbarer Identität zu verleihen, also ein Identitätsprojekt in sehr offensichtlicher Weise zu gestalten, die eine Geschichte des Raumes und Formen geographisch-kultureller Determinierungen verbindet.

Eine Konstante dieser kruden, aber wirksamen Werbekampagne waren die klimatischen Verhältnisse. Bereits 1872 veröffentlichte der Journalist Charles Nordhoff seinen Bestseller *California for Wealth, Health and Residence*, in dem er das Leben in Kalifornien in solch glühenden Farben schilderte, dass das Buch einen wahren Touristen- und Siedlerstrom auslöste.

> It is generally acknowledged that some very respectable people live in California; but we who live on the Atlantic side of the continent are sorry for them, and do not doubt in our hearts that they would be only too glad to come over to us. Very few suspect that the Californians have the best of us, and that, so far from living in a kind of rude exile, they enjoy, in fact, the finest climate, the most fertile soil, the loveliest skies, the mildest winters, the most healthful region, in the whole United States... [I]t is, in fact, the best part of the American continent, either for health or for profitable and pleasant living in any industrious pursuit. (118)

Wie gut, dass unmittelbar nach Erscheinen des Buches die Southern Pacific Railway 1876 einen Anschluss an das Schienennetz zwischen Los Angeles und San Francisco herstellen konnte: dass Nordhoff.

damals Journalist der *New York Evening Post*, auf der Gehaltsliste der Southern Pacific stand und gleich auf der Titelseite die Reiseroute für die von ihm beschriebenen Attraktionen entlang der Eisenbahnstrecke darstellte. Dies tat der Popularität seines Travelogues keinen Abbruch und etablierte ein pastorales, zugängliches und attraktives Bild eines mediterranen, sanften Südkalifornien, dass sich deutlich von den bisher existierenden Mythen einer unzivilisierten Goldgräberfrontier – also Nordkalifornien – abhob. Darin spielte auch der Glanz vergangener spanisch-mexikanischer Zeiten, als Feste gefeiert wurden und die Missionen der Franziskaner noch funktionierten, eine große Rolle. Los Angeles in Nordhoffs Beschreibung stellt sich als verschlafene, gemütliche Kleinstadt dar, bewohnt von Weißen, Indianern, Latinos und Chinesen, ein beschauliches Bild friedlichen Zusammenlebens, in dem *fandango* und *hacienda* neben den Möglichkeiten expandierenden Geschäftslebens stehen.

Bis 1890 kamen mehr als 130.000 Menschen auf der Suche nach einem Arkadien nach Südkalifornien, und Los Angeles erreichte 1889 eine Einwohnerzahl von 50.000 (Fogelson 21). Die überwiegende Mehrheit kam aus dem protestantischen Westen der Vereinigten Staaten (Starr 49), und eine dieser Touristinnen sollte der Mythologie kalifornischer Geschichte einen ersten Höhepunkt verschaffen: Helen Hunt Jackson.

Erfolgreiche Autorin von Romanzen und Gedichten, begann sie sich (angeblich bei einem Bostoner Teekränzchen, bei dem zwei Urbewohner als exotische Gäste geladen waren) für das Schicksal der Urbevölkerung Amerikas zu interessieren und publizierte 1881 *A Century of Dishonor*, ein Werk, das in Intellektuellenkreisen Interesse an der Sache weckte. Auf dieser Grundlage wurde sie vom Innenministerium nach Kalifornien geschickt, um das Schicksal der Missionsindianer (mission indians), also jener Ureinwohner, die auf den Franziskanermissionen missioniert und zu Feldarbeiten herangezogen wurden und dann nach der Auflösung der Missionen (1832) durch die mexikanische Regierung zwar von Zwangsarbeit befreit, aber umso mehr ein kärgliches Dasein fristeten.[1] Begleitet wurde sie von Abbot Kinney, einem Booster auf der Gehaltsliste der *Los Angeles Times* (und späteren Schöpfer des mediterranen Themenparks *Venice by the Sea*), und sie war natürlich von Nordhoff et al gründlich auf ein romantisches Bild eines prä-amerikanischen Südkalifornien eingestimmt, in dem gütige Franzikanerpadres (bei Nordhoff sind es Dominikaner) väterlich über die Ausbeutung und Zwangsarbeit der Indianer wachen, während nebenan auf den Ranchos ebenso patriarchalisch-gütige spanische Granden elegante Feste feierten.

Jackson verliebte sich nach Lokalaugenschein der verfallenen Missionen so sehr in diese nostalgische Vision, dass sie es zunächst 1883 in dem Werk *Glimpses of California and the Missions* unter ihren Landsleuten zuzusagen als Aktualisierung von Nordhoffs Werk verbreitete. Wenig später holte sie aber schon zum nächsten Schlag aus und landete mit dem Roman *Ramona* (1884) den Megahit unter den Old California-Romanen.

Ramona glorifiziert das Leben auf den *ranchos* und *haciendas* in den 1870er Jahren. Der Roman ist einerseits eine moralisierende Kritik am Yankee-Imperalismus und den gesetzlichen Bestimmungen von 1848 (die in der Realität einem Diebstahl mexikanischer und indianischer Landrechte gleichkamen), andererseits aber – und das war die dominante Rezeptionshaltung – eine wirksame Darstellung der romantischen und eleganten spanischen Vergangenheit Südkaliforniens.

Im Mittelpunkt der Handlung stehen die edle Señora Moreno, aristokratischer spanischer Herkunft, die den Yankees trotzt, gütig über eine immer kleiner werdende Rancho residiert, die Eingeborenen durch Missionsarbeit, durchgeführt von einem steinalten Franziskaner, und anderen kulturellen Errungenschaften (wie Musikpflege) zivilisiert und in all dem die Werte des Old California standhaft konserviert; ihre Ziehtochter Ramona, ein Halbblut, jedoch als edle Señorita erzogen; und der edle Indianer Alessandro Assis (dessen Namen nicht nur Assoziationen mit italienischen Tenoren erweckt, sondern der tatsächlich ein begnadeter Geigenspieler und Sänger ist, dessen Musikalität die idyllische Gemeinschaft des Rancho erfreut). In den Worten Helen Hunt Jacksons:

> The señora Moreno's house was one of the best specimens to be found in California of the representative house of the half-barbaric, half-elegant, wholly generous and free-handed life led there by Mexican men and women of degree in the early part of this century, under the rule of the Spanish and Mexican viceroys, when the laws of the Indies were still the law of the land, and its old name, ›New Spain,‹ was an ever-present link and stimulus to the warmest memories and deepest patriotism of its people. (zit. nach McClung 95)

Es waren schöne und glänzende Zeiten... Vor den heranrückenden Yankees ist die Liebe zwischen Alessandro und Ramona jedoch klarerweise zu einem tragischen Ende verdammt, der zweite Teil des Romans ist der Flucht der beiden durch eine immer enger werdende Welt der missions und Ranchos in den Süden des Staates (bis zum unausweichlich tragischen Ende Alessandros) gewidmet.

Der Roman war ein durchschlagender Erfolg, mehr als 600.000 Exemplare des Romans wurden verkauft, nach dem 2. Weltkrieg waren bereits 135 Auflagen erschienen (McWilliams 74). Zum perfekten Zeitpunkt herausgebracht (als sowohl die Promotionskampagne als auch die Zuwanderung, die auf genau den gleichen Mythen beruhten, gerade ihren Höhepunkt erreichten), erschien eine Flut von »Ramona merchandising«: Ansichtskarten, Touren zu »Ramonas Geburtsstätte,« »Ramonas Ranch« usw., zahlreiche Spekulationen über die Identität und den Verbleib der »wirklichen Ramona,« zahlreiche Neuauflagen und Folgewerke und eine florierende Heiratsindustrie an der angeblichen Stelle, wo sich der edle Alessandro und Ramona angeblich das Jawort gaben, zementierte den Mythos.[2] Auch die Filmindustrie nahm sich des tragischen Schicksals und der Nostalgie vergangener Zeiten an und produzierte mehrere Filmversionen, und die Werbeindustrie war ebenfalls mit dabei.

Ramona erwies sich als Onkel Toms Hütte für Kalifornien. Der mediterran-spanisch-katholische Landschaftsgarten, den *Ramona* herbeizauberte, passte wunderbar zum selbsternannten Eden der protestantischen Anglos, dies ist nur scheinbar ein Widerspruch: »Ihre [Jacksons] implizite Strategie ist es, die Gesellschaft mit der Landschaft zu identifizieren, und so der relativ stabilen Qualitäten des Klimas, der Landschaft und der Vegetation den sentimental-tragischen Handlungsverlauf einzuschreiben, sowohl was das Schicksal des Liebespaares Ramona und Alessandro als auch den Untergang ihrer Kultur betrifft« (McClung 77).[3] Der Ramona-Stoff und die gesamte (v)erträumte nostalgische spanische Vergangenheit, die *ranchos*, die Missionen, edle Granden, gütige Padres und ihre treuen Missionsindianer boten eine verwendbare Vergangenheit, romantisch-elegisch, pastoral und Sombero-verziert. Das spanische Element lieferte genug von Europa, um der kulturellen Distinktion dienen zu können, und war weit genug weg, um das tatsächliche Elend sowohl der Urbevölkerung als auch der Latinos übersehen zu können. »*Ramona* erreicht für die Region, was *Vom Winde verweht* für den alten Süden bewirkt: es liefert eine beruhigende Rekonstruktion von Geschichte und versichert eine noble Vergangenheit« (Fine 34).[4]

Als der Boom 1888 seinen ersten Knick erlebte (Klein 28), griff man umso entschlossener auf die bewährten booster-Mechanismen zurück, veranstaltete Ausstellungen über dieses exotisierte Kalifornien im Osten bis nach Chicago, und dabei erwies sich der Mythos der spanischen Nostalgie im Land des Sonnenscheins als immer wieder revitalisierbar. »Die Imagination zu verkaufen war Los Angeles' Webersche Modernität, das totalisierende Mittel, das erklärt, wie Raum verbaut und gesehen wurde,« meint der Stadthistoriker Norman Klein (30).[5] Hier spielte wiederum die Publizistik eine entscheidende Rolle, vor allem in der Gestalt von Charles Fletcher Lummis und seines zwischen 1895 und 1909 erschienenen Magazins *Land of Sunshine* (später *Out West*), das sich der Erschaffung und Perpetuierung einer spezifischen kalifornischen Identitätskonstruktion als Teil einer Kulturlandschaft des Südwestens, also der ehemals spanisch/mexikanischen Gebiete, verschrieb. Der Missionsmythos war dabei der Angelpunkt der konstruierten kulturellen Identität, sowie das Klima für die konstruierte geographische Identität, Los Angeles die selbst deklarierte Hauptstadt dieser Region.[6] Propagiert wurde von Lummis und seinem Kreis eine angloamerikanische Zukunft als Erbe und Konservierung einer spanischen Vergangenheit, und das durchaus in einem rassischen Sinn: die angelsächsische Rasse, so befand Lummis, hätte hier ihren Bestimmungsort, ihren Lebensraum: »Der ignorante, hoffnungslos unamerikanische Ausländer, der die Städte des Ostens heimsucht und zum Großteil kontrolliert, ist hier fast unbekannt,« bemerkte Lummis 1895 in einer seiner unappetitlichsten Äußerungen (Starr 89)[7] – übrigens eine Situation, die die Filmindustrie wesentlich verändern sollte.[8]

Ein anderer unermüdlicher Booster, der Historiker John Steven McGroarty, machte aus der Fiktion Geschichte in seiner für lange Zeit als autoritativ geltenden Geschichte Kaliforniens, *California, Its History and Romance* (1911), nach den Worten Kevin Starrs das »vielleicht letzte der großen, in Kommission entstandenen Photoalben, die lokale Potentaten verherrlichten, die bereit waren, die Publikationskosten zu tragen« (Starr 87).[9] Aber diese angeblich autoritative Geschichte Kaliforniens war nicht der einzige Beitrag McGroartys zum Mythos Südkaliforniens. Sein Hauptbeitrag bleibt wohl das Mission Play, das zwischen 1912 und 1929 2,5 Millionen Zuschauer anlocken konnte und mehr als 2600 Aufführungen erlebte.

Die Idee eines Missionsspiels ging auf General Otis und den Unternehmer Frank Miller zurück, der unter dem Bann des Missionsmythos in Riverside bereits äußerst erfolgreich ein Themen-Hotel im immer populärer werdenden *mission revival*-Stil führte. Das Mission Inn in Riverside, begonnen in den späten 1890ern, war damals der wohl bedeutendste Schrein einer spanisch-italienisch-mexikanische Phantasie kalifornischer Vergangenheit.

Dies inspirierte die Idee eines Mission Play, das im wesentlichen von Otis, Miller und McGroarty nach den Passionsspielen Oberammergaus, versehen mit einer Prise Ramona, konzipiert und 1912 erstmals in einem eigens dafür errichteten, nahe der Mission San Gabriel gelegenen Theater, das immerhin fast 1500 Besucher aufnahm, uraufgeführt wurde (vgl. Starr 88ff; McClung 89). Ein riesiges historisches Spektakel mit 300 Schauspielern, Chorgesang, Musik, Umzügen und Tanzeinlagen, wurde das Stück begeistert aufgenommen und ganz im Sinne Ramonas als romantische Mythologie begrüßt. McGroarty wurde zum *poeta laureatus* Kaliforniens gekürt, von Spanien zum Ritter geschlagen und zweimal zum Kongressabgeordneten gewählt.

Die konstruierte spanische Geschichte unter Ausblendung der real existierenden Latinos (die gleichzeitig immer bemerkbarer – und immer häufiger deportiert – wurden) funktionierte noch immer, allerdings wurden immer häufiger die Mexikaner, nicht mehr die Anglos, für das traurige Schicksal der Padres verantwortlich gemacht. Gleichzeitig traten in der Rezeption immer stärker die protestantischen Werthaltungen in den Vordergrund, für die die katholische Vergangenheit gnadenlos usurpiert werden konnte. Das Missionsspiel zelebrierte die Werte einer protestantischen »muscular Christianity,« die Werte der Ordnung, Betriebsamkeit und Arbeitsethik. Das Missionsspiel salbte den *boosterism*, die Chamber of Commerce verhalf wie seinerzeit die Franziskaner einer Bevölkerung, die der Lenkung bedurfte, zu einer besseren Gesellschaftsordnung:[10] produktiv, stabil, konservativ und fromm (protestantisch).[11]

Seit der Jahrhundertwende zählen folgerichtig pseudo-mexikanische Fiestas zum Kulturprogramm jedes Rotarierclubs in Los Angeles. Ebenso konnte das Thema in der populären Imagination weiterleben; in den 20er Jahren vor allem in Form des maskierten Rächers Zorro, der Ramona wenn nicht ablöste, so zumindest durch einen aktiveren (protestantischeren? weißeren?) spanischen Helden ergänzte. Basierend auf einer Kurzgeschichte des Screenwriters Johnston McCulley, *The Curse of Capistrano* (1919) und dem darauf basierenden Roman *The Mark of Zorro*, enthielt der Mythos alle Elemente, die *Ramona* so populär gemacht haben, den edlen Don spanischer Herkunft, den gütigen Franziskanerpadre, die fügsamen und zahmen Eingeborenen und – ganz im Sinne der Anglos – die üblen Mexikaner, die diese Welt – allerdings noch erfolglos – bedrohen. Doch auch der Stadtplanung kam der Mythos gelegen: Man promotete schamlos das »historische Zentrum,« die Gegend um Olvera Street, renoviert als historischer Themenpark, als »fiesta pueblo,« ein Ort, wo Amerikaner »spanisches« Essen vorfanden und Geschichte erleben konnten, wo der Camino Real seinen Anfang nahm.

»Das katholische Spanien wird verehrt dafür, Südkalifornien als Ort definiert zu haben, aber die wahren Erben sind protestantisch und weiß« (McClung 82).[12] Harry Carr, faschistoider booster und White

Supremacist, schreibt in seinem *Los Angeles: City of Dreams* (1935) unter dem Titel *Romance and Tamales*: »Old Los Angeles [was formerly] a dirty alley, abandoned to slums and desolation. Then we picked up our (!) traditions« (zit. nach McClung 83). Die Plaza-Kirche des Pueblos schmückt Carrs Umschlag als romantisches Symbol einer Kultur der Frömmigkeit und wird dem Mythos entsprechend als »Mission Church« bezeichnet.[13]

Gerade um Olvera Street macht sich jedoch auch eine subversive Komponente der ambivalenten Vergangenheitskonstruktion bemerkbar. Nahe der wirklichen Hauptstrasse mexikanischer Öffentlichkeit am Broadway (wo die Fassaden allerdings viktorianisch sind), entbrannte in den achtziger und neunziger Jahren des 20. Jahrhunderts ein Streit um symbolische Anerkennung, dessen Ausgang noch nicht absehbar ist. Während die Stadtväter ein französisches Restaurant und ein italienisches (!) *heritage museum* anbringen wollten – fröhlich-kulinarische Yuppie-Multikulturalität in Gehdistanz der Banken und Anwaltskanzleien des westlichen *downtown* um Bunker Hill und California Plaza –, kämpften Latino-Aktivisten um ihre Murals, ein Museum für sich und machten das touristische Highlight der Missionskirche zu einem Refugium illegaler Immigranten (Klein 61).

Der Kampf um symbolische Sichtbarkeit ist auch ein Kampf um öffentlichen Raum, um ein *support system* und ein Stück genuiner Gemeinschaft, das aus seiner touristischen Vermarktung heraus usurpiert wird und dem die Ledergürtel-Märkte des Olvera Street

Market daher nicht unbedingt im Weg stehen; die Tatsache, dass die Vermarkter eines kulinarischen Multikulturalismus »historisch« durchaus recht hatten – als Olvera Street für das historische Erbe Anfang der dreißiger Jahre reklamiert wurde, war es eine ethnisch durchaus gemischte Nachbarschaft, nahe, aber nicht im barrio – spielt in diesem Fall keine Rolle. Bedeutung, schreibt Meaghan Morris, ist das Ergebnis sozialer Verhandlungen, nicht semantischer Definitionen (23)[14] (oder realer Geschichte); für den Kampf um die semantische Besetzung, und damit auch den realen Raum, ist es die erinnerte, nicht die »reale« Geschichte, die Bedeutungen und damit erlebten Raum schafft. Populäres Gedächtnis schreibt realen Orten einen historischen Raum ein, den sie niemals bewohnten, Nostalgie überzeugt gerade, weil sie nicht wahr ist, weil die Ereignisse der Vergangenheit vergessen wurden. Simulation, der historische Themenpark ist in diesem Sinne keine einfache Kopie, sondern eine verschwommene Stelle zwischen dem (materiellen) Signifikanten und der Erinnerung[15]; und dieser Trick öffnet die produzierte Vergangenheit, macht sie der Aneignung und Umdeutung zugänglich, der Aneignung durch Gruppen und *communities*, die die Orte real bewohnen. Die Latino-Bevölkerung reokkupiert heute in einem sich als aggressiv multikulturell vermarktenden Los Angeles des späten 20. Jahrhunderts, in dem zunächst Fiestas sehr bequem hineinreklamiert werden können, einen Raum, der historisch nicht der ihre ist, indem sie den hegemonialen Symbolhaushalt der Anglos aneignet. Der Kampf ist jedoch nicht entschieden, das Cinco de Mayo Festival oszilliert unstet zwischen Gemeinschaftsstiftung und touristischer Aneignung.

NOIR

I drove east on Sunset but I didn't go home. At La Brea I turned north and swung over to Highland, out over Cahuenga Pass and down on to Ventura Boulevard, past Studio City and Sherman Oaks and Encino. There was nothing lonely about the trip. There never is on that road. Fast boys in stripped-down Fords shot in and out of the traffic streams, missing fenders by a sixteenth of an inch, but somehow always missing them. Tired men in dusty coupés and sedans winced and tightened their grip on the wheel and ploughed on north and west towards home and dinner, an evening with the sports page, the blatting of the radio, the whining of their spoiled children and the gabble of their silly wives. I drove on past the gaudy neons and the false fronts behind them, the sleazy hamburger joints that look like palaces under the colors, the circular drive-ins as gay as circuses with the chipper hard-eyed car-hops, the brilliant counters, and the sweaty greasy kitchens that would have poisoned a toad. Great double trucks rumbled down over Sepulveda from Wilmington and San Pedro and crossed towards the Ridge Route, starting up in low low from the traffic lights with a growl of lions in the zoo.

Behind Encino an occasional light winked from the hills through thick trees. The homes of screen stars. Screen stars, phooey. The veterans of a thousand beds. Hold it, Marlowe, you're not human tonight.

The air got cooler. The highway narrowed. The cars were so few now that the headlights hurt. The grade rose against chalk walls and at the top a breeze, unbroken from the ocean, danced casually across the night.

I ate dinner at a place near Thousand Oaks. Bad but quick. Feed 'em and throw 'em out. Lots of business. We can't bother with you sitting over your second cup of coffee, mister. You're using money space. See those people over there behind the rope? They want to eat. Anyway they think they have to. God knows why they want to eat here. They could do better home out of a can. They're just restless. Like you. They have to get the car out and go somewhere. Sucker-bait for the racketeers that have taken over the restaurants. Here we go again. You're not human tonight, Marlowe. ...

Malibu. More movie stars. More pink and blue bathtubs. More tufted beds. More Chanel No. 5. More Lincoln Continentals and Cadillacs. More wind-blown hair and sunglasses and attitudes and pseudo-refined voices and water-front morals. Now, wait a minute. Lots of nice people work in pictures. You've got the wrong attitude, Marlowe. You're not human tonight.

I smelled Los Angeles before I got to it. It smelled stale and old like a living-room that had been closed too long. But the coloured lights fooled you. The lights were wonderful. There ought to be a monument to the man who invented neon lights. Fifteen storeys high, solid marble. There's a boy who really made something out of nothing.

So I went to a picture show and it had to have Mavis Weld in it. One of those glass-and-chromium deals where everybody smiled too much and talked too much and knew it. The women were always going up a long curving staircase to change their clothes. The men were always taking monogrammed cigarettes out of expensive cases and snapping expensive lighters at each other. And the help was round-shouldered from carrying trays with drinks across the terrace to a swimming pool about the size of Lake Huron but a lot neater.

The leading man was an amiable ham with a lot of charm, some of it turning a little yellow at the edges. The star was a bad-tempered brunette with contemptuous eyes and a couple of bad close-ups that showed her pushing forty-five backwards almost hard enough to break a wrist. Mavis Weld played second lead and she played it with wraps on. She was good, but she could have been ten times better. But if she had been ten times better half her scenes would have been yanked out to protect the star. It was as neat a bit of tightrope walking as I ever saw. Well it wouldn't be a tightrope she'd be walking from now on. It would be a piano wire. It would be very high. And there wouldn't be any net under it. (Chandler 441-4)

In den zwanziger und insbesondere den dreißiger Jahren entsteht – auch als Reaktion auf die eben dargestellten Mythologien – in der literarischen Strömung des *noir* eine umfangreiche Gegenbewegung, ein Gegenmythos, der Los Angeles als Ende des Traums, als dezentrierte Stadt ohne Zentrum, unorganisch und Ort der Vereinsamung, Selbsttäuschung und des Verbrechens darstellt: Los Angeles as urbane Hölle einer verdrängten Mittelklasse.

Der archimedische Punkt der urbanen Kritik an L.A., der Ich-Erzähler (Verbrecher in der Todeszelle oder Detektiv) ist weiß, männlich und einsam, ein desillusionierter, zynischer, leicht homophober und rassistischer, jedoch schwer sexistischer Flaneur im Auto, in einer Stadt, in der sich Gemeinschaft und Solidarität in Korruption und Verbrechen aufgelöst haben, so wie sich die Stadt selbst in ihre suburbs, die Architektur in die Stukko-Fassade, die Neonlichter oder – ultimative Metapher – die Filmkulisse aufgelöst haben.[16] Die eklektischen und exotischen Phantasien der Architektur eigneten sich die noir-Literaten und Filmemacher, auf der Suche nach bourgeoiser Authentizität, als Bilder und Beispiele des Mangels ästhetischer – und damit moralischer – Kontrolle an (Fine 20). Der Mann, der die »mean streets« entlang geht (bzw. fährt), verkörpert die ohnmächtige, teils sich in Gewalt entladende kleinbürgerliche Frustration einer Stadt, die der protestantischen Kleinstadtethik ihrer Gründerväter entwachsen ist, das verallgemeinerte kleinbürgerliche Ressentiment gegen den Einbruch des Traumes von Südkalifornien. Was kritisiert wird, ist das künstliche, aufgesetzte, Geschichtslose; was aufgedeckt wird, ist das Wahre (in Form einer – meist persönlichen – Geschichte): es sind nicht die Rackets, die das Verbrechen verursachen, sondern persönliche Traumata.

Diese sozial und historisch sehr spezifische, literarisch und filmisch jedoch unglaublich gut verwertbare Vision (nicht zuletzt in Europa), konnte sich als dominanter Mythos etablieren. Noir L.A. ist seit den 1930ern eine vermarktbare Ware, in den Worten von Mike Davis eine transformationelle Grammatik, die jedes der zauberhaften Elemente des booster-Arkadiens in sein düsteres Equivalent verkehrt (Davis 38). »Für [Nathanael] West [Autor des Romans *The Day of the Locusts* (1939)], wie für Chandler und Huxley und praktisch alle Autoren, die ihnen in den folgenden Jahrzehnten nacheiferten, stand die Phantasiearchitektur der Stadt nicht nur für das umfassende Bild einer Absenz ... sondern auch für eine Projektion, oder Externalisierung des zwanghaften Rollenspiels der Menschen, ihres Scheiterns daran, reales

Leben und Phantasie zu unterscheiden« (Fine 20).[17] »Es ist im Grunde ein Mythos über weiße, männliche Panik – der weiße Ritter in der brodelnden Hölle urbanen Verfalls« (Klein 79).[18] Aber bereits in den dreißiger Jahren ist noir mehr als das, mehr als ein Gegenmythos einer bestimmten Stadt: Los Angeles ist DIE Stadt. So wie Adorno die Zukunft des Kapitalismus in Los Angeles, Kalifornien und Amerika zu entdecken vermeinte, so wird Los Angeles für Philipp Marlowe zu der Stadt an sich, zur Metapher einer Gesellschaft *gone awry*.

Manche Interpreten von noir gehen noch einen Schritt weiter: Noir als die Präfiguration der postmodernen Stadt (oder ist es: des postmodernen Blicks auf die Stadt?) Für Fredric Jameson zeichnet sich im L.A. Marlowes die postmoderne Vieldeutigkeit einer ausgehebelten Gesellschaft des Spätkapitalismus bereits ab, dieses Los Angeles ist »bereits ein Mikrokosmos und eine Vorschau auf das Land in seiner Gesamtheit, eine neue Stadt ohne Zentrum, in der die verschiedenen Gesellschaftsklassen den Kontakt zueinander verloren haben, da jede in ihrem eigenen geographischen Segment isoliert ist.«[19] Daher gebe es, so Jameson, für Chandler keinen privilegierten Blickpunkt, und eine Figur – eben die des Detektivs – »muss geschaffen werden, um sie der Gesellschaft als Ganzes überzustülpen, um ihre separaten und isolierten Teile zueinander zu führen« (625).[20]

Ich bin mir da nicht so sicher. Die Metapher des Stadtdetektivs, des Mannes von Welt,[21] ist eine durch und durch moderne, nicht postmoderne, Figur, die Figur des Utterson im *Strange Case of Dr Jekyll and Mr Hyde*, der die Türen aufbricht, die verborgene Wahrheit ans Licht bringt und damit sehr wohl einen Standpunkt, einen – sehr klassen-, rassen- und geschlechtsspezifischen, »Wahrheit« im Sinne der Anamnesis beanspruchenden – Blick eröffnet. Wie im Ramonamythos, nur projiziert auf Gegenwart und Zukunft, wird L.A. konstruiert als Bild des Anderen, bestimmt durch eine Absenz (eines Zentrums, eines authentischen Stils, einer Tradition, einer Gemeinschaft), eine Projektion, die völlig eurozentrisch und modern ist.

Und dieser Blick stellt die Stadt als Objekt dar, das aus seiner Vergesslichkeit herausgerissen und – ganz im Sinne des industriellen Manchester als, wie Engels meint, ungeplante Wildnis – behandelt, kuriert werden muss, natürlich ohne Miteinbeziehung dieses »Anderen,« ihrer tatsächlichen Bewohner, und natürlich am besten von der Chamber of Commerce durch die Schaffung von »Business Improvement Districts,« von gated communities und von Autobahnen, die schmucke postmoderne Gebäude von Slums abschirmen. Tatsächlich beginnen sich in den dreißiger Jahren neue Strategien der Stadtplanung breit zu

machen, in der es nicht mehr um Beschönigung und Verschönerung geht, sondern um die Lösung einer als Problem wahrgenommenen sozialen Krise, und das ganz im Sinne des hard-boiled Detektivs durch Gewalt. Überwachung, Spiel mit kleinbürgerlicher Angst und law and order-Denken sind hier bereits grundgelegt.[22]

Eine Stadt auf eine gewisse Weise zu sehen heißt, in einer gewissen Form an ihr zu handeln. Neue Formen der Planung in den 1930ern basieren auf Perzeptionen einer urbanen Krise, die unmittelbar aus den *mean streets* herausgewachsen ist und von dieser Mythologie unterstützt wird: Los Angeles hatte in den 1930er Jahren ebenso wie heute ein klares, erkennbares downtown, in dem elegante Geschäfte, Banken und Rechtsanwälte residierten, funktionierende neighborhoods, und eine mit anderen Städten vergleichbare Verbrechensrate (vgl. Klein 84). Noir-Visionen entwurzelter kleinbürgerlicher Intellektueller halfen jedoch, es zum Inbegriff einer anonymen, de-zentrierten, chaotischen Stadt des Verbrechens zu machen, vor deren imaginierten Bewohnern man sich durch Festungen und *gated communities* schützen musste, eine Stadt, die ihre Stadt-haftigkeit als Ding-an-sich verloren hat (*suburbs in search of a city*). Hier hat die soziale Imagination Grundlagen einer Rhetorik geschaffen, deren reale Baugestalt als »Festung L.A.,« die Mike Davis so überzeugend dokumentiert ist. Die städtische Planungspolitik operiert seit den 1930er Jahren auf der Basis einer sozialen Imagination, die die Kehrseite der Vision nostalgischer Geschichte, die sich in der Realität nicht einlöst, darstellt. Auf dieser Vision konnte, genau wie in Europa, eine totalitär-planerische Stadtgestaltung im Sinne Le

Corbusiers zurückgreifen. Möglicherweise findet daher im noir-Mythos nicht die erste postmoderne Stadt ihren medialen Ausdruck, sondern wird durch den Mythos selbst der Perzeption der Moderne zugeführt.

*

Heute präsentierte downtown sich als eine Reihe millionenteurer Hochhäuser wie das Bonaventure Hotel, California Plaza usw., ein zunehmend dichtes Geflecht selbst-referentieller, nach innen gewandter und durch Passagen verbundener, von der Strasse jedoch fast hermetisch abgeriegelter Gebäude darstellt, leicht westlich vom historischen Kern. Die von Mike Davis beschriebene »räumliche Apartheid,« produziert durch den Harbor Freeway (wie praktisch das gesamte Autobahnsystem fertig gestellt in den 1960er Jahren), der eine wesentliche und effektive Barriere gegen die Immigrantennachbarschaften darstellt, ist jedoch mit der »Wiederherstellung« der »öffentlichen Sicherheit« am Fuß des Hügels, im mexikanischen Viertel, nicht mehr notwendig, schließlich ist Los Angeles multikulturell (Touristenmotto »Around the World in Thirty Blocks«) – Pluralität und Desintegration, der angebliche Verlust des Zentrums der Moderne, wird in der Zelebrierung der Multikulturalität, die in bewährter Weise ihre Akteure ausschließt, oder doch lieber importiert, zu einer neuen Tugend. Dennoch ist die unsichtbare Grenze zwischen Anglo-Land und Lateinamerika zumindest für die Einheimischen fast unüberschreitbar.

*

Spätestens seit Raymond Williams ist es eine konventionelle Weisheit, dass eine Stadt wie ein Text zu lesen ist. Mir erscheint diese Textmetapher zutreffend, aber nur unter dem postmodernen Verständnis ihrer prinzipiell unabgeschlossenen Fähigkeit, gelesen zu werden, Bedeutung, Gemeinschaft und Identifikationen zu schaffen, eine kulturell produzierte Konvergenz von verorteten Erinnerungen und Traditionen, deren Kontingenz sich dem »Image,« der Authentizität entzieht, kurz: eine Art zu sehen. Dieses Image, die hegemoniale Interpretation der Sinnangebote, ist höchst relevant, nicht nur, wie Saskia Sassen meint, für die Konkurrenz der Städte in einem globalen Markt, sondern auch für die tatsächliche Gestaltung des Lebensraums und letztendlich für *spatial justice*. Das Bild einer Stadt, die Metaphern bestimmen nicht nur, wer Touristen anzieht, sondern wo Autobahnen gebaut, Zäune errichtet und Zugangsmöglichkeiten, öffentlicher Raum

und Orte der Solidarität und des Widerstandes geschaffen oder verhindert werden. Kristin Ross schreibt, dass »die Reproduktion sozialer Produktionsverhältnisse der zentrale und verborgene Prozess der kapitalistischen Gesellschaft« sei, und dieser Prozess sei »räumlich.«[23] Die Geschichte von Los Angeles, die Geschichte seiner Repräsentationen gibt diesen Reproduktionen Form.

Los Angeles heute zu sehen heißt weniger, ein Ramonaland oder noir zu sehen (obwohl beide Komponenten weiterwirken), sondern Sushi-und-Tamales-Multikulturalismus, postmoderne Architektur, Amerika und Disneyland in einem einzigen Bild vereint, mehr denn je ein Bündel an einander widersprechenden Zuschreibungen. Es ist zweifelsohne die am meisten vermittelte Stadt (und da habe ich Hollywood noch nicht einmal erwähnt), deren konstante Dekonstruktionen mittlerweile auch ein fast schon selbst-referentielles System immer clevererer akademischer Diskurse darstellt. Dennoch: Bezieht man den strukturalistischen Gedanken, dass kulturelle Formen immer die imaginäre Auflösung realer Widersprüche darstellen, auf Räume, dann wird die politische Komponente dieser Repräsentationen offensichtlich. Wie immer vermittelt Los Angeles ist, es ist auch der Ort vielfältiger, realer und wichtiger sozialer Auseinandersetzungen und Verhandlungen eben dieser globalisierten Imaginationen um räumliche Gerechtigkeit und Mitbestimmung; und damit möglicherweise um die Zukunft der Stadt.

ENDNOTES

* Accompanying photos were taken by the editors.

1 Nach der Annexion Kaliforniens durch die Vereinigten Staaten waren sie von allen grundlegenden Rechten und von der Staatsbürgerschaft ausgeschlossen.

2 Natürlich durften auch eine Dramatisierung nicht fehlen, deren Uraufführung am 27. Februar 1905 am Opernhaus in Los Angeles stattfand (McWilliams 75).

3 »Her implicit strategy is to identify the society with the terrain, and thus to imbue the relatively stable qualities of climate, landscape, and flora with the nostalgia generated by the novel's sentimentally tragic course of events, both in the lives of the doomed lovers Ramona and Alessandro, and in the decline of their civilization.«

4 »*Ramona* does for the region what *Gone with the Wind* did for the South: provide a comforting reconstruction of history, confer a reassuring sense of a noble past.«

5 »Selling the imaginary was L.A.'s Weberian modernity, the totalizing device that explains how space has been built and perceived.«

6 Es ist bemerkenswert, dass Los Angeles zu diesem Zeitpunkt Bestandteil dieser Kultur/Naturlandschaft sein konnte. Erst der städtische Anti-Mythos, noir, zementierte eine Sonderstellung der Stadt, eben als Kontrast zu Städten wie Santa Fe, die aufgrund ›intakter‹ Tradition noch ein Zentrum hätten.

7 »The ignorant, hopelessly un-American foreigner which infests and largely controls Eastern cities is almost unknown here.«

8 Noch deutlicher war sein booster-Kollege Joseph Pomeroy Widney; nach dessen Beitrag zum Mythos, *California of the South* (1888) wird Kalifornien später für ihn zur Destination der auserwählten angelsächsischen Arier in seinem Schlüsselroman *The Race Life of the Aryan People* (1907), vgl. Fine 42.

9 »perhaps the last of the great commissioned mugbooks glorifying local worthies willing to underwrite the cost of publication.«

10 »In the final moments of the revised Mission Play, the dying Spanish heroine, shot accidentally by Indians, tells an American that California's glory will re-

turn only at such a time as the Americans restore a cross to every hill. The Mission Play, then, is a rather obvious but effective parable on Protestant piety and the work ethic. The mission myth baptized boosterism. The new Franciscans were the members of the chamber of commerce; the workers of Southern California were their Indians – needing tutelage and occasional chastisement, but capable of productivity when carefully supervised. As in the mission days, Southern California was being put to use in the Lord's name. A better order – productive, stable, conservative, pious – was in the making.« (Starr 89)

11 Dies mag zwar nicht ganz den Intentionen des Autors entsprechen (der zum Katholizismus konvertiert war, vgl. McWilliams 79), erklärt aber die Popularität des Stücks im protestantischen Los Angeles (während die katholische Kirche selbst praktisch keine Rolle im Ramona-revival spielte). Carey McWilliams wies 1946 darauf hin, wie häufig das Wort »mission« in Firmennamen vorkommt und dass »in the days of the Dons« oder »in the footsteps of the padres« gebräuchliche Redewendungen in Los Angeles wären, während in San Francisco fast kein Interesse an den Missionen bestünde.

12 »Catholic Spain is revered for defining Southern California as a place, but its proper heirs are Protestant and white.«

13 Tatsächlich war Los Angeles selbst niemals eine Mission, und die Bewohner des Pueblos Reina de Los Angeles, dessen langer Name ebenfalls mythisch ist (McClung 76), mussten bis zum Jahr der Unabhängigkeit Spaniens 1822 nach San Gabriel, um einem Gottesdienst beiwohnen zu können.

14 »›Meaning,‹ I take as a matter of social negotiation, not semantic definition.«

15 »The past is not the issue at all; it serves merely as a ›rosy‹ container for the anxieties of the present« (Klein 11). »The audience already senses, very consciously, that it is false, but buys it anyway, simply as the thrill of sharing in the magic trick... Simulation is not a copy, but a blur between memory and signifier« (Klein 12).

16 Die moderne Architektur von Schindler oder Neutra ist in dieser spezifischen Aneignung von Los Angeles, dieser partikularen Form von Imagination nicht sichtbar, ebenso wenig wie die Downtown communities, die John Fante oder Charles Bukowski in ihrer Wino-Literatur beschreiben.

17 »For West, as for Chandler and Huxley, and for virtually all the writers who followed in the next few decades, the region's fantasy architecture stood not only as the consummate image of absence... but also as projection, or externalizaton, of the compulsive role-playing of characters, their failure to distinguish real life and fantasy, living and performing.«

18 »It is essentially a mythos about white male panic – the white knight in a cesspool of urban decay; about desire turned into a slot machine. Despite its origins as social realism in Hammett, the hard-boiled story cannot help but operate, very fundamentally, as white males building a social imaginary.«

19 »already a microcosm and forecast of the country as a whole, a new centerless city in which the various classes have lost touch with each other because each is isolated in his own geographic compartment.«

20 »must be created who can be superimposed on the society as a whole... to tie its separate and isolated parts together.«

21 Among the throng but not of the throng (wie Oiseau in Allan Rudolphs *The Moderns* meint).

22 Und dies entspricht ganz dem Konzept der Modernität bei James Donald, »the

concept offers one way of telling the story of how we live in the present« (24), »an array of questions« (21).

23 »The reproduction of the social relations of production is the central and hidden process of capitalist society, and... this process is spatial« (Ross 56).

REFERENCES

Chandler, Raymond. *The Chandler Collection*. Volume One. London: Picador, 1983.

Davis, Mike. *City of Quartz: Excavating the Future in Los Angeles*. New York: Vintage Books, 1992.

Donald, James. *Imagining the Modern City*. Minneapolis: University of Minnesota Press, 1999.

Jackson, Helen Hunt. *Ramona: a Story*. Boston: Little Brown, 1951.

Jameson, Fredric. »On Raymond Chandler.« *Southern Review* 6.1 (1970).

Fine, David. *Imagining Los Angeles: A City in Fiction*. Albuquerque: University of New Mexico Press, 2000.

Fogelson, Robert M. *The Fragmented Metropolis: Los Angeles, 1850-1930*. Cambridge, Mass.: Harvard University Press, 1967.

Klein, Norman. *The History of Forgetting: Los Angeles and the Erasure of Memory*. London, New York: Verso, 1997.

McClung, William Alexander. *Landscapes of Desire: Anglo Mythologies of Los Angeles*. Berkeley: University of California Press, 2000.

McWilliams, Carey. *Southern California: An Island on the Land*. Salt Lake City: Peregrine Smith Books, 1995 (1946).

Morris, Meaghan. *Too Soon, Too Late: History in Popular Culture*. Bloomington and Indianapolis: Indiana University Press, 1998.

Nordhoff, Charles. *California: For Health, Pleasure, and Residence: A Book for Travelers and Settlers*. New York: Harper & Brothers Publishers, 1872.

Ross, Kristin. *The Emergence of Social Space: Rimbaud and the Paris Commune*. Houndmills, 1988.

Soja, Edward. *Postmetropolis: Critical Studies of Cities and Regions*. Oxford: Blackwell Publishers Inc., 2000.

Starr, Keven. *Inventing the Dream: California Through the Progressive Era*. New York, Oxford: Oxford University Press, 1985.

Contributors / AutorInnen

Andrew Colin Gow, Associate Professor, Department of History, University of Alberta

Hilje van der Horst, Onderzoeksinstituut OTB, Technische Universiteit Delft

Susan Ingram, SSHRC Postdoctoral Fellow, Department of History, University of Victoria

Markus Reisenleitner, Associate Professor, Department of Cultural Studies, Lingnan University, Hong Kong

Eva Schwarzmann, Doktorantin, Institut für Geschichte, Universität Wien

Cornelia Szabó-Knotik, Professor, Institut für Analyse, Theorie und Geschichte der Musik, Universität für Musik und darstellende Kunst in Wien